A Random Soldier

The Words He Left Behind

A Random Soldier
The Words He Left behind

Lance Corporal Richard "Chad" Clifton
Terri Clifton

First Edition

Eastwind Press

Printing History:
First Edition Eastwind Press 2006
Eastwind Press
ISBN-10: 0-9785300-0-4
ISBN-13: 978-0-9785300-0-6

Library of Congress Control Number: 2006940080

Dedicated to all of Chad's heroes...

"All the guys I know who have paid the ultimate price. Especially those who didn't want to be here, but were brave enough to do what we do anyway. I'll never forget what it was like, and when I tell a story, your names will be in it. Not covered up with some super-patriotic bullshit, either, but for how it actually was."

Foreword

This is a true story.

It feels strange writing that-by now, I'm so indoctrinated into the world without Chad that it feels more like religion than a true story. Other times, it feels like forensics: all the picking apart, labeling, wondering at the uncanny design of something horrible. Something devotional. Church of Chad. He would have loved that.

But you need to remember: this is a true story. This was a boy, age 19, not a symbol, not a martyr. He was someone you could have talked to and immediately forgotten, he was someone who could have (and probably did) cut you off in traffic. He was someone who you could reach out and touch. Feel skin.

Reading it, it's hard for me to place myself physically beside him. Thanks to the memory we're damned to-a closed book, something that can't be revised-I can't see myself as anything but a spectator, looking at Chad and seeing the colossus/jackass/genius/bastard/angel he was. It's hard to see myself as part of this history, someone that stood next to him in the lunch line. Reverent to a fault, I can't see myself as that lucky.

I'm biased, though, I've known him for years. I can't meet Chad as you'll meet him, in profile, in relief. It's easier for me to remove him from the world without risking the ultimate mistake of tangling him up in politics, cause, or motive. It's harder for you. I'm sorry. But you have to try.

The fact stands: I was there. I saw this. I bear witness. This isn't stars-and-stripes. This isn't Oprah's Book Club. This is nobody's symbol, nobody's cause. This is mine, and now, its yours.

This is a true story.
Incredible.

Rob Kunzig
Lewes, Delaware 2007

Introduction

I wanted to publish Chad's writings on their own as a stand-alone book, but going through them I realized they would need to be placed within the context of his life to have meaning. To do that, I would have to open up our private world. I wasn't sure I could. Rich, Chad, Ryan and I were a self-contained unit. The four of us were very close. Our entire life together as a family has always been a gift. It was a gift that we guarded and cherished, held close and safe and shared only in glimpses. And now it was to be opened up, looked at, pondered over.

Why do such a thing? Why not gather the tatters of our wounded hearts, the reams of memories and experiences and dreams, and take them some place safe and dark? Close the curtains on the world and grieve. It would have been so much easier, but I had made a promise.

That last summer when Chad was home on pre-deployment leave we spent a lazy afternoon on the swing in the backyard. We talked for hours about everything until we got around to the what-ifs.

"What if you get killed?" I asked.

"I can't promise that won't happen, Momma. You always told me never to make a promise I couldn't keep." he answered.

"I know all that but I really need to know what to do."

"Just be strong for Dad and Ryan. They'll need you."

"What will I need to do for you? I won't know what to do without you."

"Just don't forget me."

"No one will forget you, Chad!" I answered with impatience.

He was quiet for a minute and then said softly, "That's my biggest fear, you know. Maybe I'm crazy, but it's not the bullets and bombs or dying on the other side of the world that scares me. I'm afraid I won't make it home to tell the story. What it was like and who I was and what I learned. It'll all be lost and no one will ever know."

"They will Chad. If you don't make it back I'll tell them. I'll tell your story."

"You promise?"

"I promise."

So here I am, writing the story I hoped and prayed I'd never have to tell. I don't know for sure that I am capable of conveying fully who Chad was. I don't know that I can succeed in showing you the good and the bad, the simple and the complex, the warrior, poet, son, and friend. So I will open my heart and ask you to open your mind. We may find him there. I hope so, but either way I have to try. I taught him to never make a promise he couldn't keep.

Terri Clifton

Introduction

I'm going to take the liberty of a free form forward, allowing myself the luxury of speaking directly and literally to the intended reader.
The intent of this memoir is to paint a picture of how I came to be in this position, perhaps as a memento for my friends and family, or maybe because I feel the need to impart whatever wisdom I have gained to someone who may accidentally find himself in my footsteps. It's kind of hard to fall into them, so it's desperate when you struggle to get out.

Feel free to psychoanalyze this entire piece trust me, I've been over every sentence a hundred times in my own mind, analyzing why I put it a certain way, or why I have this or that issue.

Normally, revealing these kind of details would be devastating if I allowed anyone to read them, but death is fortunate in that the perception of self doesn't matter, even for the painfully self aware

Let me put it simply. I believe I'm going insane. Functionally, ever so slightly, out of my mind. The same ever-present self awareness that gives me mirror-like insight into my motivations and actions also creates a duality that rips my soul to pieces. All my dreams are empty. I have no faith in anything but my own will. And yet, as I write this I am sure I won't live long enough to experience any of them.

Chad Clifton

Part I

All That Came Before

"You must have chaos within you to give birth to a dancing star."
Nietzsche

Chapter 1

Raising Chad was never an easy task, but it was always full of joy. He was born an old soul, and seemed to have a sense of the importance of life from the beginning. He was born without the ability to be oblivious. There was never a time when he wasn't trying to understand himself and the point of life. He was precocious and bright and engaging. He charmed everyone he met and soon became adept at getting his way even if it meant working hard for it.

At four years old he asked me when he could have a skateboard. I told him, when he learned to read. I was thinking in terms of a time frame. Chad saw it as an obstacle and set about overcoming it. Over the next months he taught himself to read on his own. I got him the skateboard. After that, Chad was rarely without reading material. He started his day with breakfast and a book. By fourth grade he had read all of Dickens. He loved reading, going from literature to sci-fi to history. The history of warfare captured his attention and he read every soldier's biography he could get hold of.

But Chad had been drawn to all things military long before he puzzled out the letters that made the words that told the stories. Hearing the theme song for the TV show M.A.S.H. as a toddler would send him running to his Pop-Pop's lap. My Dad had gone to Korea at age seventeen, was wounded near Pyong Yang in a mortar attack and spent several months in Walter Reed Medical Center recovering. I rarely heard him talk about the war, but he and Chad rarely missed an episode.

As time passed it was other shows about war. Almost all of them were inappropriate for his age. He begged to be allowed to watch Platoon and I only agreed when Rich said he'd watch it with Chad. The Rolling Stone's "Paint it Black" had been his favorite song as long as I can remember. G.I. Joes were his favorite toys. He had hundreds of plastic Army men that he and Ryan would spend hours playing with in the backyard or vast dirt-clod bases in the farm fields. Years later we still find them.

It wasn't obsession. Chad's interests were many and varied, but it was a constant theme. It never wavered.

In fifth grade Chad met Rob and they remained best friends for all of Chad's life. Rob was also interested in all things military and also very bright. It was in ode to their epic battles that Chad wrote "Plastic Men", his first real short story. Written in pencil on notebook paper, it hasn't survived the years very well.

Plastic Men

"Commence Fire!" The small group of army men opened fire upon the three year old cat, Tails.

With a leap and slash from her long white claws, three of the small green army men were knocked over and one had a small gash on the helmet. Invisible little bullets pounded the black and white fur of the cat, making her retreat back to the litter box.

"Back to plastic men! Someone's coming!" Screamed Sergeant.

"Chad, I thought I told you to get these army men off my kitchen floor!" yelled his mother in a most exasperated tone as she entered the room.

"Coming Mom," Chad rushed in to gather the army men into a small fishing box, "I wonder how they got in here," he thought to himself, not remembering when he could have placed them there.

"One more thing," Mom said, "stop terrorizing that cat."

"But Mom, I…" he never finished his sentence because he would only get in more trouble for talking back.

Once he got to his room, he shut the door and began taking inventory of the men. With some glue, he managed to fill in the gash on the helmet of one man who was in the kitchen battle.

Chad was 12 years old, about 4'7" and had short dark brown hair. He was advanced for his age, and he and a friend, Robert, collected army men. Together they formed a sort of chess game with them and came together for an annual battle of strategy. He and Robert wanted to be career military.

§

The middle of his story has faded. I hadn't looked through Chad's school things in years and by the time I did it was lost. The summer after he was killed, we were going through his room, deciding what to store, when I found it. It was the ending I found hardest to take.

§

There was a ripping sound, and then a heap of cloth fell upon the men. A paratrooper medic had been caught in a tree above and just now came loose landing on the men. He administered some antiseptic to the sergeant's wound and managed to stop the plastic flow.

That afternoon, Chad found the men, gave the other three a proper burial sensing they were dead from their numerous wounds and light green color. They were also in a curious position Chad always wondered about.

Later that day after Chad had won, he held a medal ceremony for the seven men that showed valor and courage. The Sergeant lived on for many more prosperous years as a head officer in Chad's army.

Fifteen years later that same box was passed on to his first son whose exploits are still talked about today on the lips of every army man created.

§

As Chad grew, his interest in history and warfare never waned. In order to support him, we tried to learn along with him. If he was to make this decision, it would be an informed one. We visited the USS Yorktown in Charleston, SC when he was nine. His response to all the memorabilia and displays was mature and solemn. He took the time to read the letters and ponder the personal effects of those who had served in WWII. A couple of years later, we took him to Arlington National Cemetery. It was important to us that he understand where the road he was determined to go down could lead. It was there that Rich and I had a glimpse of a future we wanted to avoid. Chad had wandered ahead of us about thirty yards. He was completely absorbed. He stopped and turned a slow circle, taking in the rows and rows of stones naming so many fallen soldiers. For a second the world shifted. Had I glimpsed the future or just my fear? I looked at Rich and he took my hand. We didn't say a word. The whole thing had shaken me. Later I talked to Chad.

"I don't want you to die in a war, Chad."

"Can't say that I won't, Mom."

"I don't want the damned flag, Chad. If you get killed, you just tell them to keep it. I won't take it."

"No Momma. You have to take the damned flag!" It was a conversation we repeated countless times.

The War in Vietnam and the American culture surrounding it seemed to attract Chad most of all. He read everything about it that he could get his hands on, and we talked about it often. I told him of the impressions I could remember from my childhood and he educated me on the facts I was too young to have picked up on. The Vietnam War wasn't something I had ever studied. Perhaps being so close in time it wasn't a subject covered in depth by any history class in school. Chad taught me quite a bit. My opinion in the beginning was shamefully uneducated. I had no real grasp of either the history or the politics.

I was whole-heartedly against the draft. One day we were discussing draft dodgers. Chad's opinion of those guys was exceedingly low. I told him I wouldn't have gone if I were drafted. It wasn't a just war, or a war for survival like WWII. It was wrong. Chad was appalled. I'll never forget the look he gave me. I had shocked him. His answer was just as stunning for me, because it wasn't something I had ever considered before and it changed everything for me. He looked at me very seriously, straight in the eye, and said, "If you didn't go, someone else would have to go in your place. Could you live with that?"

Much of Chad's middle school years passed as they do for most adolescents. He studied Tae Kwon Do, played paintball, joined the wrestling team. Life was good. Our family was solid and we were happy.

At the end of seventh grade, Chad got his first dose of politics. He had been accepted as a Student Ambassador and was to spend most of his summer in Europe studying other cultures and systems of government. We thought if he was eventually going to go out into the world as a soldier he should see it first as a peacemaker. He thought he could bring back some of what he had learned and benefit his school, so he campaigned and wrote a phenomenal speech. I snuck in the back of the auditorium to watch him deliver it. He was great! Then his opponent came to the microphone and spoke one line. "If you elect me, I'll get a milkshake machine in the cafeteria." Chad lost the election and all interest in politics. I told him he shouldn't give up and he laughed. "I don't ever want to be the kind of person that can win an election, Mom. I want to do something that matters."

When Chad went to high school he joined the JROTC. He was the shortest kid in school and had to have a uniform ordered for him. He didn't care. He was so glad to be on his career path, and he and I had finally reached an agreement. He was going to get a college degree before he got shot at. That meant either an Academy or a ROTC program at a University. He had the brains and the grades. He was well rounded and physically strong. He was on track to get what he wanted, and I had bought time for him to think it all through.

The JROTC program offered opportunities to explore, so he took advantage. He joined the rifle team and the raider team, and involved himself in every activity he could. I had hoped getting to play soldier would get some of it out of his system. I was wrong. His first summer camp for the program was at Ft. Indian Gap. He was fourteen.

§

JROTC CAMP VIGILANCE
Cadet Chad Clifton
Days 1-4

These last 4 days have been hard, but I'm not quitting. We run a good deal... hmm... a lot, but I'm getting stronger.

I'm tired, I'm cold, and ticked off, but I can function. The drill instructors seem to find it funny that I am so short, and yet, I act 10ft tall. They talk to me and say weird stuff, like "I told you not to come back." So, I reply, "Sorry, Sergeant, I just can't get enough." They love that kinda' stuff.

Sleep deprivation, food I can't taste, more running, muscle failure, dumb leaders, yet so much easier to deal with than grades in school. I'm eatin' it up.
Cadence: A is for Airborne
            I is for In the sky
            R is for Rangers
            B is for Born to die

June 21, 2000
23:00 Zulu

What's my mental state right now? I can't really say. I could be over the edge, but I'm starting to like the push-ups, the running, and the pain. I know I'm alive when my arms strain and my muscles fail, when my legs are burning and a Sergeant is screaming in my ear.
There is a big difference between my spiritual warrior self and my physical soldier. The warrior screams, "Rage, push harder!" and the practical soldier groans, "Short cut?"
I'm a changed person, now. I don't wanna go back. I think this is something I've gotten the most out of. Most blow by it as a cool deal, but I've taken it seriously.

Mom, Dad, Ryan,
Hi guys! I miss you over here. Camp is tougher than you would think. You should see the muscle definition I have now (thanks to 600+ sit-ups).
The company I'm in is Charlie Company. We are the best. Alpha and Bravo might as well drop out now.
I've gotten used to military wake-up calls, but I still want to smash that stupid bugle. It's true what they say, that the military gets more done by 7:00 AM than most people do all day.
How are you guys doing? Don't worry about me; I'm a military

machine now. Little sleep gives snappy reflexes. I don't even think too hard anymore. I eat this stuff for breakfast.

The mountains are really beautiful, but the weather is usually foggy or rainy.

Right now, I'm prepping our barracks for inspection, but they changed the linen (or rather we did) and we can't do anything else.

Later, we have raider challenge orienteering. Finish the course of finding markers in the fastest time. My team is mostly Raiders like myself, but we are trying to not have to take this asthmatic fat girl on the 3 mile hike/walk/run.

I have to fall in soon so I'm going to stop writing. This may or may not get to you in time for it to be relevant, but I just wanted to write.
Hi Ryan, I'll be home soon.

Love you, Chad

June 26, 2000

Haven't been able to write for a while. We went to Dorney Park (much fun) and came back to a paper bag lunch for dinner. After this delicate cuisine, Sergeant Karr decided to run us through the activities that we do tomorrow.

Sergeant Wishop tries to make camp fun, but I don't think Sgt. Karr wants anything but the win. I want it too, but not to the point of exhaustion when simple tasks become difficult.

Cadets who complain and cry and can't fall in should be shot or sent home, one or the other. They are driving me crazy. I want to do this, they don't. See my conflict?

When I get back, I'm going to have a real meal and stare at my own room.

I miss my family. I miss the food, the companionship, the lack of structure, and I miss being yelled at by sane human beings. Playing with Ryan, talking to Mom and Dad, and I think I remember something called entertainment. We do weird things here for entertainment; we sing and have push up competitions. We have cards to play with when we have the energy.

The rappel we did was fun. Jumping ten feet out and twenty feet down on a 65ft wall gives you a lot of confidence. The first step seems to be the hardest.

§

Chad only ever had one other goal in life besides being a warrior and that was being a writer. He constantly explored the world and looked inside himself and wrote about what he found. His tastes in literature ran the gamut. One day it would be Hemingway, the next Sun Tzu. He convinced his Honors English teacher to let them study Machiavelli's The Prince. He thoroughly enjoyed a good sci-fi novel. Nietchze competed with Kerouac for space on his bookshelf.

The summer he turned fifteen, he and Rob joined a writer's group comprised of professionals and serious amateurs. Meetings were held weekly at the coffee shop and bookstore where they worked in Dewey Beach. They were by far the youngest members, but were soon embraced by the group. They discovered they had real talent. It didn't take long for them to move on to visions of being the next Kerouac and Ginsberg. They were the new beatniks. Lattes and leather jackets. They were aiming at being the greatest literary minds of their generation. I had hope that this was a shift in direction for him and was thrilled. He soon disabused me of the notion. "I don't want to be a writer with no experiences. I want to be a great writer, but I have to live first."

Those days were the calm before the storm, and they were sweet. Endless summer days by the ocean, watching sunsets over the bay. Teenage nights on the boardwalk and all the time in the world.

§

In the following stories/reflections, the reader will find the clumsy, stumbling, beginnings and ends of countless would-be books.

The author reserves the right to a mature use of "flavored" language and the right to scrap unfavored characters with any act of wanton violence or well timed heart-failures.

Those seeking a psychological profile may indeed find a richly imaginative, darkly poetic, stunningly urbane, utterly suave, author but those Freudian idiots who think otherwise can indeed throw themselves into some dark, Stygian abyss. And no, that was not an outburst triggered by some repressed psychological fear of sexual inferiority. Humph…

Chad Clifton

WARRIOR SHADOWS

The sharp, pungent odor of Cordite fills the jungle, accompanied by a rough staccato of small arms fire, the harsh sound muffled by the soft pattering of rain on shiny green leaves.

Shouting. Half uttered screams of women and the desperate cries of wounded children. Cries dwarfed by the following detonation of a plastic explosive that obliterates the village.

Silence returns to the forest, a blanket of calm to smother the chaos of destruction. No bird calls for its mate; no frog croaks its throaty song, no animal dared to move from its hidden shelter.

Six shadows slither through the underbrush, barefoot, covered in war paint and mud, their muscular arms gripping the steel and plastic instruments of their trade, the objects both foreign and familiar to the war torn forest. A column of smoke trails behind them, and a knife snakes out from a battered sheath to slash the thin monofilament wire that would have shattered the silence in another hellfire explosion.

God himself couldn't disrupt the wordless synergy of these solemn warriors as they slip quietly into the murk of the river Styx. Bodies clad in tattered camouflage and olive drab bandanas, laden with ammunition and grenades, move effortlessly into the water, barely rippling its obsidian surface, a mirror for the professional murder carried in their souls.

Possessed by demons, these soldiers live their own legend. The men with green faces have gone to war.

§

"Erin " was Chad's first attempt at a novel, which he worked on as part of his writer's group. He wrote and discarded many chapters. These are what remain. What is marked as Chapter 5, though numbered by Chad, does not appear to be meant to follow Chapter 4 and is set much later in the story.

§

ERIN

Erin-Chapter 1 Introductions

Stubs of candles hiss and pop, wax dripping slowly to the gray cement floor where several figures huddle over legal pads and tattered leather-bound books.

One of the figures looks up at the sound of boots near the doorstep. Several hard thumps, muted as if the knocker is wearing heavy gloves, resound off the thick wooden door.

"Martin, get the door." A small, composed man in his thirties, Duncan McDougal glances up at a co-worker and gestures with his glacier blue eyes and a slight nod towards the door. He runs a hand through his matted red hair and rubs his weary eyes, glad of an excuse to look away from the parchment unrolled in front of him.

A dark hooded figure glides forcefully into the room, unhindered by a startled Martin, shaking the snow from his heavy cloak. "Hello, brother."

"Erin." Duncan's mouth seems to drop away from the rest of his skull, hanging open in shock at the apparition before him.

The figure pushes back the drenched cloak, soaked from the raging snowstorm outside, revealing a pair of disarming emerald eyes and closely cropped black hair.

"Good to see you alive." It was all that Duncan could say, their differences rising up like demons between them.

"And you," Erin's deceptively smooth voice matched his wiry figure, muscled, but not what one could call large or dominating. His very presence in a room commanded attention, for no other reason than he seemed to exude confidence and character, something his thin, waspish brother secretly despised him for.

"I have come to ask a favor..." Erin's voice trailed off with the note of a snake charmer putting a serpent to sleep, a maneuver designed to soothe and quiet the room, full as it was with scholars. Even the candles seemed to cease their angry snapping.

"Yes?' Duncan had certain immunity to his brother's mesmerist tricks. One must remind oneself, he thought bitterly, the man is only human, however much he would have us believe otherwise.

Erin watched, his gaze cold, as Martin closed the door and sat down next to a severe looking girl, who appeared to be in her twenties. He winked at them both.

"Yes?" Duncan repeated.

Erin beckoned to the girl and asked her name as she came to stand next to him.

"Sarah, this is very important. Do you know what language this is in?" Erin withdrew a small book from the folds of his cloak, wrapped in oilskin, journal sized, obviously very old, and turned to one of the hand-written pages.

"Of course," She leaned closer to see the writing. "Aramaic." She pronounced, somewhat triumphantly.

"Let me see that." Duncan snapped, grunting as he got off the cold floor and stood next to them, glaring at Sarah as if she had committed some heinous crime by not deferring to him first. "Yes," he said, confirming the startled girl's statement. "That is Aramaic."

"Thank you." Duncan was genuinely grateful, immediately spying the quality of the pages, scanning the text within.

"Yes, I... "Erin cut off his sentence and glanced over his shoulder, his gaze drifting outside into the snow. He reached for the door and eased it open.

"Shut the door, Erin." Duncan was becoming nervous.

Two men in white uniforms with gold trim and embroidered crosses appeared in the doorway behind Erin, their finery dulled by the damp.

"Good evening, Mr. McDougal. You act so brave, yet still you run from Gods will." One of the soldiers jibed from behind the stock of an assault rifle.

"Not very clever are you? All that time to think, and there you are, and here I am, and that's all you could think of?" Erin's back was still turned away from the two soldiers, his hands hidden in the folds of his thick cloak.

"You arrogant little-" As the soldier raised his rifle to hit Erin in the head, a small knife blade flicked out of Erin's cloak, a crimson stain spreading across the soldier's uniform just above the heart.

The second man never drew his pistol, an arrow protruding from his back, the soldier dying in silence, surprise lingering in his lifeless eyes.

"Thank you, Luke." Erin spoke softly to the figure emerging from the trees, bearing a crossbow in his arms.

Luke nodded silently as he disappeared with the two bodies.

"Get out!" Duncan shook with rage, everyone's attention focused on him.

"But, Duncan, I- "Erin looked hurt, his grin wiped away.

"Duncan…" A pretty, blonde female reached out to calm him.

"Out!" Duncan screamed again.

"Fool. Sit here, brother, wasting your life. Write a book, damn you, do something. Tell your theories to the world, risk something for once. Would mother want you to waste away in this infernal basement? Would she like that?"

Erin lashed out at Duncan, reminding him of their pagan mother and her love of life and human experience. He knew this would hurt Duncan more than anything else.

"I see." Duncan had sobered quickly, his spirit wounded.

"No, you don't." Erin turned and disappeared into the storm.

Erin-Chapter 2

A frantic techno-dance mix pulsed its way through the club, a giant mosh pit, writhing it's own path through the night. Glow sticks and strobe lights confused the seething mob of party-goers, allowing Erin to lose himself in the music.

One arm around a pretty girl in a tight, black leather miniskirt, another hand in the air, Erin moved with the rhythm of her body and the waves of sound that pounded in his ears.

He did not think, but let his body take over. Time was of no matter. He was not hungry, not thirsty, had no where to go. He could party for days.

Hands on Celia's thin waist, he steered her towards the crowded bar through the frantic mob, now jumping and grinding to a Moby tune.

"Vodka shot and a margarita with salt." He ordered the overworked bartender's assistant. It was hard to hear, but that was the point, Erin realized.

Draining his shot glass, he paid for the drinks and left to lose himself in the crowd, but Celia held back.

"What?" Erin wanted to go back, not drink himself to death.

"You want to go back to my place?", she yelled, but it came out a whisper in the pulse of techno and funk.

"Damn straight." Might be good, he thought, I need to relax.

Outside, they hopped on Erin's black ninja bike and drove to her apartment on the outside of London.

Her apartment was more of a suite; she worked as a waitress on an expensive yacht for a rich eccentric who liked room-service and dark-haired females.

"I don't feel very tired. I'm going to get a shower, okay? Erin, honey?"

Erin appeared from behind a decorative pillar in the living room. He had been in flats before, even owned one across town, but the small steps leading down to a mess of cushions, squared in by four pillars, facing a huge picture window with a view of Thames… it was too much.

"Okay… go ahead." This was a trap, it had to be. She was making this way too easy for him. She could just be easy, he thought, but the apartment was ridiculous.

Celia's nude body dripped water on the stone tiled floor as she emerged from the steaming shower. Her long black hair hung plastered to her back and ample, supple breasts. Her soft skin was white and damp, starting to develop bumps in the cold air.

Wrapping a towel around her shoulders, she stepped out into the dark, richly appointed master bedroom.

The towel dropped away as she slid into Erin's warm embrace. Falling on top of him on the silk bed covers, she felt a cold barrel press against her temple as a strong hand gripped her waist to him.

She felt a momentary urge to scream, but fought it off. Years of reporting had tempered her nerves to an edge harder than most men.

"Well, that's different." Celia attempted humor, to lighten the situation.

"I thought I knew you. You're with CNN, huh?" Erin's face remained cold and impassive.

"I'm just the pawn-" Celia was stopped short.

"In a game for how many? Not just for two, no, you couldn't afford this by yourself."

"No one else knows, I swear. It's a friend's flat, I just wanted to borrow it for a little while." She feigned innocence, her hand moving across his taught stomach muscles.

"Wrong. Try again." Erin rolled over, pinning her with his weight.

"I want to know one thing, Erin McDougal. Why did you blow the Vatican?

"Now, now… are you always in a rush?" Erin saw his advantage and would use it.

"Tell me, and I'll tell you whatever you want to know."

"Would you believe it was a botched job?"

"Come again, Erin?" His eyes glimmer, even in the darkness, Celia thought.

"The job was botched. We didn't do it… not directly."

Erin-Chapter 3

A thin black cord dropped from an ornate silver grate in the stone ceiling of the Vatican libraries. Row upon row of immense book shelves lined the walls and formed a labyrinth of the gray slate floor.

Erin was chilled beneath his black cargo pants, combat boots and the black knee-length trench coat he wore over an army green T-shirt. Strange, he noticed, it's not damp. It must be climate controlled, reason told him, but the obvious use of technology bothered him.

Erin dropped to the floor first, holding a bag packed with ammunition and a gray crossbow for quickly and silently retiring unwanted observers.

The four other men followed behind, dressed as Erin, covered in black. Michael was the youngest, tall and skinny, raised by nuns in an orphanage. His reason for participating was based on a simple belief that knowledge should be placed highest. He was the scholar in the raiding party.

The others toted snub-nosed assault rifles, all of them hardened veterans who now worked for Erin's private military corporation. Each had been chosen for their background in intelligence, and loyalty, whatever the situation. They were all orphans like Michael, anonymous to the world. No one would miss them if things went wrong.

In reverence, they stood in awe for several minutes, running their gloved fingers over the centuries old manuscripts. As they began to creep along the rows of books, heading towards a large, illuminated dome in the ceiling, several men began packing books into their duffel bags, removing ammunition and placing it in pockets.

Erin stopped, signaling with a hand motion, stopping the column and bringing the men back into reality. Now fully alert once more, safeties clicked off and magazines were loosened in pouches. All had heard the footsteps and odd humming.

Pedin sat in his study, writing the eulogy for Pope Claudius. The poor old man had days to live; perhaps hours before the cancer that racked his frail body would consume him.

He looked down in grief at the blank paper before him, wondering what one could say about the death of a Pope; like the death of a God. He was a god, really. He sat in his pristine city, worshipped and revered by the starving commoners that huddled around the gates, hoping for the blessing that would allow their souls entrance to Heaven. Yes, a god.

Maybe he wasn't so real for the people who were not near him. Catholics in America are more removed than those in Russia, or those small numbers in China, who lived and died for the banned religion everyday. Even the mixed cultures of South America, half a world away from the Vatican, practice Catholicism with more fervor than American Catholics. Americans are their own gods.

Pedin's thoughts had begun to wander as one of his robed aides walked reverently through the door. It was James. Pedin couldn't stand the gossipy little twit.

"Yes?"

"Archbishop, your eminence," James began, flatteringly. The title of 'eminence' was usually reserved for the Pope. "We missed you at supper."

"I am fasting. Get to the point."

"Yes, your holiness," James' face wrinkled up and his lips drew tight, as if about tasting something bitter. "Forgive me if I speak falsely, b-but this is what was told to me."

"Please, do get on with it James. I have work to do. Consider yourself forgiven and go on." Pedin was quickly becoming annoyed.

"Your reverence, a manuscript has just been uncovered in the libraries… written in early Aramaic. The scholars have said…" James stopped briefly. "The scholars have said that it is very old and…" James paused again, melodramatically.

"They say that it is signed by Joshua." He finished the last sentence so quickly that Pedin asked him to repeat himself.

"Joshua, sir. It is signed by Joshua."

Pedin studied James' face for a minute, looking him seriously in the eye. "Are you sure?"

"That is what was said, sir."

The Archbishop folded over in hysterics. "Oh, that's great, James. That is very rich." Pedin struggled to regain his breath, bursting into fits of laughter between sentences.

"Sir?"

"Oh, James," Pedin recovered from his laughing attack, sitting upright at his desk. "James… poor boy. You have played the fool. What is today's date?"

"It is December the twelfth, Archbishop Pedin." James face reddened, obviously left out of some exclusive joke.

"Yes, dear boy, it is. It is a joke that the scribes play every Christmas. You see…" Pedin told James about a tradition in the church and sent him away.

My, he thought to himself, that was quite the close call. No matter. The manuscript was probably a fake… probably. Pedin got up and walked to the Pope's chambers, his mind weighing heavily on the subject.

Archbishop Pedin knelt; palms pressed together, wrinkled face set in mock concentration as if in prayer. Truthfully, Pedin was praying, not for the life of a dying Pope, but for forgiveness. Why, he thought, should I need forgiveness in carrying out God's will? The answer came to him instantly. Because, he chided himself, because I am not without ambition.

Pedin was deeply disturbed as he entered the Pope's spartan chambers, adorned only with a rosary hanging on a peg by the bedside, a small writing desk, and the bed on which a frail old man lay dying.

"Pedin, true son." Pope Claudius murmured. An interesting term, Pedin thought as he crossed himself and knelt beside the bed. True son. How touching. "I must tell you about Fredrick."

"Yes, I know. I shall take the best care of him, though I think you are not so far from meeting again, you know. None of us are growing younger."

Fredrick was Claudius's truest friend, an aging, unassuming mute priest that worked diligently in the Vatican library, cataloguing the countless unread books and documents stored there, transcribing them excitedly whenever something new was found, bringing it loyally to the Pope. "He will retire soon, I think."

"No…" The frail man rasped, his cancerous lungs rattling. "You must protect him from the One."

Pedin rarely cursed, especially in public, but he almost did so now. Yes, he knew what Claudius meant, however ominous. Only an hour ago, after dinner, did the report reach his ears. Bound in oilcloth, written in Aramaic, scribes had found a journal, rumored already to be of great importance. Pedin had passed it off as trash, the kind of forgery that was seen everyday, more heretic slander to him. The old Pope's wits had not fled with his health, and it worried him that Claudius was so concerned.

"The One we talked about." Pedin inquired. He began to doubt the Pope's sanity, a sad realization that after years of intelligent rationalization and pious duty, even one so strong as Claudius could lapse into senility. He spoke of the Antichrist.

"Everything will be fine, Claudius. Speak no more of it. I will see him right away." Pedin bade the Pope a long, solemn farewell, kissed his ring, and left the room damning his luck.

Slipping between two shelves, Erin raised the crossbow and braced it on another bookcase, peering intently into the scope, ready to kill the unsuspecting visitor.

Sitting in a large, wooden chair, behind an even larger oak desk, a frail old man in faded robes scribed away at something in front of him, an intense look on his wrinkled face.

Erin's finger tensed on the trigger. He had just clicked off the safety when the relic suddenly looked up, eyes wondering at the apparition before him.

The crossbow jumped with released tension, pinning him to the chair. He gurgled once as his mouth fell open. He did not scream because he had no tongue, no doubt removed to keep silent his vast knowledge pertaining to this place.

"Let's go!" Erin pulled back, eyes lingering on the grotesque scene. Quickly, he ran up and snatched the two books the man had been working on so intently, turning away to speak to his men.

"Sir, you'll exit first." Donahue, a dark-haired Irishman like Erin, both stated and inquired of his superior officer.

"I'll excuse your insolence, Donahue, but I prefer to leave last, thank you." Erin grinned. They played this silly, amateur game every time. Amateur, Erin knew, but a show of loyalty nonetheless. He would stop that next time.

Michael piped in. "Sir, I think you should go first, seeing as we have the good weapons." He gestured with his gun.

Erin smiled at Michael's use of "Good weapons", but he thought he heard boots scuffle close by. He would go first and scout the way into the city. It was the only way his men would move.

Erin climbed up the rope, entering the stone sewers no longer used in Vatican City. The rest of the team could use their GPS gear to get out, and Erin would scout the way.

He walked for about five minutes, pausing occasionally; to make sure he had not heard gunfire below.

Erin had just removed his crossbow from his back when the shock wave hit, knocking him flat. Erin smashed his forehead violently against the stone, barely hanging on to consciousness.

The heat wave followed, singeing his body and pushing him into a wall, bits of debris floating in the air. Ash, paper, and crumbled stone-dust filled the passage, choking him.

Shivering with sudden cold, he clutched his bundle to him, pain throbbing in his forehead, memories of Michael's youthful face and the smiles of Donahue and the others, playing in his mind. Erin cursed himself as the darkness seeped into his brain, a welcome escape from reality.

Erin-Chapter 4

Bailey's Tavern was in an uproar, occupants yelling curses and arguing at a television perched above one corner of the bar.

"Shut up, or go home!" Pete Bailey bellowed over the din, quieting the crowd with only a few murmured curses in his direction.

An emergency newscast had interrupted the Friday night rugby game.

"About nine o'clock this evening," a mild female voice played over scenes of smoke and wreckage. "A small explosion shook the Vatican complex. A small portion collapsed in on itself, destroying a small park and lightly damaging nearby buildings, shattering glass windows and setting ablaze an underground storeroom believed to have housed precious religious relics."

"The explosion is rumored by some to be an accidental gas explosion caused by the build up of sewer gases in tunnels that run underneath this area, though the extent of the damage seems centered to one locality."

"Others," The voice continued. "Blame protestant radicals protesting the build up and escalation of the political situation in Northern Ireland by Cardinal Pedin, who has officially begun to raise a volunteer militia in Ireland to support the IRA. The Pope sanctioned this action several weeks ago, after an altercation between IRA protestors and English police.

"Still no word from the Vatican itself..." Bailey muted the volume as the newscast signed off and surrendered their attentions to Rugby.

"Damn," Bailey thought out loud, taking a long swig from his mug and staring off into the crowded bar. "It's begun."

Erin-Chapter 5

The war was over.

Erin hung his head between his knees, cramped in the darkness of the ship's hold, alone with the rats and smuggled cigars, the cocaine and the untaxed coffee.

Dark, humid air, heavy with the smell of decay filled the mercenary's lungs. He tried to focus on his breathing, afraid to stop because he might forget to start again.

A voice from someplace deep inside the folds of his memory called to him. His mother's voice, from a time long ago forgotten, a childhood Erin did not remember. A simple scene played out in his head: dinner in a tidy kitchen, a summer time breeze passing like spirits through the house. His mother had loved fresh air.

Erin awoke suddenly, jolted out of his reverie by a change in direction and speed. Over the dull throb of the engines, he could hear voices on the deck above.

Painfully, Erin stood up, stretching his back against a steel bulkhead. He checked the date and his small corner with the dull illuminated face of his wristwatch for the hundredth time.

Erin's perception of place and time was horribly skewed, passing in and out of consciousness for the first week of his two week voyage on the oil tanker Tal from the east coast of Brazil, through the Panama Canal, to where he was headed, Puerto de Sole, on the western coast of mainland Mexico.

The ship had finally slowed to under five knots. The ex-marine found his thigh length wet suit and rubber bag with his only remaining possessions, climbing the steel rung ladder three stories to freedom.

"War challenges virtually every other institution of society-the justice and equity of its economy, the adequacy of its political systems, the energy of its productive plant, the bases, wisdom and purposes of its foreign policy."
Walter Millis

Chapter 2

Chad had spent his lifetime preparing for war, not just a military career. It didn't matter that the world seemed peaceful and secure. He was going. We knew he would. We had no idea how it would come to pass.

The morning of September 11, 2001 was as beautiful as they come. Rich and I had our coffee out on the deck, savoring the last of summer. There wasn't a cloud in the sky. We weren't even aware that the World Trade Center had been hit until we came in and I turned on the computer. I thought at first the news was wrong, it couldn't be what it seemed. Turning on the television we saw the second plane fly into the tower. Amidst the horror playing out on the screen in front of us, it seemed my mind separated into categories of *Oh my God*, and *What this means for the World, What this means for our Country. What this means for Chad*. I looked at Rich and said, "Nothing will ever be the same again."

This meant war. It came like a bolt from a perfect blue sky.

Twenty minutes away at his high school in a beautiful little historic town by the Atlantic Ocean, Chad was in the first days of his junior year. Watching the coverage he turned to Rob and said "Looks like this is my war." Nothing would ever be the same again.

When he stepped off the bus that day he was angry. The administration at the school had switched television coverage away from the attacks to avoid upsetting the students. Coming up the driveway his frustration burst out. "Just who in the hell do they think will be fighting this war?"

It was only a few weeks later that Chad took part in the National Youth Leadership Forum for Defense and Intelligence in Washington, DC. The forum is a gathering of some of the finest young minds in America with an interest and aptitude in protecting our national security. Our country was still in the early days of trying to assimilate the tragedy. It was strange to be driving him through the city to attend the forum. The Capital, the

Washington Monument, we had seen them many times. It was different seeing them now. The Pentagon still showed its blackened wound. Chad was pissed. In the days that followed, excellent opportunities were offered by the representatives of the CIA, FBI, Defense Department and others. They fell on his very deaf ears.

It was Quantico that captured his full attention. He called home full of the experience. He joked after spending the day with Marine Snipers, "Mom, they're short and weapons-obsessed just like me." It was playful, but he was telling me he had found what he was searching for. When he came home, something had changed in him.

The rest of his junior year he was restless. His grades slipped. He completely blew his AP History class. I was furious. History came so easily to him. I didn't know until much later that the rebellion was two pronged. Firstly, his teacher had called him out in front of the whole class as a warmonger. She was apparently anti-military; consequently anti-Chad. Secondly, he had found a way out of the deal. It didn't matter that he was in line to attend the Naval Academy in Annapolis. He had figured a way out of the deal we had made. If he made himself ineligible, he could sign up as a grunt Marine. He didn't want the war to be over before he got there.

I was blown away at his stupidity. He was disappointed in my inability to understand. We fought loudly and often. After several months of it, I was exhausted and he was desperately unhappy. He played lacrosse, worked his job at the coffee shop and bookstore, and hung out with friends, but he had changed. When summer came and he didn't snap out of it, I finally confronted him.

"I don't know how to help you or even what's really wrong," I said.

"I have to do this, Mom, and you and Dad don't get it. You've always been there for me, and now when it matters, you're not."

Just after his seventeenth birthday, Chad announced that he'd asked a Marine Recruiter to come to the house. Being quite naïve of the process, I thought he was coming to provide Chad with information on the Marines. Chad already had all the details he cared to know. He wanted in on the delayed entry program and for that he needed our consent and our signatures.

Sgt. Green arrived and gave his presentation. He touted the educational package, showed us brochures. He began talking specifics about the various jobs available to Chad, Military Operational Specialties. I could see where Chad was herding us and I wasn't going there. Not infantry.

"Sgt., have you seen any of Chad's test scores? His SAT or his ASVAB?" I asked. If looks could kill.

"No ma'am, I haven't."

If Chad hadn't been so mad with me his expression would have been comical, but he was livid. I explained to them both that there was no way

I was signing anything yet.

"Once you've looked at his scores, come back and we'll talk some more."

When Sgt. Green returned, Gunnery Sgt. Wally came with him. They had checked the test scores and were honestly intrigued as to why Chad was choosing this entry into the Corps. It was obvious he had choices.

"We've got plenty of trigger fingers, son; we need your brain." said Gunny.

We looked again at the possibilities. It took a third visit before he chose Public Affairs as his MOS.

I was happy because he'd be writing speeches for Admirals, serving his country with the words that came so easily to him. He was already seeing himself as a war correspondent, M16 and a camera.

"But remember", said Gunny, "Every Marine is an infantry man first."

I looked at Rich and nodded. This was as close as we'd get to keeping him safe. Chad would do this with or without us. We said okay, and Chad beamed. I understand now the reason for that smile. He knew we were behind him and he was wise enough to know how important that unconditional support would be, to all of us.

It was signing the papers that made all the difference. He signed his name and his world changed. We signed ours and the weight of it lifted from his shoulders. Now he could do what he needed to do and he had us behind him.

The relief of going unhindered in the direction he was pulled made him buoyant. He had his senior year and he used it. He had a new job at an internet café, his friends, his car. He began to train physically and worked hard with his trainer, Rick. It seemed he threw himself full force into everything, making sure he paid attention so he could remember. At the same time he was in a holding pattern. He was biding his time till his real life began and using the chance to try to understand what he was leaving behind.

Over the course of that year we watched the build up to war in Iraq. This would be his war.

§

Instant Message Conversation between Chad and Rob
Early September 2002

a random soldier: hey man.

It's Rob: Yo! What's up?

a random soldier: Sippin a latte (organic soy of course). Listening to
                  Oakenfold.

It's Rob: techno?

a random soldier: What else would it be? Chill out techno though… Very
                  artsy. LOL

It's Rob: ha-ha… Goes with the soy, huh… Sorry, Organic soy.

a random soldier: better

It's Rob: Guess who I'm going to see on Friday.

a random soldier: Who?

It's Rob: Incubus.

a random soldier: Ew. Loathsome, over produced noise incorporating
                  nothing but Melodrama and rappish 3 chord
                  melodies…

It's Rob: Bravo! That was good, Chad.

a random soldier: Feeling pretty contemplative. I just produced the
                  coolest, most thought out techno song in the world.
                  It's got vocals, a killer chill progressive beat… I just
                  have to talk Char into doing the vocals for me, cause
                  female vocals are bangin'. I think I have a future as a
                  dj.

It's Rob: Or a bullet sponge. He he… I like that phrase… you just want
          her to be bangin, Chad.

a random soldier: That would be a nice side effect of the E. and the music
                  and my talents for both… That's why ex and sex
                  rhyme.

It's Rob: hahahahahah Beautiful.

a random soldier: I feel like I'm having an enlightened day… rainy
                  outside… feeling lucid.

It's Rob: Pre-Cal in front of me, feeling trapped. See also: doomed,

It's Rob: fucked.

a random soldier: You'll never smile again?

It's Rob: Yeah, probably.

a random soldier: Homecoming is October 4. I need to ask someone.

It's Rob: I'll go with you, Chad, we could make a statement.

a random soldier: But the whole subtle breakup of C and B might take a
                  couple weeks, if you work it from B's angle…

It's Rob: Just ask C.

a random soldier: and K turns me down like every time I ask her to go
                  someplace… I wonder why, cause she's the one that
                  initiated the hook up and I'm just trying to get back to
                  that… Small goals… Baby steps, man. Oh shit. I saw
                  One Hour Photo last night! Fucked up movie.

It's Rob: Really? I was gonna go see it. We saw Full Frontal instead. You
          like Coldplay much?

a random soldier: No. And Robin Williams was great in the movie. I still
                  don't understand it.

It's Rob: It looked super creepy.

a random soldier: But I think I liked it.

It's Rob: Still debating that?

a random soldier: Yeah. Andy liked it.

It's Rob: Who'd you all go with?

a random soldier: Me, Drew, Stephen, we saw Andy, Mark, Amy, etc…

It's Rob: ah… How are things? Life?

a random soldier: Things are pretty trippy here in DE… life is improving
                  with it's approach towards church dances and
                  Homecoming season…

It's Rob: Yeah? "Mellow, man, we've got ourselves a nice, mellow war
            today…"

a random soldier: Oh, and I bought a strobe light.

It's Rob: Oh.

a random soldier: That was cool.

It's Rob: It was… That's one of the greatest things said in that book.

a random soldier: Yeah. I think her Mom hates me. That book was cool. I
            love how we can carry 5 convo's at once…

It's Rob: Yeah we can. Why would she? Have you even ever talked to her?

a random soldier: I've talked to her… Apparently, K has let her in on
            some of our more… uh… sadistic conversations.

It's Rob: Oh, dude, that's not good.

a random soldier: Like, last years character bashing pieces…

It's Rob: That's worse.

a random soldier: Um, yeah, so I don't know if her mom… ah fuck it. I've
            always been in love with that girl cause she can control
            me and I've just gotten used to rejection from her. I've
            stopped caring if she returns it or not. It doesn't matter,
            'cause her reaction won't change anything.

It's Rob: That's very interesting, actually.

a random soldier: How so?

It's Rob: It just is.

a random soldier: I see it this way…

It's Rob: It's like you come back to it because it's familiar, almost
            comforting.

a random soldier: Yeah. It gives me purpose, right? I think so. It boils
            down to me having nothing to drive me, no ambition

a random soldier: that other people have, and it kind of gives me a reason
to shoot for something…

It's Rob: But why her? Because you know you can't have her?

a random soldier: Think, dude. I have no reverence for money cause my
parents have it. I don't want a career cause I hate
people with careers. I just want to find something that
means anything. Fuck me; I'm a merc in every sense.
I just need a cause bro.

It's Rob: I know how you feel, It's like that here… everyone seems to be
on that divine path to success, they're taking the steps and
trotting the trots, neither of them having any notion of where
they're dancing, or with who, or why.

a random soldier: See, but I don't do that. I don't claim to be a rebel in
any romantic sense, but I don't have an objective and
I'm not naive enough to find religion and I'm too smart
for life in the food chain. So if I waste away with drugs
and music or a broken heart, at least I can say that I was
devoted to something… Know what I mean?

It's Rob: That's very interesting. Yes, I know exactly what you mean.

a random soldier: So I keep going back to her, not because I'm "in love"
with her or even that I find her attractive. I just need
something to hold me in bounds, a kind of sanity
check. You've read Howl. I'm trying not to be one of
"the greatest minds of my generation… wasting away"
with insanity. Reality is blurred. I need something to
hold on to as real, even if it is painful. I think what I
feel for her is real. Nothing else matters because it's all
here, in the physical. She is real.

It's Rob: That's great, Chad, that's good stuff. You can really make
something out of that.

a random soldier: I hadn't thought of writing it down before now. Rob, do
you know why I started taking ecstasy?

It's Rob: Why?

a random soldier: I heard that it kills memory, a kind of amnesia. Kind of a random soldier: a self-med to stop thinking all the time.

It's Rob: You don't have anything that bad to have to forget, Chad.

a random soldier: I do nothing but think, though. It's not about
                  forgetting. That's the last thing I want to do. I just need
                  to be grounded in the here and now. That's why.

It's Rob: Why?

a random soldier: Because I stop thinking and just drift.

It's Rob: You just got sick of expectations, wanted something of your own
          but couldn't find a single god damned thing.

a random soldier: Do you know how that is? Just to stop, and appreciate
                  the false existence we all cling to. Just to be.

It's Rob: Very Zen.

a random soldier: I think it's no coincidence that we met, you and I. I
                  think we are the greatest of our generation. But I have
                  found my own fatal flaw; I will self destruct. You've got
                  to keep this in your head, so that if whatever happens
                  to me 10 years down the line keeps me from being
                  recognized someone has to know…

It's Rob: I won't forget you.

-The Best Progressive House Song In The World-

I dance and watch and watch you dance
Here next to me…

Wondering what it is you see
Your pupils the size of pills
In ecstasy
Dancing next to me

Your heroin eyes see what I can't see
You're long gone standing next to me…

Leave me far behind
Wondering
What it is you need

To stop the bleeding
And just...
When you've left it all behind
When you've out run all the pain
It catches up to you
And we fall like rain...

Nietzsche

"If you gaze too long into the abyss, the abyss also gazes into you." Rain beat down outside the dirty windows of the café, pounding a rough staccato on the tile roof and eroding the cobbled streets, just as it eroded everything in town. The names, the faces, the memories were washed away with every shot of Jose Cuervo and every night spent face down on a bar top.

"Who said that?"

"Nietzsche." Boyd coughed violently into his fist, a tremor enveloping his body. He sniffed and wiped his glasses on his shorts.

"We need to go home, man. This town was fun for awhile." Roy looked bleakly at his friend, eyes weighed down and looking distraught.

"For what? This place is purgatory, bro, judgment. Its here, its now, it's who we are. Part of the fucking system, assigned our little roles and our little emotions and our little meaningless choices that compose our tiny pathetic lives. Cogs in one larger, useless machine bent on self preservation." Boyd coughed again, not as hard this time.

He stood up from the scratched table and shuffled to the doorway, lighting his cigarette. He gestured wildly with the cigarette, illustrating some silent point to himself before clearing his throat and continuing. "Our lives are brief and futile. We are products of our environment, predestined by our surroundings to make the choices we think we make, just along for the ride when we think we're driving."

"You're drunk, cantigo."

"Not just us, not just here. What does Joe mother fucking computer technician, who lives his entire life in Pittsburgh, and works for some company providing tech support, ever live for? Satisfaction of a job well done? Simply to exist. We seek to avoid suffering but we persist in living. We pursue a false hope. Even with money or affluence we only abate suffering, only set aside mental anguish for a short time. Relief, without meaning."

"That's fucking cynical."

"Why do you think there's religion, Bro? We aren't born with it. At some point it was invented to keep us from wasting away. Look around you man. We live in a text book description of post modern era nihilism. We all know it doesn't count for shit. Some people accept it and move on, sidestepping the actual meaning and import of it all. See generation X. Extreme everything because there's relief in thrill, close to death.

Our quest for better narcotics is symptomatic of the same problem. They leave us blown away. The perfect drug is a pill that you swallow and forget who you are. Online gaming, virtual reality, same concept… all the clues are fucking here for us. The cards are on the table. All the cards are on the table. We want to burn ourselves out. We shouldn't be, my friend, we shouldn't be."

"Dude…"

"God is an abstract concept. God can't save us now. God never could. We're alone with each other. This gun in my hand, the round in the chamber… my impending death… pointless. As little effect as a grain of sand hurtling through space, perhaps less so. Where does time start, where does it end? We can not grasp infinity."

§

March came. The war began. Everyday we were tuned to CNN, watching bombs light up the night sky. We watched our military fly across the desert, meeting no resistance to speak of. Back home we had no idea that security was being sacrificed for speed. No one told us there weren't enough troops on the ground to make a peace. Our guys were headed to Baghdad, and there would be flowers in the streets. We had been through Desert Storm. It would be like that. Quick. Easy. We hadn't yet become familiar with the term insurgency. We hadn't grasped the horror of IEDs.

§

Journal Entry
April 5, 2003

These past few days have moved slowly. There's nothing to break the boredom. Lacrosse… a very temporary distraction. Short burst of aggression followed up by… work or going home.

Ironic, isn't it? That I, of all people, have nothing to do. I always imagined (don't we all) that my life would be brief and to the point. It probably will be. But I never imagined there would be so much wasted time between now and then. I mean, all I'm doing now is killing the days until I can get on with whatever is in my future. It's not that I hate where I am; quite the contrary. I love it, but there has to be more to it than this. A twelve year old could take my classes and do my job, it's that easy. So what's the point? I ask myself that all the time.

I used to fill this gap, this absence of meaning, by creating it and adoring this or that girl, despite any flaws. There was at least some factor of goals or achievement there. Something to think about, keep me focused, but that created its own problems.

Want. We all want something. To be happy. In the end, everything we do is to achieve happiness, through education, then the acquisition of wealth, then what in retirement? Who can say, but all we want, at any given point in our lives is happiness and meaning. Everything revolves around these points.

So my lifestyle is wanting of meaning. I have all the things I need... good family, money, decent car to go places in... but no one that I can feel close to, no one who's friendship is justification for staying. I stay because I have to. Don't get me wrong... I know lots of people, I have many friends and several close friends... but as far as I know they are people who I will probably never see again as long as I live and for the most part, I don't really care.

But there are always exceptions. They (the exceptions) would be my best friend, who I have known for half of my life and all of my important years, and one random individual thrown in near the end of my time here... the only two people I feel are capable of properly understanding me, and who understand time and how it's so valuable.

My best friend, away and off to school, departing early from this place, finding his meaning. The girl... nothing to me and everything to me at the same time. She's an enigma. I truly can not decide if she's a figment of my imagination that I subconsciously chose to fill my mental void, out of boredom and dependency, or if she might actually be the sign I was looking for... I know the connection, a sense of effortless, complete understanding is there... but I doubt myself. I could just think there's a connection because... no reason for that. In all aspects we mirror each other. I couldn't make this shit up if I was trying.

So where do I want it to go? I want it to end perfectly. As my last weeks creep ever closer, I want a brief, quiet, perfect day where we come to a perfect and absolute understanding of each other... two people, each one afraid for the other, to meet for the last time at the point of separation. For them to look into each others' eyes and see themselves. To know companionship, to know heartbreak, and overwhelming and total understanding... finding that perfect match and then leaving, never knowing if they will see each other again after the initial separation. I want us to be that way because I can see it happening, fate unfolding the master plan in front of our eyes, begging us to finish it, and to finish with style, this tender dance of life and aging and experience and death... it's waiting for us to step in and complete the masterpiece, the greatest love story and tragedy of all time, carried out unnoticed by the rest of the world. So now I'm asking... will she see it in time to let it run its course?

§

On April 10, 2003 the first soldier from Operation Iraqi Freedom to be buried at Arlington National Cemetery was laid to rest. Four days later, the first Marine from this war is buried there. The flag draped coffins were coming home, but our nation was not allowed to see them.

At the beginning of May, Chad was getting ready for his Senior Prom. We sat down to watch President Bush give a speech from the flight deck of the USS Lincoln. The country heard that our mission was accomplished. The President had said so. And he would know, wouldn't he?

Somewhere between prom and graduation Chad came to me and said he was going to try to get his leave date changed. He was scheduled to leave for boot camp just days after graduation. It sounded great to me. He would have a chance to enjoy a bit of summer before he left. What I didn't know was that it would cause him to lose his MOS and he could go into infantry. He, however, knew exactly what he was doing.

§

Journal Entry
Spring 2003

I don't remember when we first met. A few years ago of course but no specifics. Years passed quickly and we barely had a second thought about each other, friends by association with other friends.

But somewhere it shifted. One obscure weekend, a random night when we suddenly became aware of the wasted time. A connection, an unquestioning understanding for a few hours… things that would occur to me too late. This girl, who by accident or fate, had become an overnight best friend, she got it. It blew my mind.

So now with my remaining months counting down to weeks, I'm struck by the timing of her friendship. Why now? Of all the times to be making new friends, new people to trust… now isn't a good time.

There must be a reason. Some answer, something to learn from each other.

The potential is enormous. Life is short, especially mine, and I'm convinced the entire situation is set up to illustrate some principle if we open our eyes and look.

I've spent entire nights thinking, debating the point. It could be nothing. It could be everything. I've read philosophy, studied religion for awhile. Read up in psychology. The only words of wisdom I found were this; Humanity is a state of suffering. Everything we do for pleasure is punctuated by the misery of survival. We breathe not because we want to, but because it hurts too much not to. This principal applies to our entire lives. Education, success, material wealth… all symptoms of trying to be happy, to avert suffering…

With that new focus I reach my conclusion. We should stop looking at people objectively, ignoring their failings, and wonder what it is that they are looking for.

So why her? Why now? I didn't need to be here again… she scares the hell out of me. Sometimes she's a mirror for myself, other times a direct opposite. But the timing is uncanny. I'm so afraid right now, terrified in a way tanks and bullets will never touch… I want to run away, before I get myself hurt. Thirty more nights and I'm safe.

I've watched my death
A thousand times
In my nightmares
In my mind
But I stay here, still alive
Nothing can kill me
I know because I've tried
Born to hang
So I can't drown
I wish this ride were over
I'm so strung out

Don't touch me
My mind is fragile
I am so weak
Like porcelain
Can't stand on my own
I crave an addiction

I've watched my death
A thousand times
In my nightmares
The end of my life
But I'm still here
I'm still alive
Nothing will kill me
Because I've tried

Every night I pray for an end
But morning always comes
And I'm still in bed
So I get up and progress

Journal update
Spring 2003

This girl, a random snag in my otherwise welcome departure, a sudden and unexpected companion, who I will only know a short time…

She is nothing and everything to me. I've known her for years, mostly as an acquaintance, not really a friend… and now as we're counting down our months into weeks, our weeks into days… we recognize an odd connection, this unwelcome familiarity similar outlooks, same interests, compatible tasks… thrown in at the end where it should be a beginning; time is precious. And we hesitate.

Ocean Vignette

If the human experience is cyclic, and all things in time will come to repeat themselves, the value of the individual can only be judged by the changes in perception that mark point from point, beginning from end.

My first came as we stood listening to waves crashing into the jetty and the rain drops hitting the boardwalk. In turn, the three of us smiled or smirked or grinned, intensely aware of each other, linked by the stark reality of the moment. The smells of damp cigarettes and perfume mingled with salt on the frigid breeze.

Standing on that beach in the dead of winter, every sight and sound imprinting itself in my memory, I thought of Kerouac and his lost beat generation. Despite half a century of revolution and evolution, the spirit of youth remained unchanged.

He, she, and I were nothing new, but everything was new to us. We felt nothing original, but we felt it for the first time. We clung to that minute, that snapshot in time, in the place we had grown up because we were growing up and couldn't stop the change.

<u>Untitled</u>
Fell in love with this girl
She was my whole world
But we were just friends
And that was the end
That was the end of my world

Hill 656
Introductions

The reinforcements arrived around noon, ferried from some distant firebase by helicopter. They made a clean insertion to Hill 656, drawing only a few mortar attacks from the surrounding jungle.

Captain James Burheizt, referred to as Captain Jack by his soldiers, waited for the new platoon to set their gear down and settle in before he spoke to their lieutenant, who was busy trying to call back a Huey still carrying one squad's M-60.

"Problem, LT?"

"Sir, Lieutenant Mike Sanders, sir. We're just having a small issue… Well, a big issue with a fly boy who won't turn around and bring back our guns." Sanders looked flushed under his helmet.

"Give me that radio, please," Cpt. Jack took the handset from the young officer and began to reason with the chopper crew.

"Listen up you mother fuckers. You turn that bird around now and drop off those munitions or I will personally see to it that you fly deep reconnaissance missions from now on, clear: Maybe scope out some enemy gun emplacements for the grunts?"

The pilot quickly turned around and they could hear the distant thump of the chopper turning back.

"Welcome to Hill 656, soldier."

Chapter 1-Sunrise

Dawn came, especially stunning as the light filtered through the smog and jungle haze. The colored remnants of smoke grenades hung in the distance. Nick, Shader, and Leonard all sat on ammo cans, cooking breakfast as the sun came up, spilling light on the hill and over the valley below.

"Good morning, ladies." Lt. Sanders strode up to the trio, pulling his flack vest on over an olive drab shirt.

"Hey man, nice pants. I have some just like those." Shader cracked, the other guys giggling like little girls.

"Aw shit, you guys high already?" Sanders shook his head.

"Nah, lieutenant, we don't smoke no more, remember? We just hallucinate twenty four hours a day." This brought more laughter.

"I don't know if it's the stress of combat or the bug spray, but you people are some crazy mother fuckers." Sanders sat down on a can and took out a permanent marker.

"What's up, Lt?" Nick asked, sipping instant coffee from his canteen cup.

"Looks like we'll be here awhile. Digging in won't be a problem, though, cause we're pulling security for the Army Engineers," he held up his helmet, on which he had inscribed the words 'Born to Kill'. "And you're my personal fire team."

All three grunts fell into hysteria at Sanders helmet, a tribute to the 80's movie Full Metal Jacket, which every Marine in the Corps had seen at some point. Then they sobered up some, proud that their leader had chosen to "walk through the valley" with them.

The troops fell over laughing when Sanders pinned a peace symbol to his jacket.

Jungle Morning
Prologue

Fading smoke grenades cast a rolling red haze over the barbed wire, mud, and pungi sticks that separated Firebase Delta from the surrounding jungle, the only distinction between two identical and continuously embattled sides... In the morning they would count the bodies.

Chapter 1- Introductions

Jungle mornings brought back heat, the air sponging up the night's rainfall and carrying with it the stench of rot and humidity. Air strikes had been the soldier's only recourse, preferring the harsh chemical burn of Agent Orange defoliant and napalm to the smell of the native soil. The whole country stank of it.

Reginald was lounging in his hammock when the first mortar shells began to burst in the mud. He yawned, bored, watching idly as the explosions shook dirt from the sandbagged and reinforced bunker. The roof above was also reinforced and about five feet beneath the hills surface. He smiled darkly, blessing the Army Engineers who had built this place. It took a minute to remember that they had also been wiped out to the man.

"Yo."

James nodded his head and removed his helmet, sitting back warily on his bunk. "Sup."

"Nothin, Vibing the body count."

"How many?"

"Thirty-four."

"Sweet."

Reggie looked up from his open Penthouse, watching as four more soldiers stumbled in and passed out on hammocks and bunks.

"They're coming off patrols..." James said, uninterested.

"We're getting short."

Almost as Reggie finished, they heard the thumping of a supply chopper coming in, followed by rockets from another helicopter's gun platform, trying to suppress anti-aircraft fire from the woods line.

"Well, I'll be damned." James put his helmet back on, picked up his M-4 and went to meet the reinforcements.

Jonathan was carving another notch in the stock of his .308 Remington, a total of 53 confirmed kills, just in 6 months. It was some kind of record, he knew.

Able
Sometimes at night
I pick up my phone
I check my old mail
Just to hear your voice
I play these messages
Over and over again
I play the hollow words
Over and over again
And all these empty moonlit hours
They pass me by with a maddening cycle, Jekyll and Hyde
I've tried drinking
I've tried porn
I've tried not thinking

I've tried scorn
You alone pacify my mind
I play these messages
Over and over again
Scribbling my soul
By indiglo light
I write you epics, I write you lies
I spill on the altar of these pages
Ink like a strangers blood or cheap wine
Words given to you, my sacrifice
So drink up the phrases
To ease my mind
Tell me its genius
Mark my eloquence
Are you embarrassed
Tell me you're sorry
You didn't know, but you're blameless
Under your breath
Under duress
Tell me you're sorry
Say it's my own fault
You're not divine
(Though I'm not wise)
Maybe I'm jaded
Maybe you really are
Fucking right
I get crazy
Late at night

§

Chad was thinking ahead. His mind was running all the scenarios. He would leave. What would be back there when he turned that last time to look over his shoulder on his way out? Would what he gained be worth what he had given up?

He believed in the future. He foresaw a time he would come back and walk the road not taken. Or maybe he didn't and that's why he wrote about it. Either could be true. I do know he saw the blessings of his life. He took a good look at the people he loved, the place he'd grown up in, and in his own words knew his life was "almost perfect." Did he still have his demons? Don't we all, if we're honest with ourselves?

§

Coming of Age Story

I've always placed more faith in the trap of Americana than man, government, or God.

After graduation, the speeches and empty traditions, our indoctrination into the hollow religion of maturity, and the tossing of caps, he, she, and I separated with a few tears, a few jibes, and last minute confessionals. It was safe, then, to admit to lost love and lost time, because we knew it was over.

Life sent us packing. My best friend to the city, my lover to college and into the arms of someone else. We were all so empty, trying to cope. He tried to find solace in his books. I tried to find redemption in the war, and she tried to ignore feelings she didn't believe in. In every way we distanced ourselves from our past, rejecting what had been without accepting what was. We were lost.

We agreed to meet for coffee in the same shop we had all worked in, this time five years down the road. It was unlikely that any of us would show, too impractical for us to take time out of our lives and go back.

He was sipping a soy latté when I arrived, still sporting khakis and size-too-small black tee, a throwback, pretending as if his good looks hadn't faded. We smiled large inane grins of camaraderie, remembering childhood arguments and high school jokes. We talked for a while about his next novel and his kids as I told him stories about war and far away deserts.

She walked through the open door with practiced importance, blonde hair pulled back in a conservative ponytail, business-like short skirt revealing legs that hadn't lost their firmness, expensive blouse unbuttoned just enough. She needed to prove to us how much she had grown.

Conversation stopped between my former best friend and I. He looked at me with pain in his eyes. I nodded back, knowing his thoughts as my own.

More small talk. She was indeed successful, pointed it out, and rubbed it in a little. No harm there, we thought, and I told her about my commission and he talked about his Pulitzer. We all rubbed it in a little.

We exchanged contact numbers, hugs and handshakes. Only an hour or two had passed while we reminisced. We may not have been content, but we had lives to go back to.

 She pulled away in her import, my old high school buddy and I standing in the rain, laughing seriously about how poetic everything was. It felt right to end everything there, where it started. I told him I was sorry it had turned out this way. He said he was sorry too, because he still dreamed about her, and how he loved his wife. I pretended like I knew what he meant. The regret had been there a long time and we were less bitter, so we smiled and looked into each others eyes, saw the pain in our reflections, and had to turn away. We were twenty-three. Our affair with youth, with that last sentence of the first chapter of our lives had ended there, in a wet parking lot, watching the sunset over the bay.

Senior Yearbook Info
Chad Clifton
Activities: JROTC, Lacrosse, Viking Ventures, Ink, Acting, Paintball
Future Plans: Enlisted in USMC, seeking commission as officer, hoping
to "save the world"
Best Memories: Not doing homework, laughing about it, getting lost on
the way back from CR, paintball and video games with
the crew, summers in OC, senior year.
Senior Will: Whoa, it's not like I'm dead. But if I have to… to my brother
Ryan (ha ha… freshman) I leave random parties, school
lunches (buy the Oreo things), my useless lax gear, summers
in Ocean City (H2O & Coma, bro), but not my car.
To all next year's seniors, I give you this advice:
A street race in the rain is bound to cause pain.

Journal Entry
Exact date unknown

Raining outside today. Thinking back on the past two weeks; a car ride in bad weather, in and out of traffic. God knows what will happen next. She, me, some thoughts like daggers thrown… my old best friend and my newest companion. One forgotten, the other discovered, now contented to be alone with each other.

It's wrong, but I'm laughing at myself. Leather jacket, macchiato in hand, notebook… sitting at a table by myself in a Starbucks, watching people, watching rain, watching people in the rain. The image of everything I can't stand and my rain soaked reflection telling me this is who I am.

That, Alannis, unlike 10,000 spoons, is truly ironic.

Some kind of swing music in the background, and I'm still here, reasoning with myself, trying to get a grip. Helps me stay grounded, just passing my time here before work. By myself, I'm reminded of all the things I like to do, most of them on my own. Just like this. Just like everything I do.

"Your silent screams/ keep me wide awake"
"I like to watch the night/ turn into day"

Thoughts of you
I'm not dark all the time
But you're staring at my darker side
Perhaps you'd like to talk some other time?
No, well then I'm not responsible
For making you cry

<u>Student</u>
Learning
But not learned
Because you are
Not a master
Of regurgitating
The ideas of the professor
Professor
Your diploma is the
Death warrant of
Creativity

<u>The Free Form Essay on Human Nature of Which No Sense Can Truly Be Made</u>

Sucking shots of dark espresso bent over my notebook wishing I was listening to John Mayer, pondering Kerouac's subtle genius and the self induced serenity of this point in my life, so surrounded by the chaos of existence in which I have become the point of all that matters, a fulcrum on which everyone balances precariously. Out of habit I read this paragraph twelve times before I finish this idea, crossing out a redundant "life" to allow "existence" and adding punctuation to my thoughts, wondering if anyone gets the double meaning in this sentence… Let me help you… I crossed out life (a redundant one, like so many) to allow a more pure existence.

I pause and reflect on the ink stain on my shirt. It annoys me, but I don't know why. The stain really doesn't change anything, yet I curse and worry if my mother can remove the stain.

It's human nature to control everything… I could not control the pen. Infuriating.

To further illustrate my point; when we are angry, what is the cause? When we are depressed and at our bleakest point, what does it stem from? A lack of control. Road rage, homicide, rape, theft, virtual reality, the players of our generation in an attempt to control that which we have no hold on.

The stain remains, and I sip my espresso, bent over my notebook, wishing I was listening to John Mayer.

Control. Is my sudden calm, this sedated view on the world a product of total control or my acceptance that I have none?

All this espresso is making my handwriting erratic, making me not want to write.

Now, though, I have the inspiration back, as I realize that I can't control my handwriting and it doesn't really matter.

Serene once more. But out of ideas. Not to be deflected, I'll save this moment in my head for when I care again.

<u>Untitled</u>

Every minute of every hour of every day of my life had lead to that final

July night, sitting at the edge of the water, my feet buried in white sand. All the paths and trails of boyhood had brought me to that place and time, that instant in which neither title; boy nor man could be ascribed. My identity lay in what I had succeeded in, failed at, and hoped still to accomplish. One road would lead me away.

She sat down beside me. Silently, looking out across the ocean, searching for something she couldn't find.

I smiled my ironic smile, looking over at her, trying to find something to say. She was wearing my hooded lacrosse team sweatshirt over a bikini top and shorts. I loved it when she wore my clothes.

"You're leaving tomorrow," she said. "Will I see you before you leave?"

She knew the answer; we'd been over it before. "No, I'm leaving for Baltimore when I get up in the morning."

"Oh." She looked at me, looked into me, and pretty eyes welling up with tears. "We just have tonight."

"Yeah." I would have said more but I didn't have to. I just kissed her, pulled her close to me and it was enough. Most high school couples would have done the same thing, but our bond had always been different. The friendship had started only seven months before, and the relationship only six, but the connection had been instant, never forced.

We were losing each other and we knew it. It was like watching flowers wilt and die, only sadder still because the beauty in our love was permanent if only it could be kept together. By the time I got back from recruit training, she would be in college. A few months more and I would probably be off to fight a war. I wondered how long it would take us to recover. One month? Two? Six? She would get over me sooner than I would get over her. She'd be in a new place with lots of guys to fill the void. I would be in some desert shooting people. Such was life.

My best friend joined us, handing me a beer. He was like me, aware of the finality of what was happening, leaving two months after graduation, not to return for another three, and then gone for an indefinite amount of time. He nodded his head and stared up at the hazy summer stars, smiling with me because it was sad.

My girlfriend, more like the love of my life, got up and walked back to the party. She knew we'd see each other later and I needed some time. God, I love her.

"You okay, man?"

"I think so." I told him.

"Shit, man, you're really leaving." My best friend, like a second brother to me, was as dazed as I was by the stark reality of departure.

"I know."

"You're really in love with her, aren't you?"

"Aren't I always?"

He laughed. "Yeah, that's true."

"I say goodbye to my family tomorrow. They'll be there when I leave." I told him to get it off my mind.

"That's going to be hard."

"Yeah. But I have tonight, and only tonight, to party with you guys." I gestured back towards the party on the dunes, comprised of my closest and oldest companions.

"Righteous." He laughed. That was my word.

We got up and finished our beers, walking back to my circle of friends, wondering what it all meant, what it was for, and what I was leaving behind.

§

Summer was good that year. The party in the backyard combined Chad's eighteenth birthday with his leaving for boot. Before we knew it, August had arrived.

We took Chad to Georgetown to meet his recruiter. From there he would go to MEPS in Baltimore for processing.

He had finally hit a growth spurt so I was looking up at him after the hug. Yes, he was taller and had trained his body hard in the past year to be ready, but he still looked so young. My thoughts must have shown on my face.

"It's okay, Mom. I'll see you in three months."

§

Mom and Dad,

I sat down to write you a letter, but words can't begin to describe the way I feel. Within 48 hours of writing this, and by the time you read it, I'll be stepping out to try and make something of my life. I walk into the unknown, with only vague plans and dreams, but I walk with confidence because I know you have prepared me.

I've never been a "mushy" person, or one to get too emotional, but there are some things I want you to know.

Mom, I don't even want to think about how I would've turned out without someone to help guide me and keep me from making stupid mistakes with my life. I know that you've been through a lot to make sure I've had the advantages and opportunities I needed. Things could have gone a lot differently for the both of us were you not such a strong person. I love you.

Dad, I've never gotten the chance to tell you how much respect I have for you. I may be young and I may be fearless, but doing what you've done scares me shitless. All that you did, working so may hours to support us, raising two sons, building a house, and forging an art career… I just hope that I grow up to become half the man that you are. I mean that.

I love you, Chad

"I think of a hero as someone who understands the degree of responsibility that comes with his freedom."

Bob Dylan

Chapter 3

I began to understand how difficult Marine Basic Training was in the first few letters Chad wrote. He asked me to write everyday, about anything. That simple request spoke volumes. Whatever the challenge, whatever brick wall he had decided to batter down, he had always reached inside. Now he reached out. Those thirteen weeks would require all he had and then some. He wanted it badly enough to ask for help. We couldn't do anything about the miles of running, the physical stresses, the day to day activities that build a Marine, and he already had that handled. We became his touchstone. He needed us, heart and soul, for defense from the mind games, the homesickness and the mental vulnerability that comes from stunning exhaustion. And that we could do. Go ahead and hitch your wagon to a star, Chad. We're right behind you.

§

AUGUST 9, 2003

I HAVE ARRIVED AT MARINE CORPS RECRUIT DEPOT PARRIS ISLAND, SOUTH CAROLINA. I HAVE BEEN ASSIGNED TO PLATOON 3092, INDIA COMPANY, THIRD RECRUIT TRAINING BATTALION. IN MY PLATOON THERE ARE APPROXIMATELY 70 FROM VARIOUS PARTS OF THE COUNTRY. WE WILL LIVE AND TRAIN TOGETHER FOR THE NEXT 3 MONTHS, UNTIL OUR GRADUATION DATE OF 31 OCT 03. THERE ARE THREE DRILL INSTRUCTORS ASSIGNED TO MY PLATOON. MY SENIOR DRILL INSTRUCTOR IS SSGT VILLEGAS. WE EAT THREE MEALS A DAY AND HAVE BEEN ENCOURAGED NOT TO RECEIVE FOOD PACKAGES. DUE TO THE TIME IT TAKES TO RECEIVE THEM AND THE CONDITIONS OF THE BOXES. THE FOOD IS EITHER CRUSHED OR STALE. IF YOU ARE GOING TO SEND ANYTHING YOU ARE ENCOURAGED TO SEND ITEMS THAT I CAN USE WHILE

IN RECRUIT TRAINING. I WILL BE MORE SPECIFIC IN FUTURE LETTERS.

IF THERE SHOULD BE AN EMERGENCY, THE <u>ONLY</u> WAY TO REACH ME IS THROUGH THE RED CROSS. THEY MUST VERIFY ANY HOSPITALIZATIONS OR DEATHS. I AM ENCLOSING MY ADDRESS AGAIN TO BE SURE THAT YOU HAVE ALL THE INFORMATION NEEDED TO WRITE ME. BE SURE THAT YOU ADDRESS ALL THE MAIL JUST AS I HAVE IT BELOW IN <u>BLACK INK</u>.

> REC. <u>CLIFTON, RC</u>
> USE LAST NAME, INITIALS (NO NICKNAMES)
> PLAT 3092, "I" CO, 3RTBN, RTR
> MCRD, PARRIS ISLAND, SC 29905-2003

Monday August 10, 2003
Mom, Dad, Ryan,

Wassup crackas? Very little time to write, except to say that there's a week or so delay in mail all the time. Also, feel free to send Gatorade mix pouches, cough drops, and lots of Power Bars. I need to gain about 10 pounds, no problem though.

Everything is still okay on my end, the food is pretty good, better than I expected. I'm eating a lot. We start martial arts training tomorrow.

It's not exactly pleasant here… it's almost like I was in boot camp or something… interesting note: it takes several months to get off the island if a recruit quits. It's faster to graduate, but we've had some pansies drop out anyway.

Alcatraz vs. Parris Island: PI is way more of a bad ass island. It's the king of all hells on earth, but in a productive, occasionally funny way now that we're all starting to band as friends/unit.

Better go address this. Peace out, yo…

Love,
Chad
P.S. Say hi to everyone for me.

August 11, 2003
Mom, Dad, Ryan,

Long time no see! We're all so homesick it's amazing. I've been away for less than a week but it seems like forever. You have no concept how much I miss civilian life and you guys especially.

Everything is intense here. Often stupid bullshit, but high speed stupid bullshit. In just a week they've ripped away everything we thought we were… its disorienting and values shaking. Even weak and tired now, I know that I can finish this. I am nothing. I will be a Marine.

Didn't mean to get philosophical there, sorry, I just meant that I'm adapting better than most recruits. It's indescribable, worse than prison, and like nothing on TV, but I'm doing well and as happy as and overworked recruit could possibly get. That said, I would still KILL for a steak and a Corona.

How are you guys? I can't wait to hear from you. Write in depth, I won't get bored! Has Ryan started soccer camp yet? Everything copacetic around the house? How's Duncan coping? How's the gallery? Any current news I could tell other recruits? We have no radio/ TV/ newspapers. Please write at least a short letter often (everyday?) it would help a lot.

I'll write further when I know what kind of packages I can receive. Also I will tell you some funny stories but I have to go. Almost time for the DIs to replace the Senior DI and do their thing (which includes barking orders and fucking up our stuff... lol. Its true; it's all they do.

Love, Chad (This Recruit)

Tuesday August 13 2003
Mom, Dad, Ryan,

Just another short letter from this recruit to say that training is picking up. Our platoon only has about 5 or 6 "screw up" cases (recruits that drag us down) out of about 65 of us. It tests my patience, but I haven't killed a dumb kid yet so I must be learning some tolerance.

Love, Chad

August 14, 2003
Hey,

I know I've been writing a lot about general stuff, so here's a look at our daily schedule:

03:00- wake up

Then- Clean

PT (stretch, 3 sets of max pull-ups, 75 pushups in a row, roughly 200+ crunches, 3-5 mile run)

Soon- get quarterdecked

Or- eat breakfast/lunch (we get 3 meals a day, the time just varies)

Then- Class time @ recruit training center

Then- drill for 2+ hours

Then- dinner

Then- clean up, hygiene time, possible mail call

I'd actually be having fun if it weren't for that psycho DI Sgt. Butler. Everyone else is okay but this guy is the pettiest mother fucker on the planet. I am going to kick his ass the day I graduate. I can not describe the dumb shit he does, simply because he gets his mental rocks off being sadistic. Petty bullshit. If I got the chance to knock him off a balcony or something there would be no hesitation.

I think I'm getting stronger but losing weight. SDI Villegas says that's normal and I will gain more than I lose in about two weeks.

Only ten more Sundays till graduation, you have to think of it that way to stop from going crazy with homesickness/ stress.

Hey,

I now know the date finally Thursday, Aug. 14, 2003. I only have about two minutes to write though. You guys probably still, as I'm writing this, haven't received my other letters but it helps me just to write.

I've been on this island for ten days as of tomorrow, roughly 1/8 of the way through altogether, and the fun parts start in two weeks.

Friday 15, 2003
Continuing my letter from last night

Today sucked. We got all screwed up in the sand box today for not being loud enough. Imagine lying in the sand, soaked in sweat, and performing, 5-6 different exercises at whim for about five minutes. Let me tell you, it's a good time… or not. Actually it's not all that bad; this recruit is never even sore, just tired and hungry. I eat a lot more than I did at home but we burn food like oil with this schedule.

I sat down to write this letter and had to admit to myself: I am one bad mother fucker… lol. Other guys are dying from PT and getting sick and crap and my only problem is that I'm a bit hungry. I'm doing better than I thought I'd be doing last week.

I still haven't received any mail at this point but if you've received mine then I'm sure yours is on the way. I miss you three more than I can remember missing anything. Time is probably normal for you but its going slow here. Feels like I've been here a month. Days do go by slowly, but we've been filling it with drill, screaming, drill, chow, and drill and classes. Classes are a nice break from the DIs, and the topics are relevant; Customs, History, First Aid, etc. Drill would be cool if people would manage to remove heads from asses and march the right way. We kill lots of time repeating what 90% of recruits can do the first time but 10% screw up. Chow is my favorite, unless DI Butler is there, in which case I'd rather be anyplace else. That dude is no joke. I lost my voice a little too, which means I can't "sound off" the right volume, so I end up quarter decked. I'm getting used to it.

The thing about this island is the lack of a) contact w/ real world and b) dignity. We are clueless about back home and we can't do anything right, as we are constantly reminded. Like I said though, I manage to do better than most of the recruits. As soon as mail starts coming in I'm golden. Most of the guys here don't have letters yet either. We understand though. Snail mail just sucks.

Write soon, I'll see you in October… Love you.

Chad

Saturday August 16, 2003
Guys!

So awesome to hear from you! It's Saturday night and I just got your first letter. I'm so stoked to know that everyone's doing OK. I was having trouble w/ a drill movement that my arm seems too weak to do and your letter brought me back up. I'll get that move eventually, but it involves one handed cocking of a lever that is pretty weighted.

The trip down here I can't really remember, and my other letters should fill you in up till now. Write back with questions, I don't know where to start.

This recruit's body is still adapting, and I seem to be growing because I need more food than any of the other recruits. Problem is time. No time to eat extra, so the SDI said I can go to medical on Monday and get a pass for double rations, and that I would be allowed to eat them somehow. I'll keep you updated.

We did pugil sticks today; I slaughtered my opponent. We drilled for about five hours. My arms hurt.

I got separated from the guys I left with at MEPS, but I've seen them up on second deck barracks and I have friends in this platoon. Everyone is still coping with homesickness so most people are bonding where they can.

I'm just about out of time. I'll write more again when I get a chance. Time for lights out.

Love,
This recruit, USMC
(Or Chad, though I don't hear my name much anymore.)

Sunday August 17, 2006
Hey all,

Writing this from church cause it's time we have away from the DIs. Yep, Sunday School. We take what we can get and it's better than drill, because I'm still having trouble with that one cocking movement. Drill, chow, and church are probably the things we use most to mark time.

Nine more Sundays until the week of graduation, less than two months of actual training days left. It seems far off, but the days will start to pick up in about a week or so we're told. I hope the days are moving faster for you. Shouldn't you guys be school shopping by now? I know Dad is always busy this time of year, too, with so much stuff coming. I wish I were there for all of it. Its so strange knowing that I'll be missing all these events (open house, school stuff, shows, etc.) that I've always been home for or at least aware of happening.

Enough of that stuff, I haven't told you enough about what's happening to me:

DI Sgt. Bennett- Tough, but intelligent and reasonable

DI Sgt. Butler- Biggest ass hole in the history of mankind

Senior DI Staff Sgt. Villegas- our best friend on this island. He takes care of us and keeps us motivated and sane. A good SDI.

Those three pretty much run our lives, but we spend the most time with Sgt. Bennett who teaches us drill. Butler chimes in to be sadistic when he can't shut up anymore. SDI SSgt. Villegas steps in to save us, give us letter writing time, pass out mail, and council us. He can break bad but usually doesn't.

I think this week we're doing pugil stick training, and then next week is Combat Swim Qualification. Also, we should be getting to go to a PX this week for letter writing supplies. I could still use the stuff I requested in other letters, when you get the chance.

Church is almost over now, so I have to go. Tell everyone Hi.

Love,

Chad

Monday- Fixed my drill problem. Lots of love to you guys!

Ryan,

It's Tuesday, I just got your letter and it really helped me stay motivated like you can't even imagine, I read it about thirty times. Best letter in history, ever.

No time to write now, we have to hit the rack. I'll write you tomorrow during class. Okay? Best of luck, I miss you a ton, tell the crackas I said Hi.

Love,

Chad

P.S. I did the John Wayne thing yesterday, got quarterdecked.

August 20, 2003

Ryan,

What's up Bro? Thanks for writing to me, I was hoping you would. Keep on sending stuff; it keeps my head in the game. I can't explain how stressful and hard recruit training is, because you don't realize on TV that you have to be "on" for 24 hours a day. News from home is a reality check. And yours put a tear to my eye, which takes a helluva lot.

Time is finally starting to speed up here, and days drag on less. I can't wait to get home (where I will still own you at Halo… by the way, any games I would like coming out? You're allowed to send me my PC Gamers.)

I haven't changed too much. I have a different outlook but I'm still joking and not paying attention. I'm writing this letter in USMC History class. We get like one hour of class a day on different military subjects. Most of it is fun, and it gets our butts out of drill. We spend most of our time drilling, and thinking about home.

Only two months until graduation week, or as we like to think of it, only nine Sundays; seems a lot shorter when we count Sundays. You guys should send my training schedule for the next week or so, so I can see what we're doing. They don't tell us.

In two days we are allowed to go to PX. This is good, because I've been wearing the same boxers for a couple of days after mine got lost in laundry… lol. These are a little crunchy right now.

Oh and don't worry about making the team. You'll make it easily, trust me. Don't even stress about it. They only cut fat kids and bad attitudes, even if you're a stupid freshman… he he.

Out of paper, will write tomorrow. Keep it chill. Send my love to Mom and Dad.

Love,
Chad

Wednesday August 20, 2003
Hey,

Writing in class again… what can I say, I'm just not going to start paying attention now, am I? Ha ha… Not after 18 years.

We just got done drill and sat down. We got up at 4 AM, ate breakfast, drilled for two hours. I'd rather have done PT. Rumor states we have an obstacle course later, which would explain why we didn't PT this morning. This platoon is tired and hungry. The DIs told us they know how we're feeling and it will change soon. Right now, you can't even take a piss without a countdown. We dress by the item. And Fast. I can do anything in 5 minutes. That's enough time to wake up, make a rack, and dress in cammies and boots and be online for head call. It's like living in fast forward with the volume up. The best way to describe it is imagine a big intense game of Simon Says that doesn't ever end.

Saturday August 23, 2003
Ryan,

What's up bro? I just started writing this letter, it's Saturday. I'll probably get to send it on Monday since there's no mail run on Sunday. As you can see from the training schedule we've been busier than Rob's mom on a holiday weekend.

I know you're probably about ready to start school in a couple weeks right? Some advice; Chill out. High School is not the big deal it's cracked up to be. If anything, it's more fun than grade school. You probably aren't worried about it; I was just passing on the "ye old brotherly advice." Or something.

Start thinking of things you want to know about boot camp so I can give you the dirt. Like a real version of Mail Call.

Sunday…

Just got back from church (we go just to avoid DIs) and I've got a couple minutes to finish this off.

I can't wait for family day to get here. It's a few days after your birthday so start thinking about what you want me to get you. You should have time to pick something pretty good, huh?

(Later that night)

Okay, so in the past few hours I was quarterdecked for the longest time I've ever been, so my ass is broke off. I also lost my voice again and the whole company is really sick, including me. It's from the Flu shots they gave us, so it's sucking a good amount but I'll be on the upside by the time you get this. It's probably ended as my worst boot camp day so far. That was bound to happen though.

When I get home, I'm showing you exactly what "quarterdecked" is. The mantra, DISCIPLINE: Instant obedience to ALL orders; self reliance; teamwork; the ability to do what's right or suffer the consequences of GUILT which produce PAIN in our bodies, Sir.

That's what we have to scream all the time. The most annoying shit is:

DI: Step it…

RCT: Out!

We do that 40-50 times walking someplace

Or

DI: Close it…

RCT: Up!

There are like 20 other "ditties" too, but not as frequent and angering as those. So that's been today in general. Sick and sore, and for the first day truly exhausted. Parris Island is working it's magic on this recruit. At least the sand fleas aren't as bad as everyone said.

Write me back bro.

Love,

Chad

August 23, 2003

Hey,

Just got to RTF (Recruit Training Facility) for a First Aid: Shock Class after finishing PT this morning. We did a 2.2 mile strengthening run with breaks in the middle for pushups, sit-ups, etc. Before that we did pull-ups (I did seven max sets, we only had to do four) followed by pushups (sets of twenty) and then two minutes of crunches (I'm scoring over 100 about 90% of the time now). I'm not even feeling too "broke off", as they say on this island, synonymous with wiped-the-fuck-out.

Made the decision today to pursue getting corporal in the next two years (I'll be a lance corporal in 8 months, only one step below) so I can go to OCS. I like what I've seen in the officers here and it's the place for me. I'm still happy I enlisted though. I think my experiences in the enlisted ranks will make me a better officer when the time comes. Before I came here I thought I would just bide my time until college, but now I'm serious about my career.

So that's really all that's new with me, just basically keeping my head down and trying to be as much like a Marine as possible, because once you can emulate that, you become it, and the DIs will recognize the change in your discipline and mannerisms and leave you alone. Some recruits still act like kids though, I'll be glad when we finally get taken to the sand pit again and everyone starts acting with some integrity. Immaturity is the biggest problem the DIs face; taking college kids and making them the renowned professionals the world expects the USMC to be.

Hearing from you guys is awesome. I realize there will be days you can't send mail; it's okay. Just knowing I'm not forgotten is highly motivating and keeps my head clear to focus on training.

This class is really boring, I'm glad I brought paper, it's good to catch you guys up on where I'm at. Keeps me from worrying that you're worrying. If you have any questions please just list. I'd be glad to answer it all; I can't describe this place on my own.

My MOS is Command and Control/Communications. So I can hump a PRC radio if I want, or pull another Comm job. I'll probably grab something easier than glorified infantry, don't worry. This recruit isn't completely stupid, despite landing himself in the Marine Corps.

Got to go send this, Peace out.

Love,

Chad

What's up y'all?

Got your package last night, thanks for the new inserts. I definitely needed them.

Our platoon keeps getting into trouble so I haven't had time to write at all in the past couple days. Stupid recruits ruining things for the rest of us.

Did get to the PX though so I'm good to go on skivvies and socks and tee shirts. Bought stamps and envelopes but feel free to send stamps if you want, I should have enough for a week or two.

Stress level around here has been jacked up the past couple of days. Training has been more physically intensive than it was. I woke up this morning and we went to the pit, then I went back two more times today.

Butler is pissed because he hasn't broken me yet. He tried to confuse me today in the pit by asking me a question then making us push dirt when I answered so that the platoon was against me. So, to cure the problem, I was like "Sir, Recruit Clifton requesting permission to speak, sir... Platoon, the Drill Instructor is setting us up, quit bitching." Butler looked at me like he wanted to eat me alive but couldn't, because it would have proved my point, that Butler was setting me up, so he let us go.

Chad: 1- DIs: 0... LOL sometimes its fun to be me.

Anyway, aside from that it's the same old shit here in SC. Just over two months here and I'll be home. Less than a college semester, even. Eight more Sundays till graduation week, after tomorrow. Just got to stay positive.

At least my body is finally getting used to this heat. I don't know what's up in DE, but it's hotter than balls here. Fortunately we have AC in our squad bay so sleeping is nice and cool.

...(Later that night)

Just got your letter w/ the training schedule in it. Awesome, thanks I know it must have taken awhile.

Have to jet now,

Love,

Chad

August 24, 2003

Mom, Dad, Ryan,

Que pasa? It's Sunday, 24th or something like that. Just wrote you a letter last night so you'll probably get it with this one. I just got a chance to write this because the Catholic Chaplain told us we could write home. I'm now attending Catholic Mass instead of Protestant... lol don't worry I'm not getting saved.

Went to Battalion Medical yesterday. They said I have "extension tendonitis" in my right ankle. Fortunately it's not serious, so they let me stay on full duty and gave me some pain killer/ anti-inflammatory/ muscle relaxant. Its good shit. I'm not sore at all.

Those gel inserts are a godsend; my boots feel ten times better now. I appreciate it.

Thanks again for continuing to write to me. Mail call nights are extremely motivating. Something to do with remembering why I'm here.

I think, and remembering that I'm still Chad and not 100% RCT Clifton. RCT Clifton is okay with me, but you have to hold on to your past because this island is NOT reality. It's a tricky balancing act.

This recruit's having a tired day, not sure why. Maybe cause I spent a good part of yesterday "playing in the sand" or cause we got an extra hour of sleep this morning or maybe cause we have to clean the barracks for inspection later. Who knows, days here flip from beat to motivated, seemingly at whim. I usually eat 2-3X more than the other recruits. It's a good deal, I'm already gaining weight and I've only been doing the double rations for a few days.

I was thinking of things you guys could send in the mail and I thought about the obvious: Football scores. We have no way to follow that here. How are the Vikings doing? Also any NASCAR wins (I heard Gordon crashed last Sunday?) Jokes, headlines, anything you guys want to write or print out. Like flyers for the gallery show or any digital printouts of new originals Dad does that I haven't seen. Also, family pictures, etc, etc. Family photos would be cool.

Sorry to sound all needy. I'm not bad off here, it's just that here is all we think about all day. So that gives us a lot of time to think about what we don't have.

We only have one more week of 1st Phase. It ends with Initial Drill Competition on Sunday then we start Swim Qualifications (easy) and continue on the schedule you sent me (much obliged). Things will be looking up if I can just get through this next week. After this week it will be September, so we at least get some psychological advantage of not having an entire month between now and October. Instead of being Aug, Sept, Oct… just September and October. That's a good feeling. We've pretty much survived the first month. They keep saying if we make it through first phase then we'll make it to Grass (Dry Fire) Week and Rifle Week and when we qualify that, it's the home stretch.

Write Soon, I love you guys and miss you more than you probably know. Crackas.

Chad

Wednesday August 27, 2003

Momma,

What's up? This recruit is just writing to say he received a third box of power bars (thanks again) and also that I was told to go to sick call again today. I've got a sinus infection and a ton of fluid in my left ear, as well as this damn cough. Not for you to worry though, the corpsman took one look at my sick mug and gave me meds and bed rest so I should be better by the time you receive this. Just keeping you updated. I'll survive. I have to go back for a follow up tomorrow, and the extra sleep is a godsend.

At least Phase I is over on Wednesday, then we have swim qual and "grass week" which is a lot of sitting in positions for 2-3 hours. They say it's painful. No shit? This recruit looks forward to it.

I hope you're actually receiving my letters; I'm not seeing that you've got all of them. I've sent one just about everyday.

Give Ryan and Dad my love; I know they're both busy. Gotta jet.

Love,

Chad

Monday September 1, 2003

Sup?

We don't get any music exposure here, so in protest… well, in protest

I've been singing protest music. And we all know I'm a sucker for irony, right?

Guess what I found out today? Our Senior DI was talking with us and was like, hey have any of you guys figured out that your platoon number is famous? We couldn't think of anything but apparently it's the number of the platoon from Full Metal Jacket! How groovy is that? 3092!

It's been a long easy day here on PI. Watched the sun come up over the parade field and watched it set on the other side. We've been drilling pretty much all damn day in preparation for Initial Drill-Comp. on Wednesday. We're either good or bad, but who knows? They play so many games with our heads we don't know if we'll win or get last.

Don't stop writing, I love hearing from you guys. I still miss home a ton, but the actual "home sickness" part is fading due to all the non-stop shit.

I'm feeling almost 100% better, just fluid in my left ear that's annoying, but I should be all squared away by Swim Quals. We just got our desert cammies for the Phase II training days (swim quals-rifle week) so we're starting to feel like veteran recruits; we pretty much are.

Time up, gotta jet...

Love,

Chad

September 4, 2003

Hey,

I probably won't finish this tonight since I have to post for double fire watch (it sucks, two hours... some squad leader thought I was talking, I wasn't... it's okay because next inspection time I'll casually walk by and fuck up his rack before the DI walks around... that should show the mofo... lol).

Had Pugil Sticks III today, that was fun. Heat broke today, it was about 60 degrees and drizzling, a nice change of pace. Got the stamps you sent too, thank you. Other than that, not a lot's new. Just hanging on, it's what we do here.

Oooh we get to "blouse" our boots now, which means we tuck our trousers into them so we don't look like First Phase recruits anymore. Before this our pants just hung over the boot tops and looked stupid. Now we look cool as shit. We're close to the 30 day mark now, finally. Feels like I've been gone forever. I'm basically a more disciplined, harder and less breakable version of my old self. I say "old self" because for some reason, none of us here feel connected to our old life style. It's probably on purpose, all this calculated training and all.

My hands are calloused and my mind is tired, but I'm finally feeling healthy again. Ran three miles yesterday and wasn't even touched physically. My arms are still broken down though; I can only do eight pull-ups now instead of fourteen. Our Senior DI says the muscle will build back up.

Sunday-
Just got to the RTF late. We caught the last bus to Sunday School… doesn't it figure? So I don't have too much time as usual.

Feeling a little more motivated this morning, even if I pulled a double watch last night. Today is one more Sunday down the drain. I'm just looking forward to mid-day chow cause that means the day is almost over. Today when we get back we've got to move all the racks and scrub decks and all the "Field Day" crap.

I'm also responsible for cleaning the DI office. It's not a bad job actually. It gets me out of other work I don't feel like doing. After that is chow, then probably drill for a couple hours… after that maybe knowledge time for a while with Sgt. Butler… then more drill… then chow and drill and probably hit the rack after that. Days with no training are pretty damn boring here.

Not a whole lot to do to kill time besides drill, drill, drill… all day, everyday. Snap and pop. Drill is life, hoorah…

All in all things are going as expected here. How goes it up North with you Yankees? How's school and all that stuff?

That's pretty much all the time I have. I'm going to try to write to Ryan today. Keep writing as much as possible. It's what's keeping me going day to day.
Love,
Chad

Tuesday September 4, 2003
Yo,
Just writing to check in and hopefully keep the mail flowing. God knows I rarely can find time to write anymore, we're done with almost all of our classes and have moved into "knowledge time" which is basically like taking the same 185 question test until you memorize it. So much for goofing off in class… bummer.

While the days here continue to speed up, sometimes (like tonight) I still get pretty homesick. I miss this time of year especially. Its still mid-summer weather here in SC and its September. I'd kill to look out my bedroom window at some ducks/geese/anything. I look out this barracks window and see the parade field, not quite the same view.

Just added up on my calendar, I've been here for thirty days tomorrow, only fifty days left here on the Island. That's "good trash" as they say in the Corps. Damn straight, I can live through fifty days of anything to be free again.

Odd ball note: the song "Home for Christmas" has been stuck in my brain all week. Oh there's no place like home for the Holidays… LOL. Don't ask why, its just my random song of the day.

Okay I'm just rambling stupidly; you'll have to excuse me. All this stress makes a guy loopy.

Please keep writing.

Love,
Chad

September 7, 2003
Ryan,

What up, bro? How's Freshman Year going? Similar to being a First Phase recruit probably. That's okay, I'm 2nd Phase now. I'll be done my school before you will this year, lol.

Hey, keep those PC Gamers or Xbox mags coming my way; it looks awesome in my footlocker. A little piece of home and comfort, every little bit of identity we have on this island helps us out.

We got our desert cammies the other day. I'll see if I can score you some when I graduate; they look cool as shit. I think I can get them at the PX or you can have my old ones, since I'll need new ones anyway when I go to the fleet. You'll be the envy of the paintball field. These uniforms are supposed to be hard to come by.

Tomorrow is the start of Swim Quals for us, so we've got four days of that, then a five mile march (harder than it sounds, because of the pack) then we move out to weapons battalion for one week of dry firing the rifle, then one week of firing. After that it's the home stretch. I'm pretty psyched. I miss home a lot and the sooner out of this swampy island hell, the better.

How are Mom and Dad doing? Any luck getting broadband? Good luck with that. What's new? How are the cats? How's school? You play any paintball lately? Feel free to use any of my gear that you want. Don't I owe you like a case of paint?

Shit… got to post this. DI Butler is being a jerk again and killing our time. I'll write soon.

Chad

Tuesday September 9, 2003
Hey all,

Hope you've been getting my letters, I know they're starting to become less frequent, so I want you to know I'm still thinking about home a lot, but Phase II is all about the DIs developing more discipline and killer instinct, so accordingly we have no time. It's just as bad as Forming Phase was the first three days we were here.

On the upside I met my swim requirement and exceeded it by one level. I didn't fail anything, but my MOS doesn't REQUIRE a second class classification. It's annoying because I wanted a shot at level two and one before I got to Fleet. Oh well, I can just do it in MCT after boot camp. It was fun messing around in the water with gear, so I'm good to go. Oh, and we got our pictures taken in Dress Blue Alphas today. I ordered a big package because you can't and I know you'd want me to get a lot since they can't be re-ordered. I look very Marine-like, I'm sure.

Not much else is new except to reiterate that I won't be able to write much while I'm at weapons battalion and that you shouldn't get discouraged and stop writing. It's really out of my hands, I know you understand. I was just worried that you'd think I had the time to write but was being lazy, which isn't the case. I miss you guys more than anything. We move out to the range on Saturday and stay for two weeks, but my address remains the same.

Hang in there up in DE, I've only got fifty days until Family Day. I've just got to get through the intensity of the next two weeks and I'm in the home-stretch. Wish me luck.

Lots of Love,
Chad

Tuesday September 9, 2003
Hey,

To answer your questions:
The medics gave me Amoxicillin, some nasal spray, and yes we have yogurt at breakfast which I've been eating.

Charleston sounds awesome, I can't wait. I'm thinking Old Towne for dinner (I'm getting the Super Sampler) and chill in the hot tub the rest of the night. That little fantasy is a real motivator when I'm lying in the rack trying to remember why I'm here. Every little thing helps.

I'm really touched that you guys are so proud of me. I certainly didn't expect you all to be so proud, especially since all my friends went to college and I'm on PI. You guys are the sole reason I haven't said Fuck This and quit. I really appreciate it more than you know.

We're out of time here, going to bed early to rest for the PFT on Friday.

Lots of love to you all,
Chad

September 12, 2003
Hey all,

Well, we got to Weapons Battalion today after a five mile hike in formation with packs and rifles. Pain in the ass if you ask me. It wasn't hard enough to justify the effort (does that make any sense?). The barracks here are bigger and the showers are nicer. Chow hall is also bigger so lines go faster. And I live for chow, so that's a good thing. Only downside of tonight is I'm pulling yet another double shift for talking shit to a squad leader (he deserved it, he was being an ass and forgot he was a recruit, not a DI). Whatever, I'm getting used to it by now. Still pisses me off though…

We did the PFT yesterday; I did 122 crunches, 8 pull-ups, and a 20:41 three miles. Really disappointed about the pull-ups but I do so many damn pushups in a day that it's a wonder my arms don't fall off. Run time was alright, I would have done better if I hadn't eaten double breakfast before hand. All in all my scores were really good if you were anyone but me.

This is one of those nights I find myself unoccupied and thinking about home a lot. Wondering what you three are doing at this time, different little stuff like that. Time is taking the edge off the homesickness, but it still sucks a good amount. I know its different and that if I were at college or something it wouldn't be as bad, but here… we're ordered around 24/7 and it makes everything worse because in your head you're thinking "Damn, if I were home right now, I'd be sitting down to a nice bowl of cereal and a book…" but you look up and your dumb Marine Corps ass is stepping it out in the dark with a pack on your back heading in a big circle back to your start point. Its demoralizing, to say the least, but hey it's what we do.

My MOS is Communications, which means I get trained as a radio operator but from there I can move up in fields to things like Satellite Communications and some other equally cool stuff. I'm looking forward to it. It's all based on how well I do in MOS school. Should be fun. Sorry I can't give you more details. I don't find out a lot of stuff until near graduation. Glad I didn't do straight infantry though. (Go ahead and say "I told you so"… I deserve it.)

Sunday Morning

We start Grass Week tomorrow, our first classes in Rifle Safety and shooting positions… should last like all day, good or bad I have no idea. Our PMI (Primary Marksmanship Instructor) is pretty cool. We met him on Thursday evening. We're supposed to be "snapping in" to shooting positions for 1-2 hours per day. Third phase recruits say it depends on the person but it's supposed to hurt like a mofo. Bummer. Next two weeks should go nice and slow… DIs have yet again "turned up the heat" meaning pretty much every spare moment… sucks… there's not another way to describe it.

Best part about weekends is that I usually have time to write long letters. Sorry if I ramble on but I reason that I love reading your letters so much that the longer mine are the more you get to hear from me. Hope I'm not being boring.

What else… basically everything is the same old same old. New barracks, increased stress, the new digital desert cammies… other than that boot camp is getting kinda boring. Lots of free time spent on the drill field or on the quarterdeck or in the sand pit, none of which helps pass the time. But the phrase "oh well…" is becoming a personal anthem. Hey, only the strong survive, right? Something like that.

I'm still really looking forward to Charleston too. I know it will be especially nice to " be in Carolina in the morning" if I can wake up to a hot shower and breakfast instead of five minutes of hygiene time, scrubbing the DI House (their office) and march to chow. I definitely am sending you guys a list about a week before I get home with foods I've had a craving for while in boot. I think you should expect a long, long, long list. Forty six days til' television and food and Mountain Dew whenever I want, with no one to yell at me… ah for the luxuries of civilian life. Once the count is down to thirty days I'm gonna be a happy camper.

This recruit is absolutely exhausted today and I'm going to stop here before I go completely brain dead. Lots of luck to you guys in your daily adventures, tell everyone I'm still alive and well and I say hi.

Love,
Chad

P.S. Mom, your letters are not boring. The more the better. Dad, keep writing when you get a spare moment, I know you're as busy as could be, so trust me I understand. Ryan same thing. Love you guys.

September 18, 2003

Que pasa, Cantigos?

Actually got a spare moment to write tonight, update you on the usual Simon says shit that we do so well here on the island.

It's been Grass Week for a couple days now, only a couple left to do. Its basically been eight hours a day of classes outside about everything there is to know about the M16A2 service rifle, as well as "snapping in" to positions (which hurts like I can't explain… just grab the heaviest gun in the house and sit in position with it for two hours… now at the same time attach a sling to your arm and wait for it to go numb… yeah it sucks.) My coach said all my positions are solid and when we shot at the simulator yesterday, I had one of the tightest shot groups in the platoon. Good to go there.

Tomorrow we finally get to shoot a tiny bit to zero our rifles and check sights and tight groups. We're zeroing from 36 yards because that's the sight equivalent to 300 yards (the trajectory of the bullet requires the same sight alignment at 36 as it does at 300 I meant). When we shoot for real on Monday we shoot at 200, 300, and 500 yards. I'm really looking forward to the 500… hitting a man sized target with fixed iron sights at 500 yards is one hell of a shot. Over, and over, and over. Excellent.

I gotta hit the rack. It's been a long week. Can't wait for Sunday, we're half way through.

Peace out, homies…

Sunday September 21, 2003
Ryan,

Hey bro, que pasa? It's Sunday morning, and I'm sitting in church (Jesus says hello again… lol) writing letters. One more week down, I've got five Sundays left until it's finally graduation week. That's good stuff… it's about time I got the hell out of here. How's soccer season going? Cape is representing I hope? What's the record? You playing indoor after the season's over? Hope you're having fun. We just finished Grass Week and start live fire tomorrow and fire all week until Qualification on Friday. DIs are "supposed to" leave us alone this week so we can fire well, but I think it's a setup… too good to be true. Saturday we have a six mile march back to Third Battalion Barracks. I can't wait to get back, the chow is better there.

Some words of advice that may not apply to you, but just in case; Don't join the Marine Corps, No matter what. One of my friends here in boot camp has a brother that joined because of him… I'm pretty sure you wouldn't do that, but don't go to college on a Marine Corps scholarship either. I don't want you to have to go through the shit I'm going through. In fact, that's part of why everyone who is still in training is still here… we don't want anyone else to have to do it. It fucking sucks. Just promise me you won't join the Corps for any reason, ever. Army, Navy, or Air Force… join those if you want, those are good career options… just don't join the damn Corps. Enough said.

I know you're busy (don't worry, I am too) but keep writing. I love getting cards and letters from you and Mom and Dad. I don't know what I would do without your support… I probably would have quit the second week. Good luck with all the everyday high school bullshit, I know it can suck as much as boot camp sometimes. If anybody gives you shit, just quietly take names. I can shoot stuff from a long ass distance now… lol

Peace Bro.

Love,

Chad

Mom, Dad, Ryan

Hey! Long time no write, sorry. We've been insanely busy. Lots of dumb games this week and prepping for live firing week on Monday. I'm on the last relay of the day during firing week (I shoot last, but work targets in the morning for other shooters), which means they expect me to shoot sharpshooter or expert.

Definitely looking forward to firing. It's the only thing outside of going home that's keeping me from saying fuck it. Actually…
I generally say "Fuck it" anyway but then I keep marching. It's a bitch, but yeah, shooting helps. Word of wisdom; If You Don't Mind It Doesn't Matter. These words are pure truth here. Stress and fatigue are a state of

mind if you can truly believe that statement. I know it's kept me from breaking a number of times during repetitive little game with the DIs.

On the upside of things, I'm officially half way through boot only this upcoming week, Team Week, A-line (night firing and fun stuff), then Basic Warrior Training, The Crucible, and Graduation. Thirty six days til' graduation week. That's pretty good news since its all supposed to go fast from here out. They keep telling us that and so far it's true. Man, I can't wait to get out of here. I need a beer, a long hot shower, some music, and a candy bar, in that order… lol.

I know you want to hear more about what I actually do all day, but words won't describe the intensity and lack of down time, even when we're standing still and doing nothing. Just take my word for it.

How goes the home front? Did the hurricane pass by you guys? Hope everyone's okay up there. I know we almost had to be evacuated. That would have sucked. You guys are my main inspiration so stay safe and secure; I need someone to write to me, right?

Anyways, I'm going to wrap up this letter and get some sleep. By the way, thanks for the Gatorade and magazine, much obliged. Keep sending mags; they bring us a sense of reality beyond this sand bar.

Love,

This Recruit

September 23, 2003

Mom,

Hey, how are you? I seriously wish I were home or out running some errands with you. I'd love to go grocery shopping like you don't even know. I'm still sending that shopping list when I graduate. Food seems to jump up in everything I attempt to write, sorry. What I meant when I started this paragraph was to express that I miss the little stuff we used to do and really take for granted. I miss you a lot, Mom, and I'll give you that dance to that certain song.

Your Marine,

Chad

Hey all,

Writing after a long day spent at the range and I'm exhausted. Firing week is a god send, keeping me motivated through the halfway point. I'm shooting extremely well. I did a "dumbass" thing on my last 500 yard target and turned my sights the wrong way (lol… typical). Which caused me to lose about 30 points and I still would have qualified had today been qual-day. My coach doesn't even bother to adjust me anymore since my positions are technically not USMC issue, but they work well.

I've got to go square away my crap for tomorrow. Write soon,

Love, Chad

Hey there,

Today is Friday, September 26, 2003 and as of about 2 PM this afternoon your son made it to the third (and most notably FINAL) phase of recruit training. I qualified much lower than expected on the range, with a 199 (I'd been shooting expert 220's) which is a Marksman (damn it…) but hell, I qualified so I'm not going to kick myself over it. I know I can shoot better and we re-qualify at MCT anyway so it's no biggy. Win some, lose some. We have fifteen recruits that didn't even come close to making it. Sucks for them.

Oh shit… lights in 10 min. I have to go hit the rack. Well, only four more weeks left. See you then,

Love,
Chad

Sat. 27-Sun 28, 2003
34 days remaining
Ryan
Que pasa, bro?

Just received that new PC Gamer and a letter from you. Thanks a ton, I can't wait to play all those new games I'm missing out on. Don't worry about being busy, I definitely understand. You guys are probably getting used to me being away by this point, anyway. It has to happen sometime. I'm just glad you're still writing.

There's not much time left in this place, thank God. Three more Sundays after this one before its Graduation time. I swear to God, if I still had like eight more weeks I would say I was gay just to get the hell out of here. You try to stay focused but, man, I'm telling you, you reach a point where you half ass everything and the only thing that keeps you out of trouble is… no, nothing, because we all get in trouble no matter what. Just have to keep moving and killing time til' Grad.

Hope I'm not boring you. I'm just trying to convey the mind games they put us through from day to day. Sometimes it's pointless, sometimes it's not.

Anyway, this week is team week. We get to go to the museum (very cool) on Monday, then Wed-Friday we have laundry duty all damn day. Dress uniform fitting and issue is on Tuesday, as well. Wednesday I have dental, and hopefully I won't need to get my wisdom teeth removed. That would be a bitch, and it happens to a lot of people during team week.

I'm looking forward to shooting A-line in two weeks though. Night firing and shooting through gas masks and at moving targets and all that fun Rambo shit. Sounds like a blast.

That's pretty much all the news that I have, things are boring here day to day. A lot of wasted time on the quarterdeck and getting yelled at and cleaning weapons for hours and drilling in preparation for the all important final drill. Talk about mind numbing.

Wish I had more to tell you, but I'll end it with some phrases we hear everyday…

"Ain't no fuckin way… Ain't no way"- DI Sgt. Butler

"Shut the piss up." – DI Sgt. Bennett

"Open your fat, disgusting mouths." –Both

"Where are my bitches at? Bitches!" – DI Butler (calling for whoever made his list that day)

"Don't gaff me off, ninety two." (That means don't half ass/ignore it.)

"Fine, you don't want to stand up? Sit down. Stand up. Sit down. Stand up… (This can go on like 10 minutes. Fucking annoying)

I'll write down some more as I think of them. Peace,

Chad

Sunday, September 28, 2003

Hey,

Its Sunday morning yet again. Not a lot has changed. We're back at Third Battalion finally, so that's a plus. Team week this week and A-line, its simulated combat firing and should be a good time, except we have to get up early and hop on a bus to ride back and forth from the range everyday. Only like thirty three days til' we graduate now. Getting this far is kinda cool, even if it sucks to be here. I know I had some doubts as to whether I'd make it or not. This is the home stretch (literally) now, three more Sundays. You remember when it was like ten? I don't know how I stayed motivated then.

Training is getting harder but easier. Physically it's more demanding, and mentally we're worn out, but in some ways we're so used to it by now that nothing is particularly hard by itself. The DIs say that's what is supposed to happen. After A-line the DIs are supposed to start treating us more like Marines, less like dirt. Looking forward to it, but I'm skeptical. Something seems too good to be true about that to me.

I'm so tired today. Always am, but you don't notice it when you're training. Only on Sundays because we sit down at church and actually get a chance to think.

It helps me to write all this down sometimes. There's really no one to talk to besides recruits and we're pretty much useless for understanding.

I know I usually try to write longer letters on Sundays but I'm cutting this one short now so that I can catch some sleep before church is over. I'm really wiped. I'll try to add on to this later.

Later: Sunday school, 10:15 am

Woke up after a quick power nap. Damn, I needed that.

Found out that our duty assignments for Team Week is laundry. Not hard at all. We just have to ride around in the morning and pick up laundry from whatever battalion has laundry that day, then count it, chill while the civilians wash it, eat chow, and pass all of it back out. Shouldn't be hard unless DI Butler decides he needs to baby-sit us (hopefully won't happen, but it could). I have a feeling this week will go slow though. I'll probably go to medical tomorrow because my ear infection came back in my left ear. I haven't been 100% healthy since I got here, but I need to get this inner ear bull taken care of before A-line (guns going off next to my head and etc.) and Basic Warfare Training (gas chamber). Those would be killer with sinus problems. I can tough it out through a lot of pain but I'm going to have to step back and let the corpsman decide whether or not I train this week. I'm not going to let this get worse and end up getting dropped because I wanted to look tough in front of the platoon. I'm too close to graduation to do anything that stupid. A lot of drops happen at this point in training because recruits don't go to medical. That's one of the reasons there's a Team Week. Hopefully I'll be good to go in a week.

My thoughts keep turning to going home soon. I know I say it over and over but it's really what's making our progress possible… the promise that when this is over we can go home and see our families. When I first got here and even up through most of second phase, the "light at the end of the tunnel" was something we tricked ourselves into believing was close. Now it actually is visible for us. I'm just realizing that today. On top of that, I'm kind of proud because a lot of people told me I wouldn't survive here, and I had my own doubts like I mentioned before. Now it's almost over and I've found two lights at the end of this tunnel. #1 is seeing you guys again, but I just realized that #2 is pride of accomplishment. Being a Marine hasn't meant a lot to me throughout training, but its starting to provide its own form of motivation. Yesterday I was training to go home. This morning I was training so I could go home. Now I realize that… Hell, I am pretty pleased with myself and that completing boot camp might be something I want to do instead of being a requirement to earn my freedom again.

Sorry for being "out there" again… I had to get that written down; it just occurred to me that I'm starting to give a damn about what I'm doing here. It's a far cry from the attitude I had earlier. Epiphany, anyone?

Keep writing and I'll see you soon.

Love,

Chad

Hey,

Writing this on Monday 29th, at the end of… dare I say it… a good day here on the island. This morning I got some meds from the corpsman that are already helping my ear infection subside. Went to the museum which was pretty cool (I'll take you there after graduation), drilled some, blew some time chilling around the squad bay under the pretense of cleaning, and then finished with a "relaxed" chow time and shower. Doesn't take a lot to satisfy us.

    Keep writing,

    Love,

     Chad

October 3, 2003

Hey,

I'm starting this letter on Friday the 3rd though I probably won't finish this tonight.

Just ended Team Week, which was a blast. I goofed off on easy duties all week cause I was smart enough to volunteer to work at HQ and the visitors center. The Visitors Center was cool but all the civilians looked at us like we were aliens, just because we didn't talk much (in front of them) and we sit at attention. It was different.

By the way, I probably shouldn't be writing this down, for my own safety, but a couple of my friends and I scored a Snickers bar from the candy machine (it was complicated)… long story short, it was the best candy bar we've ever had. Definitely had a good time eating that last night. Score-Us 1: DI's 0. Oh Yeah. On top of that our SDI just fed us all Snickers Bars because we shot well on the range… Sweet.

Sorry I haven't been able to write this week… every night we've had spare time but the DIs have been making us stand at attention and dumb shit until lights out, just to be annoying asses. Mission accomplished.

Other than that, its back to training as usual. We completed our last hump before the Crucible today. It was a ten mile with gear and packs and rifles as usual. Wasn't so bad as I was expecting. My feet hurt like hell but there's no blister so I'm good to go… just happy I'm done with those damn humps. Tomorrow is Sunday, so I'll probably ramble on more from church and add to this.

Sunday morning again, thank God. Get it? Thank god… lol… okay it was lame but we all laughed so whatever…

Here's the count from our end: Two Sundays until we get Sunday liberty (and Grad Week), only two more weeks of active training, and only twenty five days from today until Family Day, which I'm looking forward to more than graduation. By the time you get this I will be done with A-line. We have two academic reviews, a Company Commanders Inspection, Final PFT, and Final Drill in between training in the next two weeks. Hope it goes fast.

Of course with the end in sight, we've been talking a lot about how training has affected us. I'm not a lot stronger, but I have endurance out the seams. I can run or march or pushup forever. I weigh 120 lbs. now but I still look young (though I unfortunately have to shave now… bummer). Being relaxed on Team Week has led to a lot of introspection, and most of the "change" that we've gone through is all mental. Confidence, maturity, probably arrogance, because we all know that we can do anything the Corps throws at us, and that the next four years will make us stronger and better that the next four years would if we were out in the civilian world. Our SDI told us that boot camp isn't supposed to turn out perfect Marines, just the basic mold. Whatever. All I know is that I still feel like myself (slightly disappointed in that) but more in control. Hmm… if I had joined any other service, I'd have graduated by now. No wonder the Army has problems.

How goes the world of wildlife art? I know Dad's been painting like crazy, I'm sorry I'm not there to see the new originals as they get done. Hopefully, I'll be home on recruiter's assistance… that would put me home for the gallery show, right? By the way, tell Heather I say hi. I'm coming in for three or four iced chocolate mint lattes the first morning I'm back home. Tell her I said to be in stock. Glad to hear Ryan's doing well. I knew high school wasn't anything he couldn't handle. Hell, he is my little brother. That should speak volumes for how tough you have to be. Hey… you get first report cards back yet? Those were always fun… yeah right. If he screws up his GPA I'm going to quarter deck him. Boom, there's motivation for you. Run! Push! Run! Crunches!

I think we have like fifteen days til' the Crucible, which all Mike Company recruits are telling us is easy and overrated. They say BWT is harder because you do more physical work (low crawl, assault courses, camping outside, etc.) BWT you get to eat MREs finally, so I'm looking forward to it. Crucible they say is tiring but not really hard. I guess I'll find out.

I've probably bored you and rambled on long enough, so I'm going to stash this in my locker and get it in the mail as soon as possible. Please keep writing; getting letters at night is my main source of motivation to get through the day. You have no idea how much I miss you guys all the time. I'm constantly wondering what you guys are doing while I'm doing whatever the DIs have come up with. Thinking of you…

Love,
Chad

Sunday October 12, 2003
Hey!

Sorry I haven't written since last Sunday, we've been busy as all hell finishing up A-line, prepping our uniforms and drilling about six hours a day to get ready for final drill tomorrow. We spent most of last week doing that and studying for the test yesterday and the practical knowledge (first aid on dummies and etc.) test on Tuesday. Final PFT is Wednesday, then we start BWT. Like I said, I've wanted to write but there's just no time.

To catch you up on last week: A-line was pretty boring. Lots of waiting around to shoot, but fun once we got to pop off rounds through gas masks and from bunkers. Low-light and night–fire looked pretty cool with the flares and tracers, but it was hard to hit anything so I just rocked and rolled in the general area of my target. I qualified 8 of 12 on the unknown distance course for pop-ups as well (75-500yds).

We finished up on Thursday, came home and switched back to green cammies again and got our red platoon flag that designates us as third phase. Friday morning we did PT. I ran a three mile Indian Run with the fastest group. It slayed me but I kept up and we did it under twenty minutes so I'm pleased. I also did 146 crunches in two minutes. I just need to bust my ass in pull-ups on the PFT to get first class score.

Saturday we drilled for literally eight hours, no exaggeration. It wasn't as bad as it sounds. By this point, the entire platoon will do whatever it takes to win Final Drill. A little extra work hasn't killed us before, and hell, we're getting paid to march around and look cool. Final Drill is like the damn Super bowl around here. Once you get here for family day I'll show you HQ and the other places where platoons get pretty much immortalized for winning drill. It's major. We definitely have a good shot, so hopefully it will pan out for us.

Let's see… Prac. App. Test on Tuesday, we've been studying for that. It's all demonstration that you know how to do different kinds of combat first aid, reporting to new commands, procedures for boarding ships, general orders, etc. If we win Prac. App. and Drill, we'll get honor platoon guaranteed. That would be totally sweet.

Wednesday is PFT, pretty much self explanatory. I'm sure I'll do fine, even if not up to my own expectations. The low number of pull-ups bothers me, but I'll have to work on it more when I get home. Speaking of pull-ups, tell Rick I said thanks for the magazine (I got to keep the FHM! LOL), they definitely bring back a sense of reality. We're so isolated here it's easy to forget things you like.

That should bring you up to speed, I hope. Pretty cool that the only things I have left is BWT and Crucible, huh? Seems short for me. BWT will be two days in the field. Learning squad level and platoon level tactics and movements, and other very basic stuff to prep us for MCI and SOI. We also do the Gas Chamber (sounds fun, doesn't it?) and rappel from a wall and from a helicopter skid. There's like 200 yds of low and high crawl though, plus obstacles. It's going to hurt and be exhausting, but damn, I can't remember the last time we did something here that didn't hurt and wasn't exhausting, you know?

Thankfully all that's left after that is Crucible next Tuesday, three days of marching and obstacles and mock combat drills and etc. followed by a ten mile hike home. That's the road to everything I've worked for this past three months. I'm stoked!

That said, today's count is nineteen days until I leave this island, eighteen before I get to see you, and fourteen until I get Recruit Liberty (junk food feast for four awesome hours on base). Smooth sailing the final week, I'm so happy.

Like I said, I'm pretty psyched for the next two weeks. It will be hard as crap but easy because our goal is so close. I haven't had this much energy since I stepped on those yellow footprints. Seems like a lifetime ago. I think I've aged more in the past two and a half months than my friends will in ten years. We've been exposed to civilians more in the past couple weeks (team week, clothing issue, watching people on family day) and no offense, but you all look… different. Sort of lost and all the kids our age look stupid as hell. Perspective is everything, isn't it? Nothing has physically changed, but everything's different. Good stuff.

I can't wait until Charleston. The comforts of a hotel… that's like Disney World for a recruit. Big soft bed, hot water, colorful wall hangings, TV, room service, NO Drill Instructor, civilians call me sir, etc, etc. Most of all I get to be around you guys instead of sixty four recruits.

Just a quick note that I probably will not get a chance to write until next Sunday, due to the packed schedule. I'll spend a lot of time prepping my uniforms for Company Commanders Inspection (forgot to mention that) on Friday. That's an important one. That will use up most of my free time but please keep writing even if I can't respond immediately. I probably will stop writing after we get back from Crucible because by the time you get it, it will be family day. Also, try to be home on Sunday afternoon after the Crucible (Grad Sunday) because I bought a phone card to call home while on liberty. Tell Ry not to go paint balling that afternoon.

Lots of love to you guys, I'll see you very soon. Wish me luck.

Love,

Chad

Sunday, October 19, 2003

Sup, crackas?

Good morning, Parris Island… my last Sunday morning here before Grad. Week/Sunday Liberty. Finally. Next Sunday will be a four hour junk food feast… I can't wait.

Quickly to bring you up to speed on the last week:

Monday: Final Drill we took sixth place, but our SDI wasn't mad because he said we did a great job, it was just the scoring that was fucked. Whatever.

Tuesday: Prac. App. We placed second (Tied overall first on knowledge)

Wednesday: Took first place on PFT as a platoon

Thursday: Rappelled down a tower twice, slept in tents… been there, done that, got the tee shirt.

Friday: Killed a Brown Recluse in my tent… ick! Also, less scary was the gas chamber. I actually had a good time. They told us to close our eyes, hold our breath, and take our masks off… So about five of us (myself included) got gung ho, opened our eyes, breathed CS gas, and screamed out the discipline creed… lol it was great. Our SDI was impressed as hell. Don't worry, CS gas is harmless, it's just like military grade tear gas. Hurts like a mofo though.

Saturday: Co. Commanders inspection. We did good and we got rewarded… chose to see a movie as our present… guess what we picked… yep… Full Metal Jacket. We're a crazy ass platoon, aye sir.

I'll give you more detail on all that fun stuff when you get here next week. How awesome is that… next week! That tiny light at the end of the tunnel is a big ass hole in the mountain, now. We're done training in four days, probably by the time you get this.

All of us are hyped up to finish. The blood, sweat, and tears of the platoon are showing now as worthwhile. Pride in ourselves, confidence… its indescribable. In a few minutes I'm going and walking back to talk to some "go faster" recruits who just picked up yesterday. SUCKS TO BE THEM! They look so lost and weak and young. Poor Saps. They don't even know how bad it can get, yet.

A couple requests; could you please bring me a set of civilian clothes? Some khakis and my gray Fox hoodie or something like that. Also, could Ryan burn me a CD of all the songs by Tricky, Portishead, and Acid Jazz that are on the computer? You could bring my CD player and headphones for the ride… I haven't heard music in three months. It's really hard to understand, probably, but music is more important than you realize, when you can listen all the time. I think I sound stupid, but just trust me on this.

If you think of anything I'm forgetting just bring it, cause I'm an idiot. Oh… bathing suit. See? I forget crap.

This is probably the last letter I will write from boot camp. I get to call on Sunday afternoon so that's all good to go.

I just wanted to take a minute and thank you especially for getting me through this. It's the hardest thing I've ever done, by far, and I owe it all to my family. You can't know how important your support has been, but I do.

Dad, knowing that I did something right and made you proud… makes everything easier. I think we both know how things would have ended up if I had gone and wasted away time in college. I'm glad that I don't have to be the worthless brat that all my friends are, now. Their dads don't get to brag much, I bet.

Mom, I never realized how much we took for granted. The constant streams of mail and news from home have kept me sane, here in hell. I can't wait to just sit down and have a cup of coffee and a conversation.

Ryan, your letters as well as Mom and Dad's have helped me out a ton, but knowing that you're proud of me becoming a Marine… let's just say that every time I'm feeling like shit on the quarterdeck and I want to stop putting out, I ask myself "Would I stop running/marching/etc. if Ryan were standing there watching me?" The answer has always been "Hell no" and I never quit. I don't know why, but I'm compelled to be better because I know you expect and deserve a better example. Thank you for holding me to a higher standard.

To all of you, I'm just grateful that you all supported this decision. I know I would have dropped by now if it weren't for the words of encouragement and news that everything is okay at home.

Enough heavy stuff, now. On a much lighter note, I got more letters and magazines last night. Thanks a ton, everything helps. And Dad, the camo Nova looks cool, doesn't it?

I think I like the camo best. Really nice pump gun.

I'm trying to think of anything I missed or need to say in this last letter. I guess that's it, except to remind you to try and be home on Sunday. I will definitely call. I'm looking forward to it.

Well, that's all folks. I'm off to go back to the squad bay for our weekly slay fest, get some chow, and start packing for the Crucible (we step out at 2 AM Tuesday morning). Lots of loves, see you in about a week.

Your Marine,

Chad

P.S. Happy Birthday Bro! I'll get you something cool when I get back. Have fun!

Things to do after graduation
-Sleep
-Salt & vinegar chips
-BBQ Chips
-Corona
-Heineken
-Charlotte
-Candi
-Fried chicken
-Vanilla Ice cream
-Choc. Ice cream
-Finish game: STAR WARS KOTOR
-Read back issues of PC Gamer
-Re-activate cell phone/ voice mail
-Re-activate email
-Chew gum
-Try to forget boot camp
-Buy Supra
-Race a lot
-Watch re-runs I missed of Real World
-Kate
-Talk to the posse

-Pizza
-Spend time with family of course
-Hang out in Service B's
-Label everything I own with USMC
-Gloat to Rob
-Show Ryan quarter deck
-Make fun of "go faster" recruits… a lot
-STOP SITTING @ ATTENTION
-STOP STANDING @ ATTENTION
-STOP Eating Fast
-Eat sweet food and gum
-Tell Ryan how very proud of him I am

§

That thirteen weeks was a lifetime and a life change for all of us. At the end of October 2003 we headed south for Chad's Graduation.

When we got to the Island on family day, the realization of what recruits go through was shocking. Letters home don't scratch the surface. The first thing we saw was a DI screaming at a young man at the top of his considerable lungs, veins bulging. The poor kid looked like he wanted to dissolve into the nothingness the DI was assuring him he was a part of. I understand, now, that the breaking down and rebuilding of the self is a necessary and integral part of the training. Seeing it for the first time as a parent just made me angry. We had a few hours before we could be with Chad, so we walked around a bit and everywhere we saw recruits in different stages of training and different stages of glazed. I spoke to a couple of them on the sidewalk and then realized my mistake. They were afraid to answer me, and equally afraid of being rude. It made me anxious to talk to Chad. I knew from his letters what he had done with the last weeks; I didn't know what those weeks had done to him.

I was standing near Peatross Parade Deck when I first heard the running cadence. Recruits running was non-stop here. In just a couple of hours of being on the Island it faded into the background of recruits marching, recruits PTing, recruits moving from point A to point B. This had a different feel. The voices chanting were strong, confident. Around the corner the runners came, down the Boulevard De France, heads high, came the Third Recruit Training Battalion just as tens of thousands of Marines had done before them. This was their Motivation Run, their last circuit of the Depot. They had made it, and the power of their experience rippled off them. They were a world away from those scared recruits on the sidewalk. Everything about them said Marines.

I've always thought of myself as a patriotic American. I said the pledge in school, stood for the Star Spangled banner, and bought poppies for remembrance from Vets on Memorial Day. Nothing prepared me for watching those young men run past on the way to ringing the bell that would signal the completion of their training at Parris Island. I had never been so proud to be an American. Then, I saw Chad.

My mind had countless stored images of Chad as a baby, a little boy, a teenager. I had watched and been a part of each progression, one into the other. Now I was looking at my son the man, more amazing yet, my son the Marine, but it wasn't unfamiliar. All those years I had seen this young man staring out of my child's eyes. Okay, I said silently to him as he ran past, I believe you now. This is who you really are.

§

"No one saves us but ourselves. No one can and no one may. We ourselves must walk the path."

Buddha

Chapter 4

Instant Message Conversation between Chad and Rob
11/1/2003

a random soldier: Que pasa, contigo? I'm back, bro.

It's Rob: No way… no way.

a random soldier: way.

It's Rob: Holy shit!!!!!!!!!!! Where are you? Home? Oh my God, you're
        home, right?

a random soldier: Hell Fuckin Yeah! Corona in hand, porn on screen. I'm
        fuckin back.

It's Rob: I'm calling you.

a random soldier: Phone is dead, and don't call my home phone.
        Everybody is asleep.

It's Rob: I was going to write your letter tonight, too.

a random soldier: Call my cell tomorrow when its charged.

It's Rob: Okay, can do.

a random soldier: I've got nothing but time. Aye Sir.

It's Rob: Oh my God.

a random soldier: Dude I'm in fuckin shock. You don't know.

It's Rob: You're a United States Marine, I can imagine.

a random soldier: It was hell… Lol… But yeah.

It's Rob: You're a Marine.

a random soldier: It feels good.

It's Rob: You're a fucking Marine. I cannot believe it.

a random soldier: :-D

It's Rob: Ha-ha-ha-ha-ha! Oh my God, Chad, how long are you home for?

a random soldier: 10 days. Then MCT in Lejeune.

It's Rob: What's MCT?

a random soldier: For twenty three days. Then Twentynine Palms, Cali…
            Marine Combat Training.

It's Rob: What's your MOS?

a random soldier: Communications… Radioman.

It's Rob: Nice!

a random soldier: Attached to infantry.

It's Rob: You're gonna be with an infantry unit?

a random soldier: But I get to call artillery.

It's Rob: So wait…

a random soldier: They told me that and I was like, sign me the fuck up.

It's Rob: Ha-ha-ha-ha! Did you get taller? Do you look the same?

a random soldier: Same but older, 20 lbs heavier, and with a high and a random soldier: tight.

It's Rob: 20 lbs heavier! God, so much to catch up on…

a random soldier: Man it was fast but slow. I'm so lost here.

It's Rob: I'd imagine so.

a random soldier: Everything is awesome, but I'm so unaccustomed to all
          this freedom.

It's Rob: So many mornings, Chad, I woke up and was walking to class
          and I tried to imagine what you were doing. I'd be walking
          between classes and I'd imagine what you were doing and I
          couldn't. I'm in awe; you fucking did it. You did what I would
          have never dared to do.

a random soldier: Damn dude, you should've been there motherfucker.

It's Rob: Ha-ha-ha, oh God.

a random soldier: That's all I could think.

It's Rob: Oh God, Chad, I'm so happy. I mean, I knew you'd make it but
          it's just… excuse me while I be a total fucking idiot, ha-ha-ha.

a random soldier: LOL. Thanks bro. I'm still in shock myself so it will
          take a while to hit me.

It's Rob: I'm in shock, too. You did it, Chad. Do you realize that in fifth
          grade, from that moment, you wanted this? Jesus Christ! Cape
          has to seem so far away now, doesn't it? Fred's class, journalism.

a random soldier: Hell yeah! I don't have the words to describe it. AAF
          said it best: "I've been gone a thousand days/
          Things have changed like a decade".

It's Rob: Ha-ha-ha-ha, oh God… God, just talking to you, knowing what
          you've done seems to totally cheapen everything I've ever done
          here. It seems so much greater in worth.

a random soldier: Don't get down on yourself.

It's Rob: Oh no, I'm not, I'm just immensely proud of you.

a random soldier: I could be in Iraq in a few months. You gotta feel better
there.

It's Rob: Ha-ha, you know. I've had dreams where you came home, you
were jacked as hell, it was classic.

a random soldier: Yeah dude. Sorry the typing is slow.

It's Rob: Oh, don't worry.

a random soldier: My computer is buggin' from all the windows I have
open.

It's Rob: Ha-ha, I'd imagine you goddamned hero. What's your rank,
scumbag? They make you a Brigadier General yet?

a random soldier: PFC

It's Rob: PFC… PFC Clifton. Dear God!

a random soldier: Yep, wild ain't it?

It's Rob: Ha-ha-ha-ha, holy shit and you've shot an M16?

a random soldier: Bitch, not just shot…

It's Rob: Thrown a few grenades?

a random soldier: I can make kills at 800 yards.

It's Rob: HA-HA-HA!

a random soldier: In one shot with iron sights it feels…

It's Rob: You asshole!

a random soldier: God like, but hey I've always had a God complex
anyway.

It's Rob: Ha-ha, just a lil bit oh, wow God. We've read about boot so many
times and how many times have we written about it?

a random soldier: I know, boyhood dreams become hellish realities and a random soldier: then the payoff.

It's Rob: So wait, what are you doing in CA?

a random soldier: MOS school. After that it's Japan or Iraq.

It's Rob: I really, really hope they don't ship you to Iraq.

a random soldier: Hey if they do the it's just fate. We're all winding up
                  like we thought we would. Isn't it funny, nothing ever
                  goes as planned and it's going exactly as fucking
                  planned.

It's Rob: Is it going at all?

a random soldier: I do believe it is.

It's Rob: Ha-ha-ha! I'd imagine for you, yes.

a random soldier: So how are things?

It's Rob: Ha-ha-ha-ha! I don't even know. Awards, grades, tests, rinse,
          lather, die… You know, Chad, for what it's worth, I thank God
          that this came through, that you're alive, doing what you want,
          and that I can call you my friend. Now that the shit is through
          with, have a beer for me and I'll be back in an hour.

a random soldier: Will do man, see you then.

It's Rob: Cheers!

a random soldier: Cheers!

It's Rob: Would you still be my friend if I told you I smoked a pipe?

a random soldier: I posed with a Ka-bar in my mouth in front of the
                  mirror earlier. Call it even?

It's Rob: Even.

a random soldier: Good Shit.

It's Rob: That, by the way, is hilarious.

a random soldier: Same to you.

It's Rob: Can I express to you how it feels to be days away from 19 and having to check in at 11:15?

a random soldier: "Check in"?

It's Rob: Yes, this means that I'm in the dorm for the night and sober, at that.

a random soldier: Damn, that sucks!

It's Rob: Oh yeah.

a random soldier: I'm tired as fuck but too psyched to be at home to sleep.

It's Rob: Ha-ha, I know.

a random soldier: Hey, I went to catholic mass every Sunday.

It's Rob: You wrote my letter in catholic mass! I was so very proud.

a random soldier: Ha-ha yes!

It's Rob: BTW, I flipped at the mail hut…

a random soldier: Yeah I didn't want to write until I was sure I wasn't going to get hurt or something stupid and get sent home.

It's Rob: Ha-ha-ha

a random soldier: It happens more that you'd think most of the drops are medical.

It's Rob: How many guys did you know who got discharged?

a random soldier: Like 20. We finished w/ a platoon of 64, about 400 in the company. But there were like 60 drops from the Co. It's hard to get out, actually.

It's Rob: What happened to them?

a random soldier: If you want to quit, you're on the island for longer than

a random soldier: if you just suck it up. They're still there waiting on
discharges.

It's Rob: No shit.

a random soldier: No shit. It sucks for them.

It's Rob: You think they do that on purpose?

a random soldier: Yes! Vicious Mother Fucking Island.

It's Rob: Ha-ha-ha-ha but Christ, you made it through.

a random soldier: Somehow.

It's Rob: You fuckin made it.

a random soldier: We humped 54 miles on the Crucible. That blew.

It's Rob: How heavy a pack or just unloaded?

a random soldier: 45lbs. Just food…

It's Rob: In how long?

a random soldier: and clothes. No ammo. Two days…

It's Rob: (I've carried 45, btw, that's hardcore) Two days? Fuck!

a random soldier: Wasn't as bad as I expected.

It's Rob: Ha-ha

a random soldier: Ha-ha… Everyone suddenly wants to call me.

It's Rob: Ha-ha!

a random soldier: How little has changed… wait…

It's Rob: Well, we're all very glad you're alive.

a random soldier: I'm the new guy again right?

It's Rob: Ha-ha, seriously, you get all the benefits.

a random soldier: For real. I'd love some!

It's Rob: I'd imagine, but dude your pants would hardly be off and you would…

a random soldier: Probably, that will be fixed.

It's Rob: Well, Lejuene won't be so bad as Parris and Cali won't be bad at all.

a random soldier: Cali will be cool. Damn its good to talk to you, bro.

It's Rob: I think my friends think I'm crazy. I narrated it all from 5th grade when we went to smoke.

a random soldier: You are.

It's Rob: I know, right?

a random soldier: LOL… Why do they think you're crazy besides the obvious?

It's Rob: Because I was being rather animated, I suppose I was just very excited to have talked to you.

a random soldier: Ah, I'm touched.

It's Rob: And, of course, all of what I said was as relevant to them as to me, ha-ha.

a random soldier: No sarcasm intended. LOL… Yes!

It's Rob: Ha-ha, well thank you.

a random soldier: They probably hate you and are thinking oh, what a special jarhead.

It's Rob: Or… My roommate is an asshole…

a random soldier: That's freaking awesome. "Those attacks spiked upward recently to an average of thirty three a day. Most occur in central Iraq, but Saturday's deadliest blow came in the north, in the city of Mosul, where the U.S. military said a makeshift roadside bomb exploded

a random soldier: and killed two U.S. soldiers and wounded two others
            as they drove by in two civilian vehicles." This is not
            under control. I just read that.

It's Rob: No shit, dude.

a random soldier: My first news bite since I got home.

It's Rob: What have they been telling you? It's been a mess over there. On
            average, two a day.

a random soldier: That the ARMY is fucking up.

It's Rob: Well, they're sure as fuck right.

a random soldier: Did you know?

It's Rob: Baghdad is the world's new capital for terrorism. It's an industry,
            now.

a random soldier: Its coming through the Corps gossip fountain that its
            going to be a permanent rotation like Okinawa.

It's Rob: Oh yeah, we have no exit plan.

a random soldier: How we're still in Okinawa after all these years?
            Baghdad is supposed to be becoming a USMC base.

It's Rob: Oh, Christ!

a random soldier: That's the shit we were told before we left yesterday.

It's Rob: Dude. That's no good. But, you know I have total faith in your
            ability to be obnoxiously alive, no matter where they throw you.

a random soldier: LOL… Fuck you and thanks.

It's Rob: Well, you know I'm so encumbered (and college won't be any
            better), and if they ask me to write your fucking eulogy…

a random soldier: They might.

It's Rob: I mean, seriously, how much can pretentious young intellects
            like me be expected to do?

a random soldier: You'll have to fight my mother for it. But do.

It's Rob: Ha-ha-ha… She'd win, you know.

a random soldier: Say it was a special request that I get two because I'm
            that awesome and deserving of tribute. Well hopefully,
            um, I won't need one.

It's Rob: Ha-ha… Please, assholes like you die in bed. We'll be old men,
            drinking beer on your front porch before you're shipped back in
            a body bag.

a random soldier. LOL… Fine by me.

It's Rob: And it's all because God has a sense of humor.

a random soldier: I know. Name a son of a bitch who is more asking for it
            than me? You can't. I'm buying a ninja bike by the way.

It's Rob: ha-ha-ha-ha-ha-ha-ha-ha-ha-ha-ha-ha-ha! Pizza downstairs,
            gimme a few.

a random soldier: OK.

It's Rob: Back.

a random soldier: Cool. I'm getting a bike prolly this week.

It's Rob: A ninja bike?

a random soldier: Yeah.

It's Rob: Should I start writing now?

a random soldier: Yes.

It's Rob: Maybe I'll add in a quote from you, for added irony.

a random soldier: Ha-ha of course. I love irony.

It's Rob: "He loved Irony, he said that night, and we enjoyed a hearty
            e-chuckle. Little did we know, but we never know, do we… ahh

a random soldier: Ha-ha.

It's Rob: God, I want to be home now.

a random soldier: Good trash.

It's Rob: Yeah speaking of trash… How is good old DE?

a random soldier: Colder than SC.

It's Rob: Really? It's pretty warm today, actually. Nov. 1, and I was
        rocking shorts.

a random soldier: Yeah.

It's Rob: In other news, I've gotten into Radiohead. Hate me yet?

a random soldier: Ever listen to Portishead?

It's Rob: Heard of…

a random soldier: Radiohead is over rated euro trash.

It's Rob: Oh, but I do so adore them.

a random soldier: You would… LOL!

It's Rob: I totally would.

a random soldier: OUCH FUCK FUCK OUCH SHIT DAMN CRAP

It's Rob: I've also been prone to smoking cigarettes after study hall,
        writing disaffected e-journal entries, and criticizing my
        classmates for no reason at all Oh beautiful! What was that for?

a random soldier: Ka-bar… sharp… Dropped on my hand… OUCH!

It's Rob: Ha-ha! Did they give you one?

a random soldier: I bought one. A big one.

It's Rob: Ha-ha.

a random soldier: I just cut my damn wrist open.

It's Rob: Oh, goddamn.

a random soldier: Not even on purpose.

It's Rob: Now that's irony…

a random soldier: It fucking bit me.

It's Rob: You know he was just nipping at you.

a random soldier: For real!

It's Rob: Will you get to use it?

a random soldier: That's crazy…

It's Rob: Or carry it with you or do they give you one?

a random soldier: In my pack, too big for the waist. Be right back…
getting bandages.

It's Rob: Ha-ha okay.

a random soldier: Back. No lie, that just sucks.

It's Rob: "CHAD CLIFTON, son of Richard and Terri Clifton, died of
accidental wounds on the night of Nov. 1, 2003. Chad had
recently returned from boot camp when his wrist was cut open
at his computer. The knife was found, but cause has yet to be
determined. The dumb ass died after making it through boot.
What a jackass."

a random soldier: LOL! Profile that shit. No room in mine.

It's Rob: Ha-ha-ha, like there's room in mine?

a random soldier: Actually I'll just save this window…

It's Rob: I'll save the conversation for the novelty of it.

a random soldier: …and put it up tomorrow.

It's Rob: Yeah. My profile is too busy with quotes and bullshit. What is on
my profile…

a random soldier: Something, I'm guessing, from Great Expectations.

It's Rob: Ha-ha, oh yes, the extended tribute to the distant love. Lori and I are still together… BTW…

a random soldier: Good stuff. Brad and Kate broke up.

It's Rob: Oh really?

a random soldier: Amazing… didn't see that one coming.

It's Rob: Yeah, predictable. Somewhat disappointing. She's probably screwing some androgynous art student. Need I add pretentious?

a random soldier: My thoughts exactly. I have a Ka-Bar.

It's Rob: She might as well screw you. At least that would be original.

a random soldier: Exactly Rob. You follow my train of thought.

It's Rob: Ha-ha-ha.

a random soldier: But God is a sick bastard and justice is his favorite joke.

It's Rob: So very true. I wonder if C has hooked up with anybody at all.

a random soldier: I honestly don't care. Lots of time to think in boot camp… She my less threatening replacement for K.

It's Rob: Ha-ha.

a random soldier: Sort of a psychological other end of the spectrum.

It's Rob: She's unchallenging at least.

a random soldier: K fucked me up bad, still probably would if she were here. Damn it I'm still bleeding.

It's Rob: Still?

a random soldier: No… I mean literally.

It's Rob: Ha-ha-ha-ha! Oh perfect.

a random soldier: It's sad, the lengths to which we go in order to play word games… LOL

It's Rob: But we do it so well. So wait, when do you leave precisely?

a random soldier: I get on a bus November 10.

It's Rob: Oh, god damn it! What time?

a random soldier: Late… Around 11.

It's Rob: That night?

a random soldier: Yup. Will you be home?

It's Rob: I'm coming home… now I am. That's my birthday.

a random soldier: For your b-day? Yeah!

It's Rob: and if my parents love me, they're letting me come home.

a random soldier: Yeah man that would rock.

It's Rob: It's happening. I don't see why they wouldn't; I can drive my car back up. Yeah, I'm definitely going to come home. I'll talk to my parents tomorrow.

a random soldier: That would be cool.

It's Rob: It will happen… Ah, that's exciting! Okay, I must take leave. My friends are yanking me off to an English-subtitled Swedish movie. Now you have no choice but to hate me.

a random soldier: Yes.

It's Rob: but I will call you tomorrow.

a random soldier: looking forward to it, bro.

It's Rob: Definitely. It's so fucking good to hear from you…

a random soldier: Peace man.

It's Rob: ...and welcome back.

a random soldier: Thanks!

It's Rob: I'm real fucking proud of you!

Chad left a response to Rob's live journal:
So bleak, so nihilistic in your "literati" approach to the mundane intellectual suburbia that is collective thought... and collective thought is a wasteland because thought is full of what we know. We know nothing.

And it's so good to leave and go and come back, but you're still here, bro... in the same god forsaken places I left behind. Fuck, you need to get out.

I remember rainy days even when the sun was fucking shining and I remember sleepless nights spent alone with a bottle and a pen... the outpouring of words like blood, oozing from open wounds into the holy grail of my latest masterpiece... and as I looked down upon that page from my intellectual cross of self loathing I tried to find some redemption... it never came. I remember that.

If you didn't have the books to read and the course-load, you'd replace it with the same damn thing. The writing is all exhibitionism, putting ourselves on display. You do it cause you're good at it, for approval and for effect or maybe for the opposite of those... who's to say. You have a weblog. The books you'd read anyway because it's voyeuristic. Some novels are works of art and analogous in parts to everyone's fascinations or obsessions... I never have forgotten K and I'm years older and I've been through some shit. Fucking Estella.

It's good to be home, bro. You're the only one I know who could follow that through to the end and understand what's said between the lines. We should talk.
Chad

§

It was so good to have him home, to see the things about him that had changed, to see the things that hadn't. But we all knew it was temporary.

Ten days after boot, Chad left for MCT, Marine Combat Training, in Camp Lejeune, North Carolina. His Dad took him to meet the bus. I didn't go. He didn't need to see me cry. It was hard letting him go again. We didn't know when he'd get home.

I knew he was eager to get on with his training, but he was still shell shocked from Parris Island. I remember joking with him when I hugged him bye. "It's only three weeks. And it has to be better than boot."

He smiled, kissed me, and was gone again. All I ever heard about

Combat Training was that it was cold and he had lived in a plywood shack with rats. "Way worse than boot."

We had no contact for those three weeks. He called from the airport on his way to Twentynine Palms, California. I could tell he was excited and nervous. He had made it through the training. Now he had school and would learn the skills needed for his MOS.

There was a gap between arriving at Twentynine Palms and the beginning of the Field Radio Operator Course. Since idle Marines are the devils playthings, they gave them busy work, military style. There were whole days spent outside in formation. Cleaning already spotless barracks. He was mostly miserable which made the news that he would be coming home for the holidays all the better.

We had a great time that Christmas. We went shopping at the Mall, decorated the tree, and cooked tons of food. All four of us piled onto the couch and watched Charlie Brown's Christmas. It was a perfect holiday.

With family celebrations covered, Chad began catching up with his friends. For the first time he got a good look at the change in himself. He'd grown up so much, and what was once familiar felt strange. He loved his friends, family, and hometown just as much as always, but his life wasn't here anymore. And he wasn't that kid.

§

Journal Entry
Thursday December 25, 2003

Lying here wide awake
Open eyes staring at the night outside
Cause when I close them
I have to stare at the dark inside

It's currently 2:51 AM as I'm looking at this. Just like old times. I don't really need to sleep anyway. I'm not even thinking a lot, at least about anything important. It's Christmas day, I'm not really stressing over anything, and it's good to be home. I don't know what I'm still doing up. Scenarios keep playing out in my head, little imperfect fantasies of how things will go when and if I ever see some girl again. I'm not even going to lie… she trips me up. See, that's the thing about blogs. We always write what we're practically screaming for the world to know, but you can never come out and say what you mean.

Its cool being home for Christmas. I missed my family a lot while I was out in the field for MCT and then went to California. In a lot of ways though, I look around at my friends and I can't stop thinking how much I've changed and they've stayed the same. I love being home, but I definitely don't belong here now. Too many ghosts here, too much past. Earning my eagle, globe, and anchor gave me a fresh start. Coming back… I find myself writing and alone at 3 am, just like it used to be. I don't want to leave, but I don't want to stay.

Journal Entry
Tuesday, December 30, 2003

Just got home from Dover. It's really early. I'm telling myself there's nothing to do so I won't go out tonight, I'll just rest for New Years. That's a good idea. I hope I stay home and sleep. I'm exhausted.

Trying to come up with a good New Years resolution is hard, especially if you're as brilliant and perfect as myself. I mean, I can think of stupid things to say for a resolution. Like… Make a million dollars. But that's pretty fucking dumb. And I don't need to lose weight and I don't want to quit drinking, so the obvious ones are out. I need something original. Like, don't talk to any hookers this year. Maybe that's it. No hookers.

Journal Entry
Wednesday, December 31, 2003

Its tomorrow.

I just spent another dazed night wandering around SoDel trying to figure out what I want. Watched a movie. Drove to the beach with a couple people and walked around. It was all messed up and I felt like someone stuck me in an indie film. Not even in color. It's all so fake when you hold this up to my real life… grenades and M16's and violence and enthusiasm and serving my country… wait a second… I don't know which one is real. Which is me? Walking on some desolate beach in the moonlight wishing I were with someone, anyone to take my mind off things… or am I really the shadow in camouflage and face paint pointing my assault rifle like some damn recruiting commercial? Yeah, "Join the Marines" and be just like me. I can kill a man at 500 yards with open sights, but I can't deal with an 18 year old girl who's had me wrapped around her finger since like 8th grade. What the hell is my problem?

I want to scream. I won't though. That would be melodramatic and stupid.

Thursday, January 01, 2004
Happy New Year!

Actually, it really was. I had a lot of fun, even though I was surprisingly one of the most sober people there. I rolled in about quarter after nine. By midnight it was just getting worse for the people who were already sick. Traditional countdown (So I lost Count… twice… I can't count when I'm drinking. Leave me alone.) and Yeah! champagne. Except I don't like champagne. So I agreed to do shots of peppermint schnapps with Christin, since the vodka I was drinking was killing me slowly.

What next… I have this faded half memory of sitting in the floor with Brooke eating Doritos. I only ever see her when I'm drinking and I have this crazy idea that maybe she doesn't really exist. She's just this dark haired, thoughtful girl in my head that comes with the booze. I often tell her she should be a model, but she always says she's to short. I'm always like bullshit, you're gorgeous. And she's like no, I'm too short. It happens every time we drink. Hmmmm. Sorry Brooke, I just decided you're a figment of my imagination, I hope you don't mind.

Um… skipping over stuff… can't tell everything… Long story short I woke up this morning after staying up all night taking care of Christin. I got about two hours of sleep. Jill was being loud and wouldn't shut up cause she got lots of sleep and damn that girl talks a lot! Love you Jill! Anyway, we all woke up and went to breakfast at Crackerbarrel and I took Caitlin to Starbucks with me and we got iced chai's cause those are good and I needed the caffeine boost cause I'm just not going to sleep. Sleep is for the weak.

This year is a brand new year, enjoy yourselves. You never know what things will be a year from now, but I hope I get to spend it with the same people! You rock my world, SoDel.

Journal Entry
Friday, January 02, 2004

I'm already packed or gone by the time anyone probably reads this, so any damage done, I'm sorry you'll just have to cope with it.

Isn't it so weird, just so absolutely crazy the things that fate will throw at you at totally the wrong time? The past 48 hours of my life are completely tragic, wonderful, and bloody ironic. For the sake of still giving a fuck, I'm not going to blatantly mention names so you'll just have to figure it out… But to further my point… I meet a friend of a friend at a party, we start hanging out. She's way more fun than I had thought before. No biggy right? Well, long story made short, we have an awesome time and we both leave extremely confused.

That was the part of my New Years Story I left out on purpose. Tonight we go see a movie after dancing around the subject. It was not a date at all, just hanging out. The movie was okay.

Talking to her afterwards, and taking her home… it took like an hour, sitting in her driveway trying to figure out what to say to make things simple and better. I'm a writer. A fucking poet. Shouldn't I have something to say? No. I sat there and thought how much this sucked, and maybe I could press the issue and maybe this and maybe that and maybe maybe BLAH and then my head exploded. Not really, but I felt that way. Instead I kept my cool, I think, subtle comment here and hidden meanings there... Neither of us knew for sure what the other one was thinking, but I know we were both feeling the same things. It was all over her face and in her eyes and I could see the same bittersweet expression in my reflection. We both knew that I was leaving this morning... Nothing has ever sucked more than that. Ever. Oh, and Dashboard Confessional was on the radio. What the fuck.

Fuck 29 Palms, California. I have a love/hate relationship with that place. Currently at hate.

"God is a comedian playing to an audience too afraid to laugh."
Voltaire

Chapter 5

Journal Entry:
Sunday, January 04, 2004

What a rough day.

Last night I flew into LA and met up w/ a few of my bros from the base. We had like a seven hour wait for our shuttle bus to pick us up, so we went into the strip club across from the Hilton and spent a lot of money. This girl Talia gave me her number. I'm so not going to call. Something about dating a stripper is just wrong, even for a Marine. Lust just isn't love, and my stupid romantic ass needs something more than a good lay. Not that that hurts. But something. Anything.

In other news. Mark is wicked pissed for no reason. Whatever, my cell is always on if you want to talk man to man. Oh wait, you called me a pussy right? I guess I am, you know, since Marines are pussies and we just pretend to fight wars so that jealous college brats can sit on instant messenger and argue with text and a sense of indignation. Yeah, I'm the pussy.

I'll be home next year.

Journal Entry:
Monday, January 05, 2004

My days have started to run together into one big fucking montage (the soundtrack is most definitely that song Stupefied).

I got an IM last night from Amy declaring that she's pissed with me and that she and Mark are back together. I'm caught somewhere in between telling her that I don't give a fuck, I hooked up with a stripper I met in LA the night I left (Talia, and she's a really classy girl… no really I'm fucking serious. For a stripper? Hot Damn.), or telling her that she'd be better off in a non-mentally abusive situation. Well, Amy, I hope you got what you wanted. He got jealous and you got him back. Mission accomplished. Freaking awesome. I guess you'll get what you're asking for right? Cause I'm not one to judge. So much for that bonding thing you were talking about. All girls are the fucking same. Point in case.

In other and possibly more relevant news, I pick up with my FROC (Field Radio Operator Course) unit tomorrow morning. This is good, because we just do idiotic things all day in MAT platoon, like today's twelve hours of outside formation in forty degree weather. It was a bitch. FROC won't be a whole lot better but I will get more free time, so that never hurts. I will have room inspections every day so I have to find a new place to stash the beer.

Bought an Xbox and a TV, by the way. You can get good deals on electronics here cause everyone who leaves sells their stuff like crazy. I'm looking to buy some cheap games and have my brother ship the ones I bought while I was home.

Journal Entry:
Sunday, January 11, 2004

Not a whole lot new. Class is fun. Learned to drive HMMWV's last week, I have a test on it tomorrow. If I'm in the top ten from my class at the end of it all, I get a chance to move up to MEOC which is some kind of non-grunt job with communications and microwave radar. I might rather be a grunt though.

I just really want to get to the Fleet and be able to finally settle down in a job. I've had four different addresses in the past six months. I just want to be in a unit, even if we're going other places at the time. Japan or Iraq or Europe or on a SouthPac someplace. Soon though. I'll get there soon.

Journal Entry:
Monday, January 19, 2004

This is a time when the trigger pull is light, the knife unsheathes smoothly, and a rope hangs loosely. The only thought I have is do I dare. The only look I have is a stare. The only feeling in me is despair.

My brother, Ryan. He says it's inspired by ROB'S MOM. Yeah, he is better than me but fuck it. My poems are cool too!!!!

By the way, my brother just reminded me. New Years resolution was broken Saturday when I asked a hooker if she knew any good hotels. Don't worry, its not as bad as it sounds.

Long Weekend.
Okay first off, sorry girls… I'm not pretty anymore. Long story short, I wrecked a four wheeler at about 50 mph on Sunday in Palm Springs

and now my face is all bruised and cut up. Whatever. I wasn't getting laid tonight anyway.

All in all it was an okay weekend. We left for Palm Springs on Saturday night and got there to find out that all the hotels were booked. We looked for three hours. It sucked. Anyway, we ended up crashing in the floor with some fellow devil dogs in some hotel they had smartly made reservations for. All is well that ends well.

Want to hear some sucky poetry? Me too! My world is stuck between poetry and machine guns. I feel so uniquely cliché.

Standing here on the curb
I'm on the verge
Of something great
Wishing you were here
To share this with me

The nights are long and cold
The days are warm but getting older
Every morning I wake up
And wonder how I made it through
Another evening
I'm always on my own
But you really wouldn't know

I talk to my best friend
Call him on the phone
He's doing fine
School is hard
I guess I'm alright
I'll show him all my new scars
Tell your girl I said hello
Goodbye

Just another fucking night
Alone
Just another fucking night

Actually, I'm a lot more chipper than that but you get the drift. Sometimes things just get a little depressing, even when they're not.

Journal Entry:
Sunday, February 08, 2004

We're going out to the field tomorrow for three or four days to do practical applications on all the radios and antennas and shit we've been doing for the past couple months. I'll be out of this god forsaken desert in like two weeks. We graduate on the 25th, leave on the 26th. Thank god. If I get stationed here for good, I'm going to cry like a little girl.

Where am I going? I don't know. Initially we were told we were all going to Iraq, but now that might not be until the second rotation of Marines, who leave in September. With any luck, my papers for MSG will be through by then. MSG, the Marine Security Guards, are the guys who guard the embassies. It's a good program; I'm trying to get into it.

What else… I can't really think of a lot else. Hopefully I'll get to come home for a little while after I graduate here, but no guarantees. I do pick up Lance Corporal sometime in April, though. That's pretty much all I know right now. In the meantime I can just hope for Japan and a flight home for a week or two.

Anyway, I'm off to get some food and walk back up this hill to my room so I can iron a uniform for tomorrow's inspection.

Journal Entry:
Saturday, February 21, 2004

I leave 29 Palms next Thursday. I head to my unit 2/5 (2nd Battalion, 5th Marines) based in Camp Pendleton, near San Diego. It's an infantry unit. Right now, the unit itself is in Iraq. I'm stoked. My life is so much more real than anything I expected it to be when I was playing with plastic army men in the back yard with Rob when I was twelve. So much different than what I thought it would be when I was playing GI Joes with my little brother in my room. But at the same time, it's exactly how I planned it. Fate is fate. You can't escape it. You just have to rush headlong into it and hope to come out the other side.

And no, I'm not scared. Everyone asks me this. I'm not you. I've been prepping for this all my life.

Sorry to sound angry. It's just that everyone relates things to themselves. If you were in my shoes, if you were this, if you were that… well I'm not you. I am the only one who can make the choice. I volunteered for the unit. I volunteered for the Corps. I survived it so far. I probably won't even get a chance to see combat in Iraq, but at least I can die old knowing I had the balls to try. It's not even about honor or glory or proving anything to anyone else. It's all about me. Putting my life on the line to test my fate, to test my courage. When the needle hits 180mph, am I going to slow down? I dunno. I have to max it out, see if I've got the guts to do it. Same thing with Iraq. I could never live it down if I didn't try to go over as infantry. I'm not a hard ass. I'm probably just stupid. But ignorance is bliss, isn't it? It's not about being extreme or cool. It's about testing the limit.

I should have died a year ago on cold pavement in the rain, racing down a highway with no fear. I should have died when I lost control and hung a 90 degree turn from 2 lanes over at 90mph. It was physically impossible for me to have made that. I should have hit the pole on my drivers' side. I didn't. I was saved. You know why? If you're born to hang, you'll never drown. Fate was with me that night. Irresponsible, stupid and young. Yeah, I was. I should have thought of my family and friends. I did. In the split second I realized I was sideways on the highway headed towards a telephone pole at 90, I did. It was something I won't do again, but the guys who witnessed it will still swear to you I should have been dead. I was twenty feet and a tenth of a second from being a high school tragedy.

There's no reason in the world I'm here today other than I'm supposed to be. My point is not that I'm indestructible; it's just that I'll be fine in Iraq. I'm charmed, destined for something other than that. Trust me. I've made it this far, haven't I?

Wow, that was a depressing entry. Rather dire. But whatever. Day to day its not all doom and gloom around here. I know I'll be fine, whatever happens. I have a lot left to do. My brother and I have to party and I've got to go to college and find something worth while. I'm not going to take any risks that I don't have to take. I'm a little older and a little wiser than I used to be. I see the big picture. I just wish everyone would understand why I'm going.

Instant Message Conversation Between Chad and Rob
February 2004

a random soldier: So have you heard?

It's Rob: I have not. Heard what? About the extended deployment in Iraq?

a random soldier: I got orders to a grunt unit in Iraq.

It's Rob: No fuckin way… no way!

a random soldier: 2/5 based in Pendleton but they're in Iraq now.

It's Rob: Shit, you're going to Iraq.

a random soldier: I report in on Thursday.

It's Rob: In Iraq?? Or Pendleton?

a random soldier: I hope I catch up.

It's Rob: Christ, ugh, where is Pendleton?

a random soldier: San Diego.

It's Rob: Oh, well at least the territory is nice. Christ! A combat marine.
        PFC or did you make corporal?

a random soldier: Lance Corporal in March.

It's Rob: All right! Rock on.

a random soldier: Top of my class. I got to choose my unit.

It's Rob: And you chose a grunt unit. Jesus Christ, Chad. Ha-ha-ha… go
        figure.

a random soldier: I'm stoked.

It's Rob: Aren't you scared at all?

a random soldier: Glory, style, and balls, bro.

It's Rob: Yeah, I suppose they teach you that. Hey, did you get to blow
        shit up with a harrier yet?

a random soldier: No. I'm a FNG!

It's Rob: Fucking New Guy!

a random soldier: I'm not scared. Everything I've ever done was for this.
        It's epic.

It's Rob: Well, when you come back home after your rotation we can have
        a drink and you can tell me all about it.

a random soldier: Yes. Do you have K's number?

It's Rob: I did before my cell phone died. Sorry.

a random soldier: Fuck. I'll call her hippie mother.

It's Rob: "I'm going to war!"

a random soldier: And your daughter should have married me. lol. I'm a random soldier: dashing.

It's Rob: No, you totally need to come back with wounds. Then she can nurse you and be sarcastic.

a random soldier: Well fuck. I love u man. Don't rail against society too hard.

It's Rob: Who, me? Hey listen please, seriously email me with contact information so I can write your sandy jarhead ass. You understand me jarhead? Contact information!

a random soldier: Will do. You're writing my memoirs if I bite it.

It's Rob: Just make sure to send me shit and I totally will. I can make that shit fly, liberal arts boy, jarhead best friend.

a random soldier: At least an indi script.

It's Rob: Shit, man, I'll immortalize you with a National Book Award.

a random solder: Based on us. Ultimate coming of age story, we always wanted what the other one had…

It's Rob: It's gold.

a random soldier: It is so gold.

It's Rob: Like, honestly, I can work that so well. I actually started it in my head. First Chapter is your going away party. It's perfect.

a random soldier: I know. Mine starts with a preface. I can't end it tho… …You will.

It's Rob: Look, it will end when you come home safe and go to college and have plenty of adventures but all your limbs.

a random soldier: I hope. I'm sure it will start that way anyway. You have to write it tho. Some proof we existed if I can't write the last lines. Promise. We're linked for a reason.

It's Rob: I swear I'll do it; I have nothing else worthwhile to write about. Love, Sex, Education, alcohol, repeat.

a random soldier: Thank you. That's really my only fear. I appreciate it.

It's Rob: Don't worry. No matter what happens, you won't die. Just
fucking write to me, so I have material! Even if it's so much as a
name of the place on the map, a smell, a taste and a sight. That's
all I need.

a random soldier: No problem, remember that line about the greatest
minds of our generation?

It's Rob: Ginsberg, of course…

a random soldier: Don't let school waste you. Always live. I wish I had
the formal education you do. Your blog worries me.

It's Rob: It's not as bad as it sounds bro. It's just that nobody knows me
here and it's temporary.

a random soldier: Look how insignificant it all seems. Me especially. God
is dead but there's still experience worthwhile.

It's Rob: I… I just can't believe it, you know? My best friend is going to
Iraq.

a random soldier: Well keep your head up…

It's Rob: I will. Just… don't die, seriously, don't die. It's not worth it.

a random soldier: I prolly won't see combat. Not this time.

It's Rob: Well, good. Enjoy the territory, sample the local wares, and write
a few disinterested letters and come home in one piece.

a random soldier: I pray I do, but I won't. Not this time.

It's Rob: I can't say I'm behind you on that one.

a random soldier: Combat I mean.

It's Rob: Yeah.

a random soldier: C'mon. Tempt fate! Lol.

It's Rob: Ha-ha-ha-, right! I'll leave that to you. God knows you'll start

It's Rob: something, ha-ha-ha.

a random soldier: Born to hang, you'll never drown.

It's Rob: This is true. God damn it, Chad, you're going to die old and
saggy in your bed and I'll get drunk at your funeral and piss on
your grave and laugh loudly and see you in hell a few months
later.

a random soldier: I'll let you get to bed.

It's Rob: Yeah…

a random soldier: But yeah…

It's Rob: We prep school kids need our beauty sleep, you know.

a random soldier: We're too big for death, bro. Sweet dreams!

It's Rob: You too, honey.

Journal Entry
February 24, 2004

Lying in my rack trying to think of something to write about. Whatever
I write is bound to feel as forced, awkward, and confused as I am right
now.

I'm exhausted, physically and emotionally. I know I'm going to 2/5…
I volunteered. Hopefully, check in won't be such a bitch on Thursday. I
still don't know if I'm staying in Pendleton or going to Iraq. Either way,
I just want to do something real. I'm sick of training. This student shit is
boring.

PFT in the morning. I'll probably do horrible, I feel sick as hell. I'm
really worried about my score, its gone way downhill since boot camp or
even before. Pull-ups especially. I have to get up at like 0450. Better get
used to it.

I really want to call home. It's about 11:00 PM at home right now
though, and I'm not going to wake anyone up so I can cry about how much
of a mess my life is. Suck it up. I keep telling myself I'm on my own, that
I've done fine so far, but all I really want is to just go home for awhile. I'm
not ready for the fleet yet. I'm too strung out.

It's 8:00 PM. Way early, but I'm going to sleep. Fuck this!

Journal Entry:
March 6, 2004

Friday night was spent like a pocket full of singles in a bad strip club. Hollow, and unmemorable. We drank and watched movies. I woke up in my room, alone, clothes smelling of stale beer. It's cold in my room.

I'm watching Real World. Their problems don't add up to mine. I am self centered, and my world is stuck in 2X. Home seems long ago and far away.

I want to see K more than anything. I can feel her body, my finger tips remember. I feel stupid. It was a lifetime ago and didn't mean anything to her or did I? My picture still hangs on her wall, right next to Robs. Obsession? Define the line between obsession and devotion to an ideal, the only thing that is constant and unchanged. Not her but the idea of her.

It ruins me.

Other girls are silly and meaningless. I want K to challenge me. She never did submit. Maybe that's the intoxicating part. I would always obey if she called.

And then I realize… it has nothing to do with her. It's me. I hold nothing sacred. My vision of myself is pretty accurate, at least it was when I was with her. Mercenary in all aspects. But I felt like I needed one thing to which I would swear fealty. Somewhere I got this honor among thieves style system of morality. Like I needed to justify my absence of faith in anything else. She is faith, life.

"I have never advocated war except as a means of peace."
Ulysses S. Grant

Chapter 6

Journal Entry:
March 16, 2004

Just got done packing my gear to go to field exercises in Yuma, AZ. A month of blowing things up with aircraft. Sounds cool, but it will probably find a way to suck. Welcome to the Corps.

2/5 is hard. Unfair, and hard. I love it. I hate it. Welcome to the grunts.

It's foggy and raining here in sunny southern California. Outstanding. It doesn't matter. I'm trying to write when it's a sober night for me and I'm not so trashed that all I can focus on is how miserable some things are. I'm actually really happy here, and I've made friends, but damn if I don't get homesick sometimes.

Sorry I'm not as brilliant when I'm sober. This must make for dull reading.

New rule: Tequila and beer when it's hot, rum when it's cold.

See? I'm just that boring when sober. Stupid revelations like that ruin everything. Liquor helps me focus. Right now, I have a gallon jug of water a six pack of chocolate donuts. Fascinating, eh?

I live, eat, sleep, and breathe Marine Corps. I want to go home more than anything. Remember who I actually am.

Instant Message Conversation between Chad and Rob:

a random soldier: Que pasa?

It's Rob: You! What's going on?

a random soldier: Yes me. Freshly fingerprinted and photographed.

It's Rob: For what?

a random soldier: Some dumb ass from my unit got stabbed and arrested in Mexico, so naturally the authorities call me.

It's Rob? Shit! Is he okay?

a random soldier? And were like hey, wtf Clifton, you shady bitch what happened? And I'm all like I dunno I was drunk and sleeping deuces.

It's Rob: Wait, where was this?

a random soldier: They don't believe me. It's fucked up.

It's Rob: That's crazy!

a random soldier: I'm still in AZ

It's Rob: Like, mug shot style?

a random soldier: Yeah. It's a conspiracy… So how are things?

It's Rob: Well! Things are good, preppish. I went home for the weekend. How is the desert, Jarhead?

a random soldier: You love that phrase, don't you? Well…

It's Rob: I do. Its very civvie.

a random soldier: The desert is OK, as we would say, very "skate". Meaning, we skate through it. Easy, chilled out.

It's Rob: Good!

a random soldier: But it got stressful today. I'm going to be bitched at about 2300 tonight. Everyone will be because of said dumb ass. grrr. We'll kill him later when he recovers from the knife wound.

It's Rob: How did that happen?

a random soldier: I dunno, as I said, I was passed out in my room.

It's Rob: That's freaky. What if they carved out your kidneys and you

a random soldier: were kidney less? That would be a medical discharge, I believe, free money!

It's Rob: But no kidneys!

a random soldier: Free money woohoo!

It's Rob: They'd give you GI lowest-bidder kidneys.

a random soldier: Mine are gonna need replacing eventually anyway.

It's Rob: True… No, that's your liver. Oh, btw, my friend and I were making a top five list of military flashpoints;
1.DMZ, Korea

a random soldier: What for?

It's Rob: For fun.

a random soldier: You have no lives but continue…

It's Rob: 2. Pearl Harbor II: Mass Sampan Invasion
3. The Confederacy of Stan: Uzbeka, Afghanna, Paki, and so on

a random soldier: LOL

It's Rob: 4. Chinese westward expansion via peasants with sharp sticks
I'll leave 5 blank for you. Oh shit, I have so much work for tomorrow. I hate prep school. Let's switch places.

a random soldier: I have to get up at like 0500 and go out into the desert for three days. I'm hiking a 70lb pack up a huge ass fucking hill with a huge cliff three feet away. I'll trade.

It's Rob: Jesus Christ, never mind, hahahah, what are you guys doing?

a random soldier: Setting up communications on some freaking mountain that the helicopter can't drop us on because it would crash.

It's Rob: Jesus Christ, well, its character building Chad.

a random soldier: Yeah.

It's Rob: See this hill, climb up it; it will make you a better person.

a random soldier: It's gonna blow. LOL. Screw the hill. It will further screw up my back and knees to. I feel about thirty years old. It hurts to get up bro. Not shitting you dude.

It's Rob: Well, dude, look at what you do.

a random soldier: Eighteen years old and I groan getting off the floor. Its all fun but tiring as hell.

It's Rob: But dude, you get to say you were a Marine. Who can do that?

a random soldier: True. Yeah!

It's Rob: That's the key to any college girl's panties.

a random soldier: Ha-ha I know. Twenty-two year old combat vet goes to college w/ eighteen year old freshman. Oh fucking yeah! That's my happy thought Rob. That gets me up the hill. That gets me through Hadji's shit little town and back home. "If I'm gonna die for a word; my word is poooooooontang"

It's Rob: How true... how very true and it's going to work and college will be a Mecca of girls as old as your brother.

a random soldier: Well I don't want to know if it doesn't work. What is your motto Rob? Your American Dream, if not scoring with everything under the sun? What the hell keeps you going?

It's Rob: Well...

a random soldier: Money? Fame? Power? Sex? Glory?

It's Rob: Oh that.

a random soldier: Is means or ends important?

It's Rob: I want satisfaction.

a random soldier: What do you want? We all know that but how? We know what I want. But you never say.

It's Rob: Knowledge. The pursuit and attainment of knowledge and writing.

a random soldier: Interesting.

It's Rob: It's just sometimes I lay awake in bed and I can't sleep because my mind is racing over all the things I don't know. Books I haven't read and places I've never seen.

a random soldier: Cool. Why?

It's Rob: Because when I read books, history books, novels… I'm shown these worlds and my mind can touch it. I want to know all of that and I'm not afraid to say that there's the spiritual question. Christianity was, for the most part, unsatisfying. I want to find an answer or not. I just want to find something.

a random soldier: I'd agree with you there. I've done oodles of soul searching.

It's Rob: I want to prove to myself God's existence, and/or prove his nonexistence.

a random soldier: It's all unsatisfying. I live for experience only, but bluntly, I think I'm here because I'm here. No great epic saga. That's why I can do things with a clear conscience.

It's Rob: But, honestly why did you join? I know why Iraq and in some sense, why in general but now, in retrospect.

a random soldier: Combat is the only thing redeeming to me. To know if I'll run away, hide, shirk responsibility or will I do well as I've always told myself I would.

It's Rob: Do you run, or stand up for something you vaguely believe in?

a random soldier: I can honestly tell you I'm prepared to kill or die for the sake of it. We'll figure it out. It's crazy like that. Maybe I joined too cause I felt childishly destined, compelled to do it. Trying to be part of something a random soldier: bigger. It was stupid.

It's Rob: But that can't be all of it.

a random soldier: But I'm here now and I need this. I have lots of issues. Self destructive possibly, low self esteem, violent, over confident in the wrong places. Shit, the Corps, it's perfect for a young moron like me. If I live, I get to say it's cause I was supposed to…

It's Rob: But the thing is… you're not dumb. You're not stupid.

a random soldier: If I catch a round, I'm a hero and everyone forgets the flaws.

It's Rob: Like, college is fight or flight. You shunned it (at least in an immediate sense) It could only be a sense of duty.

a random soldier: Well, well, well… college wasn't my thing at the time.

It's Rob: College isn't a lot of people's thing.

a random soldier: I'll actually not drop out when I go this time.

It's Rob: But they go anyway.

a random soldier: I would have burnt out… for real.

It's Rob: Yeah.

a random soldier: Like actually done so many drugs… It would have been bad.

It's Rob: Ha-ha, true. The Corps as a means of self preservation? Now that's irony.

a random soldier: Yeah. I mean it's not all of it. Probably a desire to get away from suburbia as well, figure out who I am and what I am capable of.

It's Rob: That makes plenty of sense.

a random soldier: Avoid hypocrisy in my own beliefs by living them out. It's one thing to say 'kill em all' and another to do it.

It's Rob: Totally true. Wow! The ultimate test of self worth, killing
    another?

a random soldier: I guess you could say that it's all theory… mostly.

It's Rob: Something like that.

a random soldier: But we'll see…

It's Rob: My brain is less than working.

a random soldier: I'm off to pack my shit for tomorrow's hump. Adios

It's Rob: Later, bro.

§

By the end of May, Chad needed a break to clear his head and assimilate all that he had learned and experienced. There hadn't been much down time since boot. The training in Yuma and California had been intense. It was hard to explain his new life to his old friends. He came home for a few days over the Memorial Day weekend. He didn't go out with friends at all. He hadn't really told anyone he would be in town. We spent most of the time at home, doing nothing special.

We went to the grocery store to get all of his favorite foods. Leaving the store, he stopped to buy a Memorial Poppy from the Vets standing outside. The old soldier looked at him with his high and tight haircut and said "You a soldier, son?"

"Marine, Sir."

"Where are you stationed?"

"Camp Pendleton, but we leave for Iraq in a few months."

The old man looked at him and emotion played across his face. He stuck out his hand to Chad. "Thank you for your service, son."

Chad shook his hand. "Thank you for yours, Sir."

The old man looked at me. "Your son?"

"Yes."

He had tears in his eyes. "You raised a fine young man. You should be proud."

I was.

§

Sunday, May 30, 2004

Too much has happened as far as Marine Corps related stuff to update this right now. It's been a couple months since I last updated this thing. Fuck it, I don't have all night. I'm writing this from home, I came back for three days since its Memorial Day weekend and I had a chance to fly back for some quality time with the family.

I'll be back around July 1st – 16th to party it up before deploying to Iraq at the end of the month. Knock on wood. Hope I get to come home then or I will be hella pissed off. Seven months of people trying to kill me… yeah I definitely better come home first and blow off some steam.

Alice
Welcome little girl
(Shall I call you Alice)
Welcome to the big bad world
Have a cookie
Or a drink
Large or small, what do you think?
Is it too dark for you, my dear
Shall I leave a light on?
This rabbit hole is dark
And I'm late
So what's his name?

"My country right or wrong; when right, to keep her right; when wrong, to put her right."

Carl Schurz

Chapter 7

Journal Entry
Sunday, June 27, 2004

I call this... Saturday...

Sunlight. Ouch. Saturday. Food. Drive. Fast. Beach. Warm. Body board. Meet girls. People. Alcohol. Alcohol. Alcohol. Girls. Drive. Shower. Alcohol. Apartment. San Diego. Night. Dark. Cool. Breeze. Girls. 20 pack. Captain Morgan. Salute. Homeless. Dark. Girls.

Numbers. Fire. Big Fire. Cops. Fight. Alcohol. Irish dudes. Politics. Homeless poet. Yaegermeister. Nihilism. Alcohol. Navy SEALS. Marines. Girls. Alcohol. Writer. Questions. Characters. It's a stage. Sand. Fire. Alcohol. Saturday. Sun up. Go home. Drive. Sleep. Sunlight. Ouch. Sunday.

Journal Entry
Monday, June 28, 2004

Like a porcelain pistol
Pressed to my temple
Abstract and self destructive
You're the death wish I'm in love with
Slit my wrists and tie the noose
Keep looking cause I miss you
Does he thrill you like I used to
Goddess does he bleed just like I do
I used to be your sacrifice
My passion the sacrilegious edifice
You were my needle instant high

My veins blown out with sweet obsession
Denial or acceptance but never possession
So why do I objectify
Treat you like a thing…
No matter where we used to be
You are always just a dream
I need to find my favorite drug
A kiss would set my fix
Just a touch would violate my sanity
Quivers trembles rattle my complacency
Pierce the dark and give me sight
Let me see again the art I live
Exposed unclothed defenseless nymph
Your naked flesh bares my intent
Wild summer moonlit night
We'll both get off in the firelight
Flames lick the sky I taste you burning
With pagan blood a pagan rite
When I find you the circle is complete
We'll be back where we started
I'll be at your feet…

Journal Entry
Thursday, July 01, 2004

Went out cruising with Drew tonight in his SRT. That thing is a beast. I never thought I'd see a fast Neon… that just goes to show it's not the size of the engine that counts ladies; it's how you force its induction… (Okay, so only car guys will get that… screw you if you don't get it.)

Happy to be home on leave… going to bed. G'night world.

Journal Entry
Friday, July 02, 2004   12:26 am

Wow. This was my first Friday night spent entirely sober in a long time. I don't think I mind it.

I'm just trying to soak up as much "home time" as possible in my two weeks here. I can already tell that this momma's boy is going to have a hella bad time adjusting to not being able to call home every couple nights when I'm in Iraq. Say what you want, I love my mommy! Lol. I'm actually trying to imagine what its like and every time I get close it actually scares me. People trying to kill me, me trying to kill them back… I know it's what I signed up for and everything… I'm not being a pussy… I just really want to survive this thing and come home and be done with it. There are too many unknowns and I don't want this to be the last time I ever see my brother, my dad, or my mom. Fuck, that's a depressing thought. Not a nice one to have before bedtime…

In other news, I need to find a party. I think I'll go out tomorrow night. Spend some quality time with the old crew, if anyone is around.

Here's to coming home to the good life for a while.

11:36 PM

Ah… you know it's the small things that you miss the most when you're away from home. I finally spent a quiet night just playing Xbox in my bedroom floor with the family in the house. Home cooked meal and a great evening spent doing absolutely nothing. I'm going to miss the nights like this the most when I get deployed to that big fucking sand box.

Haven't seen a lot of people since I've been home. That will change. I get the feeling that we've all drifted apart so much since high school. Its natural I guess. I have more in common with my bros in the unit than I do with a bunch of irresponsible, pampered college kids who think work is a long day at their job at the beach with no tips. But those same "kids" are my oldest friends. It's hard for me to relate, sometimes, that's all…

Journal Entry
Sunday, July 04, 2004
The American Dream

Happy July 4th, America. Go get drunk and screw your friends and celebrate your right to do so. It's not your responsibility, this whole distasteful mess, right? You didn't vote for Bush. Well neither did I, but I bet your parents did. Look who joined anyway. I guess I'm just a tool, huh? Easily fooled by the government into thinking I should serve? Isn't that what you're thinking? I'm not so far off from the truth, am I? We are the weapon that is held to the throat of the rest of the world, silently patronized by the American Left and made an Icon by the American Right. SUPPORT THE TROOPS… Give me a fucking break. That's the rallying cry of the year. It's about as heartfelt as SAVE THE WHALES. Because no one really does a damn thing about it. You can't kill whales but you can kill Marines… I think if Bush decided whale hunting and deforestation were okay, someone would get pissed. But we can go and leave our homes and families for some bullshit cause… and you just throw money at the problem, send us air conditioners and cards from 2nd Grade classes that will never understand what it's like to pull the trigger. SUPPORT THE TROOPS. Your complacency kills us, not Iraqi bombs or Islamic bullets. Because you don't really know any soldiers. It's not your son or your brother, so why do anything about it? Here's a tip, America… We're not fighting for Iraq. We're not doing our "duty". We're doing what has to be done, killing and dying and suffering and bleeding on the sand thousands of miles from anything we know, thousands of miles and a lifetime from our American Dream, because someone has to do it, and some of us are strong enough, fearless enough to put their right hand in the air and sign on the dotted line so the meek can make excuses why they're not going, why the government is wrong and why they shouldn't have to sacrifice... I bet if you got a draft card you'd burn it. Because you don't HAVE to risk it, right? Hardship and brutality are so BELOW you. You know I'm right. Fear breeds this false sense of superiority. You have a life to live. Selfish, but I understand it. You've got to finish college and write that novel you've always been thinking about, and what about love? You need to get married, have kids and a house payment and a shiny new car to soak up the oil my friends get blown up to protect. You deserve to chase the American dream; don't even feel guilty, not one bit. There are always those troops you can throw cash at, because they were dumb enough or poor enough or idealistic enough or maybe crazy enough to stand up for something, even if it's just each other. But what do you know about that? Don't even try to grasp it, it's a different mind-set, those dashing young men in their camouflage. And playing GI Joe has risks. They know it when they sign up. Besides, you'd never make a good soldier, right? Bad knees? Hate the sight of blood? Couldn't kill a man? Weak in the mind? Weak in the body? Bad eyesight? You'd benefit humanity better with a degree in business or science, wouldn't you?

Whatever helps you sleep at night.

But then you see someone get their head cut off on TV and you want to kill the bastard responsible. You talk about wishing you had joined. You speak of violence you know you couldn't bring yourself to commit. You talk like a child. You want to kill him but you've missed your chance out of fear. Fear that breeds excuses you have to believe. Whatever helps you sleep at night.

9:19 PM

Insomnia is sweet.

Anyway, I went to Rehoboth with Cait and Chels and one of her friends (who happens to know Drew... small world) but I had to jet early cause I had already told Andy that I would go see Spiderman II with him and Shawn and Dave M. Good movie, by the way.

On a different note... I'm still young and stupid enough to do 120 down the highway racing Civics with the Coug'. Good to know I haven't lost my "edge". It's about the only thing I have left from the ol' days...

At 3 am you think about the way things should have been, but never got a chance to be, for one reason or another. Maybe I'll call Kate tomorrow.

§

"The time has come, the Walrus said, to talk of many things," I sat down next to Chad on the swing and handed him an iced chocolate coffee.

He smiled and finished the quote for me. "Of shoes, and ships, and sealing wax, of cabbages and kings."

We had long used the Lewis Carroll quote to start difficult or serious conversations. This was the epitome of both.

"I love you, Chad."

"I love you too, Momma."

We spent the rest of the day on that swing. That was the day I made the promise to tell his story.

"This war isn't worth it Chad."

"That's a matter of perspective, Momma."

"It's not worth the oil. It's not worth freedom for the Iraqi people if they won't know what to do with a democracy that's been handed to them. And Bush isn't the caliber of man worth dying for."

"True. But that's not why we're there. We need a base when the shit hits the fan in the Middle East, and it will hit the fan. Iraq is nowhere near the threat Iran is." he said. "And if I die over there it won't be because of Bush, or oil, or Iraqi freedom. It will be because of the apathy of the American people."

"How so?"

"They take it all for granted. This peace. Our lives. It wouldn't last five minutes without the standing threat of the U.S. Military. But our apathetic population thinks that all that struggle for freedom is something from the past. Wave the flag! They don't even want to know what we have to do to protect it." He was angry and sad.

"Why did you really join the Marines, Chad?"

"Because I can do it, Momma. If I have to, I can kill someone. If it costs my life to protect you, or make sure Ryan never gets drafted, its worth it. It's just the way it is. In every generation, some have to stand up. I'm standing up."

§

If our family had a motto, it was "celebrate life". Holidays, accomplishments, even the change of seasons were reasons to celebrate. Summer backyard parties were the times we shared our private paradise with those we loved.

This year was to surpass them all. Chad and I both had July birthdays. He was turning nineteen. I was turning forty. Most significantly, he was leaving for Iraq, and we were going to laugh and dance and sing before he went.

On July 10th we held a blow out. By sunset, the backyard was full of people and food and music. Lisa Says No was the band Rich played bass for. We made them the house band.

All night I watched Chad. He was the consummate host. He spent time with everyone, smiling, drink in hand. My God, he was dashing. I knew what he was doing. Touching base with his life. Greeting his elementary school teachers, his aunts and uncles, old friends and new, he handed each of them a part of himself. He was working the crowd and he was completely sincere.

When full darkness fell, we set off the fireworks. If it was good to light a candle and pray then maybe lighting up the night sky with color, illuminating all of us below who so very much wanted Chad to come home safe would capture God's attention.

I realized watching him that night that my job was done. He still had things to learn, but that would come from life. He was finished with childhood, and he had turned out so well. I was amazed and proud. He caught me looking and shot me a grin. He knew who he was.

Later I was standing by the bonfire when he came up and took my hand. He led me a little way off and said, "Can I have this dance?"

"Oh, absolutely, kiddo."

"It's a great party, Momma. Thanks. I know it was a lot of work for you guys," he said as we began to move.

"No problem. It's been fun." Out of nowhere there were tears on my face. He maneuvered me so my back was to the crowd. He just held me close and swayed with the music. How many times had I done that to stop his cries when he was tiny. Now he rocked me, and I knew that no matter the outcome, he was ready to walk his path.

§

"Death is more universal than life; everyone dies but not everyone lives."
                                                                  A Sachs

Chapter 8

Journal Entry
Thursday July 15, 2004

Okay, quick update… Party on the 10th was great Thanks for everyone showing me the love. (Especially Lori. Love you hun.) Boo to you Rob. Boo to you. And your artsy school. Booooo I say. Booo Hisss. Kudos to the band… you rocked.

Stopped by to see all the grandparents and family today… it's so going to suck saying goodbye to my parents tomorrow… ugh…
Gotta go take my mind off things… G' night.

Chad

§

Thursday was his birthday. We went to the beach. We bodysurfed and built a sand castle. We went out to dinner. Such a normal birthday; only it wasn't.

The next day, he had to go. We took pictures in the yard before we left for Philadelphia. We put the camera on a tripod and set the timer. I look at those pictures now and see how much fun we we're having just joking around, holding on to the best of what we were to each other for as long as we could, down to only moments now, but then it was time to go.

We were held up in traffic and late getting to the airport. It was the last flight that would get him back to Camp Pendleton on time, so Rich and Ryan parked the truck and Chad and I took off at a run. Tears in our eyes and grins on our faces we ran to get him checked in. He looked at me and asked "Are you okay?"

I said "I am if you are."

"I'm okay." he lied.

"Me too," I lied back.

We kept running. We weren't okay. None of this was okay. How could I let him go?

We got him checked in and his Dad and brother caught up to us at security. We stood around not wanting to let him go. We said our good-byes, made jokes I don't remember. Hugged and kissed him. Rich held out his hand to shake Chad's and said, "If I never see you again, you know I love you." and pulled him into a bear hug. Chad and Ryan locked eyes in a secret communication they had perfected a long time ago. We were all so close to losing it. Chad turned and walked into the security line. He got about ten steps. I called his name. He turned and looked at me and walked back. I had to hug him one more time. In case it was the last one, I wanted to remember.

§

Terri's Journal
July 16, 2004

Nineteen years ago yesterday I held him in my arms for the very first time. Today I held him for what may be the very last.

We put him on a plane to go prepare for war. I watched him make his way through the long security line. He began to shuffle his personal belongings, removed his beach necklace and stored it away in a side pocket of his backpack. A wave, he turned to go. He didn't look back. I didn't look away. Once he was through the metal detector he was beyond my reach. My heart was breaking. I saw him lift something from the tray. He placed his dog tags over his head. No longer just our son, but America's son. And he had gone to war.

Journal Entry
Friday, July 16, 2004

Saw my family in person for the last time today before I go to Iraq.

I think I'm still in shock. Sitting here on the plane trying to cope.

What if I get killed? I can't say that I'm not worried for myself, but I'm more concerned about what it would do to my family. I fought so hard to choke back the boyish tears. My parents broke. My Dad hid proudly behind dark sunglasses and my Mom just couldn't hang on. I don't blame her. I had to turn away and focus on not thinking. That last glance at my brother and parents as I walked through security… that hurt. I can't even write sensibly right now. Too emotional for style or coherence.

Journal Entry
Saturday, July 31, 2004

Back in Cali on the weekend. Finally had some spare time to update and e-mail some friends. We've been working nineteen hour days doing inspections and firing ranges, etc since I got back off of leave. We're leaving soon. I can't say when, but I can say it's down to weeks. We don't even know exactly when or how. It's stressful to say the least. Guess I picked a bad time to give up drinking...

Hmm... Only thing that's new is I ordered a digital camcorder offline tonight so I'll be sending back CD's full of video of us in Iraq once I get over there. I should get some cool candid shots and it will be nice at Christmas time to send greetings back to everybody's families. It better, cause I spent most of my paycheck on it. I just got paid yesterday... now I'm broke. I should work at Starbucks again. I made more money.

Here's to the nights (I miss you guys. Represent for me on the East Coast this fall. I'll be in the sandbox when you guys are at frat parties.)

Journal Entry
Saturday, August 21, 2004

What a seriously rough day. I wake up and no one is around the barracks to go with me to Oceanside. Okay. I go get my checkbook and ID and stuff out of my sea bag (that I never use) just so I can go to town and get a cash advance on my next paycheck, since I won't get to use it if I'm in some other country.

That said, I get to the cash advance place, and what don't I have? My checkbook. Lost someplace en route to Oceanside. Yargh... A very pirate-like YARGH! So I'm like, OK, that's bad. I call my parents and they wire me money. I have it handled, right? No. I call the bank "emergency number" to cancel all the checks I just lost, and the bank is closed. All the tellers and humans are not there. It just hangs up on me. The emergency number. Hung up on me. WTF. I guess we are only supposed to lose important things like that on a weekday between 9 am and 4 PM. YARGH. They be scurvy landlubbers' and ye will be hearin' from this salty sea dog on Monday, when I will call thems rotten scoundrels on the phone, yargh. Some nasty Union scum could be tryin to get me buried treasure, yargh... I be the James Bond of the high seas, so's you know, yarr. Me name is Bad Rum Jude. Jude, Bad Rum, Jude. YARR

Don't even ask about the pirate talk... it's a Comm thing. Yargh. I'm going back to base... I need a nap.

§

Chad had asked us not to come to California to see them off.

"I won't be able to get on the plane if you're there." he said

"Okay, but I will be there to watch you come home," I replied. If only. He couldn't tell us when they were leaving exactly. Everytime I saw an airplane cross the sky, I wondered if it was carrying young men to war. Carrying Chad.

§

Journal Entry
August 31, 2004
1732 CA time

We're about four hours into our flight over to Germany now. I've been up since 3 am and have spent a good part of the day catching up on lost sleep.

Everyone is coping pretty well, on the surface at least. A few jokes about going UA, etc., but it's interesting to see who is stressing out and who is pumped. It will start to change a lot when we get closer to Iraq.

I'm still in some form of denial, I guess. I'm stoked to be going, but I'm nervous because I could be in a firefight in the next 36 hours. It's hard to grasp the reality of people actually trying to kill you. We've had so much training that it still seems unreal in my mind. I just hope that I react the right way and that I don't get killed on the convoy into Ramadi. Mortars already scare the living shit out of me, and the ones we use for training are just flash bangs. I will probably get used to them in the future, but still… I haven't learned to recognize incoming from outgoing or how close the incoming is. I'm still a boot.

This is crazy. My old friends are all starting their sophomore year of college and I'm on a jet cruising to war with my M16 and my flak and patrol pack stuffed in the overheads and under the seat. My home is seven to ten months away. We're getting paid, but not nearly as much as the civilians are. So why are we here?

I'm here because my best friends are here. The people I live with and work with everyday. I'm here to bring my best friends home alive.

Journal Entry
September 1, 2004

I watched daybreak over Europe again, and we're about to touch down in Germany.

"Whiskey Lullaby" and "Letters from Home" have been playing over the in flight radio all night. I guess it reminds me that I've come pretty far from a small coastal high school in Delaware. It's hard to get much farther away that this. Damn, when I want to run away from myself, I do a helluva job.

Terri's Journal Entry
September 1, 2004

Chad,

While you are away this will be my means of talking to you mostly because I very much miss talking with you, and partially because I may occasionally have something important to say. So I'll just ramble on and someday you'll read it and be reminded of how much your crazy mom loves you.

I wonder where you are now. I know you have to be excited and scared. You never did like first days. This is day one for me too.

I love you,
Mom

Journal Entry
September 2, 2004

We're all chilling in a tent w/ AC at Camp Victory in Kuwait, standing by for our turn to go and get on the C130 and fly to Al Asad, an airbase northwest of Ramadi. From there most of us will stay in Junction City for a couple of days.

So everyone is pretty hyped up, even though some of us are still finding a way to sleep. I'm not really tired now.

Kuwait is flat and barren. It looks like purgatory. Endless sand, one huge staging area for the world's most powerful military force. Our strength here is unquestionable. The presence of so many Marines is inspiring. All here for war.

We saw some Army and Air Force guys in the airport in Frankfort. We smirked at their "nastiness" and the fact that they had females with them. Some Air Force E8 called me Sir. Damn straight. We're the best thing this side of Special Forces. Most of us are 18 to 23 years old, with dreams but no expectations.

§

I walked into the florist shop to buy a yellow ribbon for the tree in the front yard. The lady behind the counter said she would make one up, and asked what it was for. "My son left for Iraq this week. He's a Marine."

The whole shop went silent. No one knew what to say. When the ribbon was finished I took out my wallet.

"Oh, There's no charge!" the lady said. "We'll all pray for him"

I thanked her, holding back tears. I took a photo from my wallet. It was the Dress Blue picture taken at boot camp. I handed it to her.

"Here, have this. His name is Chad. That way you will know who you're praying for."

"Oh, he's so young!"

"Yes. He just turned nineteen." I made it to the car before I started to cry.

§

Part II

Iraq

"Men never do evil so completely and cheerfully as when they do it from a
religious conviction."

Blaise Pascal

CHAPTER 9

Ramadi is a city about seventy miles west of Baghdad on the Euphrates River with a population of about 400,000. It is the capital of Al Anbar Province. It is a sprawling ghetto, filthy and packed with insurgents. The streets are strewn with trash that may or may not hide Improvised Explosive Devices. Gaping holes in ruined buildings provide a snipers view. It is one of the most violent places on earth.

§

Journal Entry
Friday, September 3, 2004

Long, four hour convoy from Al Asad over here to Junction City, an Army base across the river from Hurricane Point and Ramadi proper. From like 3 am to 7 am. We didn't even get shot at. Boring.

I'm part of the advance personnel going over to Hurricane Point tomorrow morning around 0900. I'm so screwed up on time zones that it's really meaningless except that I know someone will wake me up when I need to be woken up.

The Army base here is okay. The chow's pretty good. It's served by a bunch of Hadjis and Kuwaitis. The Cokes and Pepsis are all written in both Arabic and English. We're drinking Saudi bottled water by the gallons a day for each of us.

The huge tent we're staying in has child sized bunks and is pretty ridiculous. Our gear takes up more space than they do. The air conditioning works when it's not 120 outside, which is only when it's dark.

I've been asleep most of the day. We all crash out during the hottest hours and start moving around at night. I'm going to wait up until midnight and go to take a shower and use the phone center. I'm not really homesick, but I want to call today or tomorrow just because.

Terri's Journal Entry
September 4, 2004

Chad,
It was so good to get your calls. I was in the gallery when you called the first time. I didn't recognize the number and your voice was so clear that I didn't comprehend that it was you right away. You sounded strong and that gives me strength.
When you called at midnight to say you were getting ready to go to Ramadi in a convoy it worried me some, but I'm okay.
I put a big yellow ribbon on the birch tree out front. You'll see it when you come home.
I Love You,
Mom

Journal Entry
Saturday, September 4, 2004
Al Anbar Province
Ar Ramadi
Junction City

Woke up about 45 minutes ago around 0500 local time, walked outside the tent to help take out the trash from yesterday and heard the coolest thing I've ever heard in my life.

One of the mosques (I think on this side of the river) was broadcasting the morning call to prayer. A lot of guys get creeped out about it, but I stayed and listened to the whole thing. It's like being in a freaking movie until you realize we really shouldn't be here. We really are occupiers, not liberators. These people are not anything like us; they just respect our guns and our technology. We are still fundamentally the enemy. It is their religion that we are fighting. We are waging war with Allah. It's Fundamentalism vs. Freedom.

Journal Entry
Sunday, September 5, 2004
Hurricane Point
Al Anbar Province
Ar Ramadi

Got here yesterday on advance party. Sgt. Gomez showed us around. This base is skate city. It's H&S Company and Weapons. 24 hour chow hall, security on the ECP and both bridges… the Comm shop is hooked up with AC and TVs and Xboxes.

The catch?

I'm going over to Combat Outpost via Main Supply Route Michigan. It's like the name says; they take mortar fire there like its cool. And MSR Michigan is a 60 mph gauntlet of death. The grunts have gotten so jumpy from all the attacks here that they'll shoot anyone on a cell phone or who starts running. That's understandable. I'd shoot the MoFos too if I had to run it everyday.

I spent most of yesterday sleeping and getting squared away. Hygiene, cleaning my weapon, doing whatever I can to stay out of 2/4's way while we change over.

I have to admit… I like it here. Iraq is a shit hole. It's hot and dangerous. It is purgatory for the mind. You are judged, and either you come out in one piece or you don't. If you fuck up, you get killed. If your luck runs out, you get killed. If you aren't going to die here, you won't.

Journal Entry
Friday, September 10, 2004
Combat Outpost

Hasn't been much to write about the last few days around here. An RPG landed outside the gym the other day and there is a sniper that shot at Ski. Beyond that nothing.

I've been skating my ass off at Retrans. I'm trying to go out and actually do something. I don't like wasting my time, screwing around, not doing anything. I've worked this hard and come this far, for what? To sit in the shade and watch DVDs and hope I don't get hit with a mortar? I don't think so.

<u>War of the Mind</u>

Sweat pooled around my sunglasses, drops rolling down the bridge of my nose and down around the straps of my helmet. The collar of my flak rubbed at my neck, leaving the skin raw and burning when sun or sweat touched it.

Sun scorched whatever it could reach. It was an active evil in this desert, alive and spiteful. This was the sun's territory and we were the invaders. Allah sent his burning arrows down with vengeance.

We sat, crunched together, eighteen of us to each 7 ton truck, soaking and burning inside our gear. More trucks full of Marines pulled into the spaces behind us. "Condition One!"

I slip a magazine out of a pouch of my left thigh and slide it into my M16. For the thousandth time I rack a round into the chamber and check the safety. I sip on some water and want to move.

The trucks start to roll towards the gate and some Army soldier calls to us,

"Kill some Hadji's for me!" One of our corporals call back "Yeah, 'cause we know you won't!" The soldier walks on and we keep rolling.

The Marines are quiet, for the most part. Tension is high. Our convoy the night before was from Al Asad to Junction City through open desert. This would take us across the Euphrates into Ramadi itself. We hit the highway with our weapons pointed out, looking as hostile behind our body armor and sunglasses as the Iraqis did in their rags and beat up cars. No one waved at us. No kids were laughing. Silent angry stares as we passed through razor wire hung on walls, trash caught up in its spikes. Sand encroached on the paved areas, the desert reclaiming its own. The city was a ghetto.

"Hey, this kinda looks like LA.", some Marine said from the other side of the truck. Everyone chuckled but this wasn't LA. We were aware of our position; we were in a war zone.

The convoy ended quickly. We made it to Hurricane Point and unloaded our rifles and packs. The tension had lifted and it was hot again. I grabbed a Sprite in an Arabic can and picked up my gear. This was going to be fun deployment.

E-mail to Rob
9/5/04 10:58 a.m.
Subject: Greeting from Hell

Que pasa?
Yo quero Taco Bell.

I've been in Iraq since like last week (its Sunday now) and its hot as balls, bro. I'm in Ar Ramadi, in the Al Anbar Province. Ghetto shithole from hell. We had a convoy the other day through town and there was only serious hate going on there. No smiling children, no waving dumb asses like on TV… just a bunch of mean looking young Iraqi males capable of causing me to have a bad day.

I love it. I'm going to a combat outpost away from the base this week with the line companies. Get some. Goodbye Comm shop.

SO… How's life back in the states? College treating you well, I hope? All that intense liberal arts educational jive? I've been keeping journals, by the way, so you'll get a decent read when I get home. I don't have all the time to type out here. Say hi to Lori for me. Pour some liquor on the ground for your homies.

Peace, bro. I'm gonna go pack up my shit. Don't do anything I wouldn't do.

Chad

E-mail Home
9/7/04 3:14 am

Hey!

We just got the "hadji net" so I should have e-mail most days. Lcpl Hauer is the greatest guy in the world. ISC is the shiznit. Unless it goes down. And then he's not.

Its okay over here at Combat Outpost. Conditions aren't as good as the firm base, but it's livable. I'd rather be out here with the grunts than at the Comm Shop. Feels some how safer.

I'll e-mail you some more later. We're going to go drop this line down to the retrans site.

Miss you guys,
Chad

E-mail Home
9/8/2004 5:31 PM

Hey,

I'm just out here doin the whole comm. thing, you know, get up, eat chow, shower, check the radio. It works. Nap. Watch TV. Etc. So far we are just trying to get an Xbox out here from supply so we can play Halo 2 when it comes out next month. I've been doing OK. I like it here. A lot. Not much to say about the night life tho… lol.

I'm on radio watch right now, making sure the damn thing doesn't go down. It just did for the first time, since we got here, a few days ago. Figures, it's like a curse, if I'm on watch, the radio will find a way to royally shit on itself and make me work.

I have to say tho, I don't feel like I'm doing anything out here. It's surreal, I'm in the middle of a huge insurgency and civil war, but I hang out all day in the shade watching DVDs with my shirt off and drinking a Sprite with ice. What the fuck kind of war am I fighting? I don't think I am. Other people are doing it for me. I know you're thinking right now, "Oh my god I don't want to think about him going on patrols… etc etc" which is fine, but I feel like sitting here waiting for the next mortar round to hit is like going to the Super Bowl and riding the bench cause you're afraid you'd drop the ball. Not to make war sound like football, but it's an inner demon I'm trying to work out here. The only person I ever had to prove a damn thing to was myself, and right now I'm failing my own test miserably. It's as much a moral dilemma as I could ever find myself in. I don't strap myself down with much morality, you know. And this is like two roads. I could sit here the whole war and never show my face outside the tent, or I could get a hold of some balls and go out and be Radio Operator on patrols… I didn't join so someone could fight the war for me.

I don't think we should allow ourselves that illusion, tempting as it might be.

For now I'll stay in the base, but I've got to work this out with myself. Maybe the first time people shoot directly at me I'll freak and never go back. Maybe I'll get off on it like the grunts and do my job. I guess we'll see in the coming months.

Here's to another night in the beautiful city of Ramadi.

Love,

Chad

Instant Message Conversation between Rob and Chad.
9/8/2004 5:40 PM

a random soldier: How now brown cow. What will tomorrow bring?

It's Rob: Holy Shit! They have computers in Iraq? I was doing reading and thinking about calling your mom.

a random soldier: Yeah! I'm here… Uh… BRB…

It's Rob: How the fuck are you accessing the internet? Okay.

a random soldier: Mortar… How crazy is that?

It's Rob: No shit?

a random soldier: Out in town, not close. We got an RPG earlier today.

It's Rob: But a mortar… where?

a random soldier: Sounds like out in front of the Hotel OP. Who knows? Fuck it!

It's Rob: Where did you get the RPG?

a random soldier: I dunno… a hadji shot it at us from somewhere. It damn near hit our gym. Sons of bitches.

It's Rob: Did it hit anything?

a random soldier: Some sand.

It's Rob: Bet he feels like a Jack Ass. Oh well, his day will come. So, fuck, how are you talking on IM? Do they have JavaBytes in Ramadi?

a random soldier: Ha-ha! No, nothing so glorious. It's a patch net we
hijacked off the Hadji network.

It's Rob: No kidding?

a random soldier: Yeah, it goes down a lot. I thought I was gonna catch a
bullet running this line, scariest thing ever.

It's Rob: Tell me…

a random soldier: How am I?

It's Rob: Yes!

a random soldier: Honestly?

It's Rob: That.

a random soldier: I fucking love it here. It's like purgatory for the mind.
You either come out one side or the other.

It's Rob: Explain that…

a random soldier: You either crack and hate this shit so much you want to
leave with a wound to get out, or you come to love it
and take pictures… I'm on the loving side so far. I
don't think it will change.

It's Rob: But you're still bucking for MSG right.

a random soldier: MSG?

It's Rob: Marine Security Guard.

a random soldier: Maybe, I might extend in Iraq. Who can say?

It's Rob: Oh, don't do that.

a random soldier: I know what MSG is jackass. I meant that I hadn't
thought about it in a while. This place is great; it's
totally forcing a new view of myself into the light that
I hadn't thought of before.

It's Rob: What view?

a random soldier: That is… I am not infallible. I could totally be wrong about the free will vs. destiny thing. Now I'd have to subscribe to the theory that if time is relative and has already happened, then we have made the choices ourselves the instant we popped into existence, based on the choices of others, leading to one end… i.e. destiny, but as a pre-calculated chain reaction. A mortar round REALLY fucks with your concept of life and death, bro.

It's Rob: Well, fuck.

a random soldier: Incidentally, I seem to be the flavor of the week.

It's Rob: How?

a random soldier: Why is Amy talking to me now?

It's Rob: Oh…

a random soldier: Oh that's right, because everyone else is.

It's Rob: Because you're not fat and you dress well?

a random soldier: Hello, I want to be special too! See Jill, he talks to me too! I'm cool right guys?! Ahem…

It's Rob: Well…

a random soldier: That bitch ruined my friendship with Mark.

It's Rob: Eh… Mark… eh

a random soldier: She is so fucked when I get the chance… OMG… anyway… You know who I miss? Three guesses.

It's Rob: K
    A
    T E

a random soldier: Well, duh, but I wasn't going to bring her up at all, spoil sport. I meant your mother. Kate is a sad given. LOL.

It's Rob: Well, of course she was going to come up. Sad soldier contemplates art student by moonlight? DUDE, learn how to play guitar that's a fortune. Right there.

a random soldier: Fuck that. Emo is dead, it died with the class of 03. Amy is apparently rooming with Jill this year.

It's Rob: She and Amy are still living together, huh? Death o' friendship.

a random soldier: Yeah, for rizzle. When do people learn? I room with my best friends all the time and it devolves to fist fights regularly.

It's Rob: Yeah but…

a random soldier: Playfully but still.

It's Rob: You guys drink. A Lot.

a random soldier: LOL Yeah, used to, those were the days. They have non alcoholic beer. We saw beer from across the chow hall… I was like… Ahhh hell no, Budweiser? The war is looking up… walked over… FUCK… its Bud NA. I actually shed a tear, bro.

It's Rob: I would too, but hey, natty light… that's all we have here. ALL.

a random soldier: Do you know what I would do for a cold can of anything with beer? Horrible atrocious things. I would lead the hordes of hell in the apocalypse; just give me a fucking beer, dude. So how's the wifey… I mean, uh, Lori?

It's Rob: She's good… actually… she's here and I have to go to dinner like, right now.

a random soldier: Hi, hon.

It's Rob: It closes in… oh, 3 minutes.

a random soldier: You two should have kids… Mkay. Bye now. Be prudent with an email.

It's Rob: I will. You check it regularly?

a random soldier: Every other day or so… depends on what I'm doing.

It's Rob: Excellent! I'll write regularly then. I'll fill you in on Kenyon life.

a random soldier: Cool.

It's Rob: If you care… if not, I'll talk about something else…

a random soldier: No I do… vicariously I go to college.

It's Rob: I have some good stories… Okay… I'll make it fun, then… until later, bro.

a random soldier: Bye.

It's Rob: I miss you a lot, in that heterosexual way… For God's sake, be safe.

E-mail Home
9/9/2004 8:48 pm

Hey all,

Just got your last e-mail. It's about 4:15 in the morning here. I'm up on radio watch making sure the HMMWV doesn't die. I didn't do much all day so I'm not really tired yet. I'll just sleep til' like 10 tomorrow anyway. This is a surreal war. One minute I'm watching a movie and sipping on an iced coke and the next minute I'm diving between the HMMWV and what is called a HASCO barrier. Think a big steel mesh tube about 7 ft tall and 4 ft in diameter, filled with dirt. They protect from mortars and RPGs pretty well. I saw one that got hit about 30 meters from us directly on the barrier… it blew the top off but saved the Echo COC. We have them surrounding our HMMWV, topped off with cammie netting that runs to the wall and gives us some shade. Between that and the overhang from the roof, it would take one helluva shot to land back here on the back side of the building perfectly where we're at. Knock on wood, but I'm really not worried about it. Those things are like the hand of God. If you're going to get one, you're just gonna be in the wrong place at the wrong time. Tactically, the retrans site isn't even a good target. The only thing it's used for is to talk with long range patrols back at the main COC over in Hurricane Point.

It's actually really chill over here, whether you believe me or not. First day I got here, we got a couple mortar shots, then the next day there was some small arms and etc, day after another mortar, and yesterday we had a RPG come close to hitting the gym. It left a big hole in the ground. I got some video of the hole. Then we went back to eating chow and watching TV. That's my war. All that's missing is the martini glass and the Air Force uniform.

The only thing remotely scary was being on the roof running this line and realizing that Hauer and I were sky lined in the evening light… We were all "Oops… Oh fuck, run." Those were the exact words. We hauled ass. Based on the fact that the sniper that took a pot shot at Ski and the CO of Fox Co. was still around. Ski and Ross and Show and Barb have all been out a lot, since they're company RO's. This whole time I've been trained to go blow stuff up with Cobras and we're not even using them so I'm stuck here, a fucking pogue, biding my time til' I go home.

Your right about one thing though. It's a long seven months. I won't rush things. But you can understand where I'm coming from, I'm sure. But if I come all the way to Iraq for this, and I don't try to test myself, I'll never live it down. Not to anyone else, but just me. For sleeping away my war. Maybe you can't understand. I don't know. The words wouldn't make any sense coming from anyone else but we've always known I had a fucked up sense of self worth anyway. Finding myself actually in combat is like a religious thing for me, I guess if I had a religious thing. Baptism of fire without the Christian overtones.

That's what you couldn't get Ryan to spill. I'm not even close to being in mortal peril of any type, and I know that's the way any parents in their right minds would prefer it, so maybe you don't get why, but I just ask that you understand I do feel this way, regardless of why. I know you can accept that, at least.

In less morbid news, we had hot wings and burgers for chow tonight. It was pretty good. My "motivation" is comprised of two things in the field… Chow and Sleep (Tactical Rack Operations). 50% is enough to keep me going, so either rack, ops, or food and I'm golden. I'm pretty motivated right now.

I'll probably get your package this Saturday or next Tuesday when they make a run over to this outpost. It's a pretty dangerous convoy and the mail takes time to sort so they make runs every couple days. I think my mail will get to the Comm Shop at HP first though, so they might send it over for me on BoxCar (it's the morning and evening chow convoy that makes the run on MSR Michigan twice a day). I'll talk to somebody from the shop tomorrow.

I'm gonna go back to sleep for thirty minutes and wake up to start the HMMWV again. G'night.

Love,
Chad

E-mail Home
9/11/2004
Subject: Re: Love and Stuff

Hey,

I'm still sitting here bored off my ass at retrans. Somebody shot an RPG over the camp last night that made the most wicked sound I've ever heard in my life. Like a jet going by, really low, except you know it's not a jet. It hit a building on the other side of the wall just over our cammie netting but it was a dud and nobody got hurt. It should have gone off; it would have taken out some hadji civilians out in town where it landed.

Seems like they've been getting pretty worked up lately. I have a feeling a lot of Marines are going to go down here soon; they know it's a new unit. I'm glad I'm not a grunt right now, actually. Not that it changes the way I feel, it's just that I think the command is about to get a harsh learning curve. I know what I'd be doing if I were the hadjis, and this is pretty par for course. Bait and retreat, bait and retreat, then finally bait and ambush.

Enough talking tactics. Someone would probably tell me to "stay in your pay grade," if they read all this. Well fuck them, I say. I'm never wrong. In other news, I'm just waiting for my mail to catch up to me. It should be sometime this week. I hope so, cause we've been eating the food that the 2/4 left us when they went back to Junction City (from all their leftover care packages) and we're starting to run out of sweets.

Sorry for the long, rambling emails, but I have a lot of time to think, you know. I miss you guys. Hauer wants his computer back so I'll probably send another e-mail when I'm on watch tonight.

Love you guys,
Chad

•

PFC Jason T. Poindexter   September 12, 2004
Company E. 2nd Battalion, 5th Marine Regiment, 1st Marine Expeditionary Force. Died as a result of enemy action Al Anbar Province, Iraq.

•

E-mail Home
9/12/2004 5:07 AM
Subject: Re: incoming supplies

Hey,

Seven care packages? Holy Shit, Batman. I don't know when my mail is going to catch up to me. Hopefully this week or something.

Ramadi has just turned into a big ass firefight, since after morning

prayers today. It's crazy. I'll write more later.
    Chad

E-mail Home
Date: 9/13/2004

What's up?
    I've been trying to get this one radio to work all day, so my mind is currently still wrapped around getting the antennae to work. I apologize for being scatterbrained.
    Ever read *Wizards First Rule*, by Terry Goodkind? Great Book. I need to find the sequel. Pretty good story. I've been reading it since I got to Iraq.
    Is everything okay at home? I notice the emails have been pretty short lately, just making sure you're not avoiding telling me something so that I won't worry. You don't need to worry about that. I'd honestly rather know. If nothing's wrong, then nothing is wrong, but I just got the impression you weren't telling me something. Like, one line emails and stuff. It's okay if there's nothing to write, it just seemed out of character.
    I'm going to go back to sleep now. Hopefully when I wake up I can fix this damn radio. G'night.
    Chad

E-mail to Rob
9/13/2004 6:33 PM
Subject: Re: Greetings from Hell

Sup killa,
    I be chillin' up this dizzite like its fucking cool, homie. Actually, we have been taking some serious shit the past couple days. Non stop Iraqi's trying to mortar us and all. That is so uncool of them. We wouldn't kill them if they'd stop shooting at us. Killed about fifteen and wounded fifty in yesterday's firefight. We can't figure out where they keep getting these guys. Hello… we kill everything we see. Obviously it's a dumb idea to shoot at Marines.
    But what makes it worth getting shot at is… Drum roll please… I heard from K yesterday! Whoooop! LOL I'm pathetic like a school boy… and now I don't have any beer to soften the harsh grating blows of reality… Wow. I suck as a person… Yeah she has that effect on me…
    I'm still out here at combat outpost. I get to go on a raid sometime in the next coming week tho I can't tell you when, for secret squirrel reasons. I'm pretty happy. Yay, blowing up things. Yay.
    How's school? Classes are FUN FUN FUN, I assume… heh. Term paper vs. Mortar attacks. Check please, I'll chance it out with the mortars.

You HAVE to write the paper. The mortar might not hit me.
Tell Lori I said hello,
     Chad

•

Lance Cpl Gregory C. Howman   September 15, 2004
2nd Battalion, 5th Marine Regiment, 1st Marine Division, 1st Marine
Expeditionary Force. Died as a result of enemy action Al Anbar Province,
Iraq

•

E-mail Home
9/17/2004 12:00 AM

Hey all,
     Just woke up and thought I'd write you an e-mail. I was racked out
cause I've been up for about thirty hours on an operation into Ramadi.
It was cool. Kickin' down doors and going through buildings and shit. I
found an AK47 but they wouldn't let me keep it... lol. Too bad.
     The op was fun but when I got back, Nelson and Hauer told me that
Commo found out I went out on an op... Yeah, he's really pissed. I'm just
standing by to be chewed out the next time he sees me. Whatever, it was
worth it. So I probably won't get a chance to go out again anytime soon...
That sucks too, cause I was doing really good. The squad I was with was
even surprised that an RO could shoot and move like the grunts. You can
imagine how pleased I am with myself, despite Commo being pissed.
Whatever. I'll tell him straight up that I didn't feel like I was accomplishing
a damn thing by sitting over at HP or back here. I'm sure they'll find a way
to use that statement against me somehow, but I don't give a fuck. What
are they going to do? Send me to the rear again where I can't possibly get
shot at or go on ops? Ooooooo. Wow, you sure showed me...
     Anyway, I finally fixed that radio. I got pissed off at making these
textbook antennas over and over so I put some wire on a rock, threw it
up on the roof, and looped it back down to the radio. It's working now, of
course. Figures.
     I am still really tired and sore. I'm going to get some chow and go to
sleep again.
     Love
     Chad

E-mail Home
9/17/2004 6:48 PM
Subject: Re: Not bad for a pogue

Hey,

Just a short e-mail before I go to bed. The radio stopped working. I've been up all night, (piece of shit!). Yargh.

Yeah, Commo chewed me out briefly today. I stood at parade rest and inserted the proper "aye, sir" and "yes, sir" where appropriate. I didn't bother to explain. He said I was literally too important to send to a line company. I offered to teach someone else my job, you know, since we have other mofos in this platoon that are ALSO ROs who would rather skate all day and waste the only fun part of the enlistment. I didn't join to play video games. Yarrgh. He said I can't go out again, ever. I tried to talk to MSgt but he had mixed reactions. You could tell he was a little pleased that I jumped the chain and said fuck it, and went anyway. But also you could tell he had to back Commo up and said I shouldn't "ever fucking do that again." So yeah, I'm on restriction. In Iraq. That has got to be some kind of record. Restricted from combat. As punishment. What kind of Marine Corps is this anyway? The Ssgt I went out with the other day invited me back out with him tonight… he said he needs a RO that can hang. I had to turn him down and told him why. He thought it was stupid too. I told him to pass word up he wanted me. Fuck you, sir; I'll skip the chain of command wherever possible. Take that, restriction.

Anyway, I started writing this e-mail for another reason… can't remember now. I just rambled my way to the end so I'll probably remember as soon as I lay down. Eh, whatever. G'night.

Chad

PS- Biggest compliment ever… Ssgt Melendes told Cpt. Welch "this kid is a killer." Oh yeah, take that Commo. I should have been a grunt.

E-mail Home
9/18/2004
Subject: Good Morning Ramadi

What's up homies?

Another long day out here killing time and screwing with the radio. I've lost track of how many times I've re-programmed that thing. Yargh.

We've got crypto change over in all the radios tonight at 4:30 our time. It will be easier tonight cause I bummed twenty bucks off Nelson and got a watch from the interpreter. I can get him back when we get our split pay on the first.

I was just checking in and saying hi. Love you guys.
Chad

E-mail Home
9/18/2004 7:43 PM
Subject: Re: Good Morning Ramadi

What's up?

Just got up. Here it's about 3:30 in the morning and I'm about to go change over crypto in all the radios. Woooooopeeee! I hate crypto day. We've got most of the RO's awake for it though so it shouldn't take forever this week.

Requests for package… if you can find green underarmor tee shirts, those are popular out here. I know the Battalion said not to get them, but Battalion is stupid and those things are great here. Just make sure they're green, not tan. Only the army wears tan. Also, that book you looked up in the Sword of Truth series.I'm desperate for a decent book. The paperbacks that people donate are sitting in a room, but they all suck. I looked through yesterday. The latest Playboy would also be appreciated. Goldfish crackers too. I just thought of those. Hopefully that gives you some ideas.

We're living in tents right now next to the retrans site. This is going to change cause pretty soon we'll get the Iraqi equivalent of monsoon season and the radios and stuff are going inside.

I gotta go change some radios now.
Love,
 Chad

E-mail Home
9/24/2004 11:15 AM
Subject: Incoming

Hey there,

Sorry I haven't emailed in the past week. Somebody got shot in the face by a sniper and they took the internet down so it wouldn't leak out before they got word passed. It's a lovely war.

Not much is new. Stood up on one of the towers today because we're short on manpower due to an outgoing op. That was pretty boring. I still have one more shift tonight until midnight.

There's not a lot to talk about here. I guess no news is good news. I've been here like three weeks now, I just realized. Time is one big flowing mess. It doesn't matter what day it is, because every day is the same routine. Sleep until its too hot to, then eat something and wait until it gets dark. Yada, yada, yada. I wish I could go out on an op again.

Sorry to be so boring. I love you guys, miss you all a lot. I'm going to go try and get some DVDs to play on our broken TV and maybe catch a nap before going on post.
 Lata, Chad

•

Sgt. Timothy Folmar   September 24, 2004
2nd Battalion, 5th Marine Regiment, 1st Marine Division, 1st Marine Expeditionary Force. Died as a result of enemy action in Al Anbar Province, Iraq

•

Terri's Journal Entry
September 23, 2004

Chad,
Who knew that when I wished for something to occupy my mind to keep me from obsessing about the war we'd be exposed to rabies? Lots of shots.What a long strange few weeks. Be very careful what you wish for.
Happy fall. Today's the first full day. Last night Ryan and I saw the first small flock of Snow geese. Today is one of those perfect golden autumn days.
I was so glad you called on Tuesday. Sorry Dad and Ry weren't here. Thank you for sharing some of what you are thinking and feeling as well as seeing. I love you so much. Nothing you go through will ever change that.
Love,
Mom

E-mail Home
9/25/2004 4:25 PM
Subject: Uncle Sam's Misguided Children

Hey guys,
To address your last e-mail; I just got another package from Mom-mom today and a letter from you guys dated at the beginning of the month. I also got some mail from Pendleton dated the 24th of last month. So mail is slow and we get it once a week out here in no mans land. Hopefully it will speed up as we get settled in. 2/4 said mail would be slow at first. Looking forward to a package from y'all. I haven't sent anything home letter wise cause I've had pretty good access to e-mail.
Not a lot going on out here. There's been some fighting but nothings been overrun (they're too scared for that) and nothings really changed. We pass the time talking about what we are going to buy for our rooms when we get back to Cali. My list so far is a TV, Xbox, a futon, a nice rug, some posters for the wall, maybe a nice floor light, some system. Oh, and a car. We have lots of spare time.
I'm storing up some crazy stories for you guys when I get back. As Marines would say… "Stand the fuck by, gents." Lol.
Glad Dad made it home safely. That must have sucked signing all

those prints. How's Ryan doing? School is probably boring as hell. At least nobody shoots RPGs at you there, right?

Incidentally, Hollywood has it all wrong. RPGs make a big white flash when they explode, not a fireball. I guess no one got the memo. There really are some things in life you could go completely without knowing.

Don't do anything I wouldn't do (that leaves a lot of room for error).

Love,

Chad

E-mail to Rob

9/25/2004 3:43 PM

Bro!

So sorry for not replying in like... ever. My most profuse apologies, you must be furious with me.

That said, I am not dead. Couple close calls, but I'm still kickin and California dreamin. I almost caught an RPG last night walking to my post. Yeah, I put a helmet on after that. And dropped my water bottle and dove for sand like it was fucking cool. Hello, dirt. Hello, RPG. Hello, blinding white flash and deceptively quiet pop. Hello, shrapnel. How are you today? Fine, just dandy. Gee, I wish I had a bunker to dive into, Hollywood style, instead of laying here with a thumb up my ass hoping I don't die... It went about like that.

So on the last e-mail you questioned my stance on ethics: Good or bad is irrelevant, Rob. Its perception that causes reality and its totally fucking irrelevant, whether it's the intent or the action. Why attempt to justify when you can just do? We strap ourselves with all these terms and emotions; good, bad, guilt, crime... all to limit what people do. It makes society work. I can shoot someone in the face and feel completely stoked that I just scored a confirmed kill. But you know how much training it takes to suck the bonds of societal guilt out of someone like that? Civilians live in a fantasy world. I used to. There's no difference between self defense and cold blooded murder, except by what you call it to help you sleep at night. Some dudes got wasted last night for shooting those RPGs. Maybe it wasn't them. Maybe they just happened to be on a roof in the general vicinity looking guilty. We all agreed they were asking for it anyway. Popped some illum and the .50 went to work. See? Murder. Defense. Whatever. Was my intent bad or my action? Well, the intent to kill caused the action. In reality our decision was based on the desire to kill, which caused the action. See, this is why they call Marines insane. We just don't play by the fucking rules. Guilt and fear are the ultimate controls. See also; religion. If God is dead then it's cause he was an asshole slave dealer. Why should I sell my soul to Him and not the Devil? There's no difference. Fuck that, I'm keeping mine. Maybe one day I'll die and go toe to toe with somebody who's all like "Hey, I'm God. Confess and be forgiven." I'll be all like… "Hey man you're dead." He'll be all like… "So are you." I should go to college, let them retrain me, shape my mind, so I can fit back into the wall, like just another brick. Thanks Pink Floyd; you guys are great fucking hippies.

Hit me back with an e-mail man, maybe some nude Polaroids of Lori's sorority,

Chad

Instant Message Conversation between Rob and Chad
9/25/2004

a random soldier: YGM, bitch.

It's Rob: Yo!

a random soldier: What's up honkie… give me your cocktail, fruit.
                  Finally emailed you back.

It's Rob: Yeah, I was getting worried. How the fuck are you?

a random soldier: I'm alright… Seen better days.

It's Rob: How's Ramadi?

a random soldier: Read your e-mail. It's okay… the usual. Highs of low
                  100's, 30 percent chance of shrapnel, bring an umbrella.
                  How's Kenyon?

It's Rob: Same. It's good mostly.

a random soldier: Awesome.

It's Rob: A little bit of bull shit here and there.

a random soldier: Do tell… you have to stand post again? I hate that.

It's Rob: Half the kids here don't realize what a fucking privilege this is,
          and it irritates me. Yeah, standing post sucks. So wait… tell me.
          How did your raid go?

a random soldier: Cool… Kicked doors… Stole stuff… It's a good time
                  you should try it. Get a gun… Rollup at like 3 am…
                  Bust the fucking door in and take whatever you want.

It's Rob: What was the raid for?

a random soldier: It's called armed robbery in the states. Here, it's a raid. Snatched some dude. But we hit the wrong building.

It's Rob: Hah! Whoops.

a random soldier: A couple of times. Eh OOHRAH Marine Corps Intel.

It's Rob: That's so hilarious. Ali don't live here no mo!

a random soldier: Seriously tho its hella fun… ha-ha… One of the grunts ran in a room yelling "room service! quef! Get the fuck down now!" LOL… laughed my ass off.

It's Rob: Ha-ha-ha-ha… Oh fuck and what's this you say about a close call with a fucking RPG?

a random soldier: He-he. Don't tell my mother.

It's Rob: I won't, but Jesus Christ.

a random soldier: Yeah.

It's Rob: Did you get those snipers yet?

a random soldier: My thesis on good/bad says fuck you ethics and no we've lost three more people to that asshole. Can't kill him… needle in a haystack.

It's Rob: Well… can you find his family?

a random soldier: Ha-ha… yes all one million of them. We work it out, you hit us the whole city pays.

It's Rob: So, besides the sniper and the RPG, how is life in sandycrotch?

a random soldier: Shaved, it works out much more hygienic that way… lol… anyway it sucks… it's cool. It sucks… I miss the states. I'm making like 1K bucks every two weeks out here… I just realized that and I thought I would remark. I will buy you a beer when I get back and we'll relate funny stories and I will end up piss ass

a random soldier: drunk in the dark by myself writing poetry on
                napkins containing vague references to Kate.
                Woooohooo

It's Rob: I cannot wait for that day.

a random soldier: But then the next day, I will throw away the napkin
                after realizing that I am a genius.

It's Rob: Because sad, drunken poetry is the best.

a random soldier: Oh it is. Especially when you try to write sober and its
                absolute shit. Rob, I cannot write sober. My writing out
                here is inane and wandering.

It's Rob: Well, it should be.

a random soldier: I have tried and failed.

It's Rob: Dude, just take notes, random, disconnected notes. Record what
        you can't have when you're stateside… that's the place you make
        sense of it.

a random soldier: Essentially that's what I do. Factual notes.

It's Rob: Then good. You're on the right track.

a random soldier: I can't get anything to sound remotely good here. I
                expected inspiration. Near death to be shocking,
                somehow interesting but it doesn't affect me that
                much. I can't write it so I pine about lost love and it
                sounds like shit too. Writer's block sucks!

It's Rob: …Well, it sounds like you just broke it… what you just said,
        that's perfect go off on that.

a random soldier: Eh… we'll see when I get back. So how's it going Rob,
                good or bad, effect or intent.

It's Rob: Oh, it goes… it's very interesting. I'll put together a manifesto
        reply-mail.

a random soldier: I'm starved for a challenging opinion. Thank you…
                Thank you much.

It's Rob: Because there's so much to say about this place.

a random soldier: I don't argue politics with anyone out here or anything really. It's like overkill. I could argue with them but most people are so complacent or stupid they don't even see this for what it is and I would waste my breath. Alas, I need to get out of the corps.

It's Rob: Well, you're not a career Jarhead so it's going to end eventually.

a random soldier: Yeah I'll be out when I'm still 21.

It's Rob: And that's pretty soon.

a random soldier: Yep, 2.5 years.

It's Rob: Well hell, it's soon enough. At least you have half a brain, dude. Gomer Pyle over there is gonna be doing this shit his whole life but—You wanted to hear about the states. I'll tell you about my little slice of it. Well, the season is starting to turn. I'm in a writing class that focuses on nature writing

a random soldier: EEW… LOL…

It's Rob: So I've been heading out once or twice a week to check out the river, woods, etc. Well, there ain't shit else in Gambier. Parties on Fridays and Saturdays, a bunch of people getting apathetically wasted, freshmen being freshmen and doing stupid things.

a random soldier: Yes. Don't you find nature writing inane? I would have to find a parallel between nature and the trappings of our culture… but continue… I love college.

It's Rob: My friends are having those token boy/girl troubles.

a random soldier: Freshman should be freshman tho…

It's Rob: Boys are wandering about, shuddering in sexual frustration.

a random soldier: That's what you do.

It's Rob: There's this one kid downstairs… I've decided he'll be my personal nemesis. He's about 6 foot and weights 90lbs. Looks

It's Rob: vaguely Italian, or Spanish.

a random soldier: Like that kid from Road Trip?

It's Rob: Wears clothes that were peeled from the top of a thrift pile. No, he looks 'artsy' and 'cool' but in that 'I take myself totally serious way, not like us. We have the 'this is just our day job' look.

a random soldier: Yeah, I'm just doing this cause it gets me laid look. I have that, but why the nemesis… Why not apathy?

It's Rob: Because he annoys me and why not nemesis?

a random soldier: Good point… Why the fuck not? So are you going to kill him?

It's Rob: Maybe.

a random soldier: Or is this a coffee shop nemesis?

It's Rob: Depends on how drunk I get tonight.

a random soldier: You write dirty lines and evil words scrawled on a notebook in a pen with good ink… and think… that is NOT who I am right? That's not me…? I do that.

It's Rob: Yeah, you do… sometimes.

a random soldier: So kill him. I bet you won't do it…

It's Rob: How much? Whatever; you make all of five dollars an hour. I won't take your money.

a random soldier: Yeah!

It's Rob: But yeah, besides that… classes are hard. School is hard. I'm on the ultimate frisbee team and I kind of suck. But the leaves are falling off the trees.

a random soldier: I really gotta get some sleep bro. I gotta get up in an hour to change encryption.

It's Rob: Oh, okay.

a random soldier: I'm out like a fat kid in a gymnastics competition…

It's Rob: With sore balls and a lot of sweat.

E-mail to Rob
9/28/2004 4:40 AM
Subject: You kicked my dog.

Wut up brah,
      Where's that e-mail you promised me!?! I freaking know you collegiate bastards have nothing to do but e-mail Marines in the middle of bumfuck goddamn Iraq. Hello, it's called a keyboard. Use it or lose it.
      Seriously though, I'm still waiting for those nude pictorials of Lori's sorority. Actually, Jill did send me a photo of her kissing Gina. Ask and ye' shall receive. I'm happy for everyone; they seem to be enjoying themselves at UD. That's what I'm here for. Somewhere down the line, the fear of narcissistic sociopathic Marines strikes absolute terror in someone and keeps the world safe. Good, my intentions differ from that end.
      I'm bored. Here we are now entertain us/ I feel stupid and contagious.
      Chad

E-mail Home
9/27/2004 2:07 PM

Hey,
      Spent all day chillin' around the hooch. They hooked up a different kind of internet connection. So, for tonight we hijacked the Hadji Net back into our hooch. It's temporary but it's a nice chance to check my e-mail.
      Not a lot going on in the past couple of days. Still pissed that I can't go out on ops. I think I rate a combat action ribbon anyway, but I want to be sure. The Army showed up today with some tanks. Don't know what they're doing. Already they messed up and left a 50 cal. in the street cause it fell off the HMMWV when an RPG hit it. Aren't Ready to be Marines Yet. Damn straight they aren't. UN-fucking professional.
      MM's last package was cool, couple powerbars, some eye drops, some mints, and some baby wipes. I should get some mail again on Saturday. That seems to be when it comes, now. We all look forward to it. I'll try to call in the next couple of days. It's a pain in the ass to get a phone around here.
I'm going to finish watching Ninja Turtles,
      Love,
      Chad

E-Journal Entry
Monday, September 27, 2004
Ar Ramadi, Iraq

Thought I'd spend a couple minutes and make at least one entry while I'm in Iraq. I can't really say anything except that it's hot and sandy and boring and dangerous. Anything else would violate operational security. We're running off a hadji network and it's unsecure anyway.

E-mail home
9/28/2004 6:11 PM

Just though I'd say hi and drop you an e-mail... so... HI!
Bored stiff and it's about 3 am. PX came by the base today so I bought some nachos and queso (lasted abut 10 mins) and a bootleg movie. That was the major excitement of today, anyway. That and the mortars... lol... some things never change. Just seeing what was new with you guys...

E-mail Home
9/29/2004 4:48 PM

Hey,
Sorry you missed my call. I'd call more often but it's a pain in the ass to go wait in line or try to get one of the 1st Sgt's to hook me up. I have no chain of command out here, really, so we're on our own for that kind of thing. No one really looks out for us like they would back in the rear. It's a pain in the ass, but I'm on libo like everyday really so I can't complain too much. I'll try to call again when I'm not feeling lazy or asleep. Usually by the time I'm awake enough to go get the phone (past 8 PM here) the hours to check it out are over and I can never find 1st Sgt. Cole or 1st Sgt. Jackson. And I hate calling earlier than that cause you'd be asleep and not really with it when I called, which is sort of a waste of a call if you aren't completely awake to absorb the full impact of my genius.
Still hoping to get some mail in on Saturday. Tell Dad I wish I were home, I'd definitely skip school to go use my Benelli, which has been used only one time... I'll break it in for real when I get out of this contract. Sold my soul for a rifle and a pair of combat boots. I alternate between a brainwashed sense of loyalty to the Corps and a reeling wave of "FUCK THIS" every now and then.
The HF radio killed the laptop tonight. It caused a lot of drama and we were all upset about it until Nelson was like... dude, what the fuck are they going to do to us if we don't get that net up tonight (which would include forcing a couple of Gunny's to give up their intel computer... yeah, right) ...the answer being... Nothing. Comm can't do a damn thing if it's not up

cause we don't have another computer and stealing one from Gunny Tracy is a ridiculous thought. We can't force him to give it up. Hello, I'm a Lance Corporal. Send me to Iraq. Do your worst. It's not like I'm allowed to leave the outpost anyway.

Love and bullets,

Chad

P.S. I got tired of writing 'love" and decided "bullets" made me sound like more of a Rambo bad ass. Enjoy my machismo.

E-mail Home
9/29/2004 10:21 PM

Yo,

I can't think of lot of stuff that I need. Magazines to read of course… Stuff, FHM, Playboy, Official Xbox Mag, etc. Food is always a great option. We have milk here (though it's dehydrated and then re-hydrated raghead milk) so send cookies and chips and dips. Also, things like those Starbucks Frappuccino things in the glass seem to survive out here, I don't know why. I saw some guys from 2/4 with them when we got here. Also, Red Bull survives as well. Just pack carefully I guess. Cereal would be cool too, like Cinnamon Toast Crunch, if you think it would get here before the Exp. date. The chow hall always runs out. Also those breakfast bar things are good. White socks. Oh, I almost forgot. Another book to look up for me… I don't know the author but it's got a distinctive title so look for it… its called Generation Kill. I saw Gunny Ramos with a copy and read the back. It looks cool. Like some innocent left wing reporter hung out with some Marines out here and got shocked at our apathy for these people. Looks like a funny book. Anything that calls us a bunch of sociopath teenagers is down in my book as a good time. I want to hear what else they say about us. I'm pretty sure the book casts Marines in a negative light because the back talks about the author riding in a HMMWV when they take fire, and the Marines aren't phased, they just jumped out and shot the shit out of everything. Sweet. It's why we make the big bucks.

Hopefully that's enough ideas for you?

Love is a dud RPG from God,

Chad

PS I'm getting creative with the signoffs… maybe I'm just tired… it's like way early in the morning here… LOL! OK BYE

E-mail to Rob
9/30/2004 7:31 PM
Subject: Breakfast at Tiffany's

And she said, what about booksandcoffee, and I said well I, think

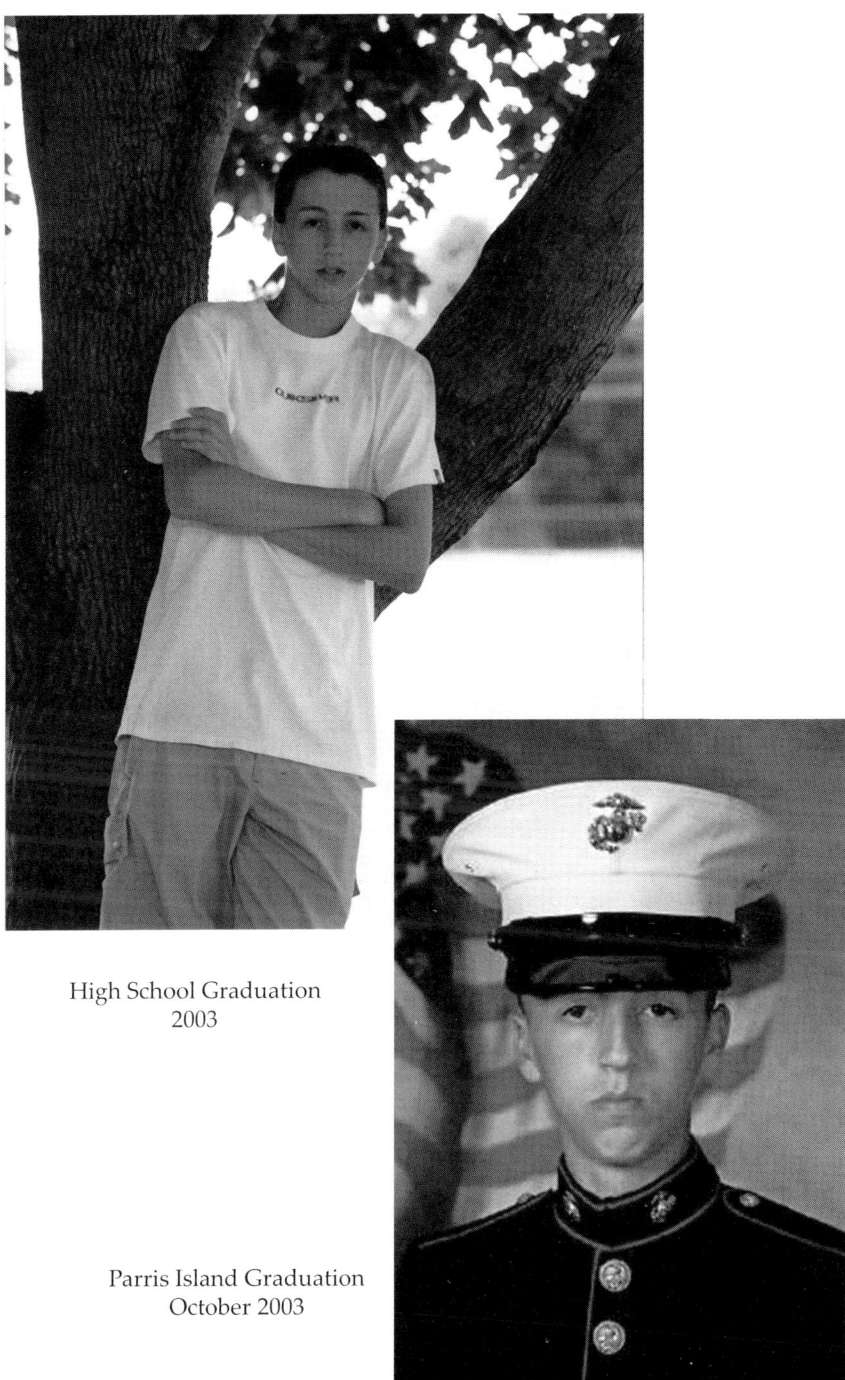

High School Graduation
2003

Parris Island Graduation
October 2003

Chad's last day home.

Waiting in a tent in Kuwait.

Target Practice

Happiness is a package from home.

Members of Whiskey 3 pray before an op.

Whiskey 3 on the streets of Ramadi.

Mike and Chad in the hooch.

Christmas in Iraq.
2004

Marines of 2/5 remember Chad at his memorial service in Ramadi.

Arlington National Cemetery. Valentines Day, 2005.
Photos by Brian Campenelli

Memorial Day, 2005

RICHARD
CHAD
CLIFTON
LCPL
US MARINE CORPS
JUL 15 1985
FEB 3 2005
PURPLE HEART
OPERATION
IRAQI FREEDOM

that's one thing we got... I think I recall we both kinda liked it.... here's to missing everything I never had and this sandy hell is worse than the inside of me crawling with nostalgia and the way it almost should have been and here's to missing perfection by just another inch and here's to the summers that ruined my life they were the best we ever had and you know it will never be there again except to tease with tattered memories and maybe it never happened except in my head... god you don't know how pathetic this is maybe you do and maybe it just isn't to wish for something so hard that you don't even want to live and the things that I have said don't make any sense...

What's up Bro?

A bit of free thought style via Kerouac. Old school Chad writing that popped out after listening to a Gin Blossoms CD at four in the morning. Makes perfect sense if you consider that it was free writing with no punctuation and no thought, just letting my fingers do the typing as it came... I rather like the sentiment it expresses, I hadn't really meant to say anything when I started it, mostly as a joke... but I like it. Missing perfection by an inch, and the goodness of it darkened the rest of the world to me. In retrospect its devastating. But I never took myself too seriously to start with. You should do more free form writing man. Keeps the art alive and keeps it from being a job. I remember why I love to write now. Fuck you writers block. Thank you old Gin Blossoms CD.

Chad

E-mail Home
9/30/2004 8:13 PM

Hey,

I'm not up to anything today. Or anytime soon. There's an op sometime in the next few days, I can't tell you when, but I don't know what's up with that feeling. I'm not going out. We did have three casualties today, though. A squad from Gulf got chewed up on foot patrol.

Got your first package today. The Starbucks Double Shots were awesome! They held up great. Same with the chips and dip.

Went in on a PS2 with Nelson today. Hooked it up and I've been playing with it since around 8 tonight... its about 3 AM right now... yeah... so I should probably get some sleep. Love you guys.

Chad

E-mail Home
10/1/2004 6:40 AM
Subject: 777

You want to hear something weird…

The number 777, which I previously had no idea what it meant, has popped up four times with enough coincidence to make me take note… in the past two days…

Once when I was working on the radio, a new error popped up: error #777 and it doesn't give an explanation. That's normal, but then I found a battery that just said 777 on it. Okay, that's a coincidence. Then Tracy gets here yesterday and asks how I like the ending in the book he gave me, specifically what happens on page 777… I never told him about the 777 thing. Then I was reading the paper this morning and the casualty list for KIAs… Number of KIAs it reported there? 777. What the fuck?

Now, the rational me is like, OK, what a weird coincidence. But then I'm like no, I should play the lottery. Or the Antichrist is coming. I say this cause I was just so curious about the weirdness I googled it…

Yeah, weird. It's also the title of a book by Aleister Crowley. What the hell. Literally. Lol.

Anyways, just thought it was bizarre and those things usually happen to you. So heads up.

Chad

Instant Message Conversation between Chad and Mom
October 1, 2004

a random soldier: Hey.

Momma: Hey.

a random soldier: What's up?

Momma: Not much. Ry's getting ready for school late.

a random soldier: Awesome… stick it to the system.

Momma: Homecoming tonight.

a random soldier: Cool, I remember homecoming game. Cory Webb passed out… on the fence in front of the state cops.

Momma: Yeah, that was great!

a random soldier: He still played Varsity Lacrosse that year too.

Momma: Talent?

a random soldier: Lewes kid.

Momma: Oh.

a random soldier: Talent was irrelevant.

Momma: Hey, did you get the package with film?

a random soldier: Nope. I got one with chips and Doubleshot espresso…

Momma: I sent it before the other one.

a random soldier: …and etc. Maybe it's backed up?

Momma: Hope so…

a random soldier: I don't know. I've been using my digital and the
                  disposables I've got. I have some cool video of a
                  medevac the other day. I called one.

Momma: Lovely.

a random soldier: Then the next one I taped. Threw smoke for one today.

Momma: Anyone you know?

a random soldier: Good times, combat outpost. One of the docs and a
                  lieutenant.

Momma: Dad says Hi!

a random soldier: Hi dad! Did you get my e-mail about the 777 thing?

Momma: Yup!

a random soldier: How weird…

Momma: Was just writing back…

a random soldier: I'm all like, not gonna leave the tent today. They a random soldier: mortared the shit out of us earlier. I'm chillin inside.

Momma: Head down kiddo.

a random soldier: Of course. Of course… I ain't skeert.

Momma: Maybe I am.

a random soldier: Nah, if I'm not scared you shouldn't be…

Momma: OK, did promise.

a random soldier: I'm a pretty good judge of pucker-Factor. Today is not a high factor… just the 777 thing that was weird.

Momma: Good to know.

a random soldier: You get superstitious out here.

Momma: Shit does happen.

a random soldier: You always hear stories of people getting warned, and its SO OBVIOUS in retrospect right… but they never saw it coming. So I conclue… *conclude.

Momma: conclueless?

a random soldier: That 777 has a 50 percent chance of winning the lottery… Play it on something with three digits.

Momma: OK.

a random soldier: What are you guys doing today?

Momma: After I take Ry to school I'm not sure… Why?

a random soldier: I dunno. I might come home for dinner and ice cream.

Momma: Dad has been craving ice cream.

a random soldier: Me too strangely… Oh that's right… I'm in a desert… that's why. Did you convert to daylight savings?

Momma: Friday Its 11 am… Not yet. Before Halloween I think.

a random soldier: oh that's my birthday… in the Marine Corps.

Momma: The witches brought you.

a random soldier: I've been in the Marine Corps like 13 months… of those… I have spent like 6 in the desert… some place or another. I don't know if I will ever adapt to trees again.

Momma: Once a tree hugger…

a random soldier: hug trees, hug dirt, whatever.

Momma: LOL Ry is taking over.

a random soldier: OK

Ry: suppizle

a random soldier: What it is nigga?

Ry: Biotch… nuttin much.

a random soldier: wut wut…

Ry: Going to school late.

a random soldier: swiizeeet!

Ry: Couldn't take the whole day off cause I wanted to go to the game.

a random soldier: Yeah!

Ry: Nothing new over here really.

a random soldier: Stick it to the system… Don't do anything I wouldn't do… which happens to include walking outside for long periods of time right now… Mortars… LOL.

Ry: ha-ha… OK

a random soldier: some teachers do suck.

Ry: Ja!

a random soldier: They think they're so great. If someone gives you shit just be all calm and be like…

Ry: Mom wants to know if the mortars are hitting the base.

random soldier: "Excuse me, you don't fucking rate."… Only a couple. They're done for the night. Counter battery fire. Annihilates everything. If they're like "What?" Just be all "Yeah. You don't rate to say that to me."

Ry: heh

a random soldier: They'll be so taken aback it might work.

Ry: ha-ha… If it doesn't work just kick their ass and take their girlfriend.

a random soldier: Two tears in a bucket, fuck it, take it to the mother fucking mike… the words of a wise man, Ssgt. Gomez. Just tell them that… confusion will ensue. You'll probably get a detention. Two tears in a bucket… fuck it… take it to the motherfucking mike. SORRY MOM. LOL

Ry: I gtg to school.

a random soldier: Alright bro. Love you. Have fun… no really…

Ry: ha-ha right

a random soldier: Actually have fun.

Ry: cyah

a random soldier: byez

Ry: Ma says bye and she loves you… Laterz

a random soldier: Ditto and goodnight.

Instant Message Chad and Rob
10/01/2004 11:16 AM

a random soldier: EMAIL ME BACK YOU FUCKING POGUE MY LIFE
IS BORING EXCEPT FOR THE MORTARS BOOT!

It's Rob: JARHEAD! HOW THE FUCK IS SANDYCROTCH?

a random soldier: Don't call it that… we call it… home. You self righteous
bastard. What's up man? I miss you.

It's Rob: I miss you too! I'm trying to finish reading some Sartre. You'd
dig this shit man.

a random soldier: Yeah? I'd dig an e-mail to entertain and delight as
well… Yargh!

It's Rob: I'm working on it! My days are fucking busy even when they're
not supposed to be.

a random soldier: I'm just giving you a hard time.

It's Rob: I've been drafting it in my head but Hey, there's a party tonight
in the DKE lounge. You should come.

a random soldier: Alright, I'll be right over. You mind if I haven't washed
these cammies in like two weeks?

It's Rob: PSH, hell no.

a random soldier: SALTY… wwwooooo

It's Rob: The republicans might make you stand outside, though Ha-ha,
ew. They don't have laundry service in Iraq?

a random soldier: No, they'd probably hold me up as an icon… support
the troops… vote for Bush…

It's Rob: Ha-ha-ha-ha!

a random soldier: Look at this poor fucker.

It's Rob: Yeah, they would.

a random soldier: He NEEDS bush.

It's Rob: Ha-ha-ha-ha! And you would so get some. We'd wash you up.

a random soldier: I could use some… nah.

It's Rob: I would have you hooked up in three seconds.

a random soldier: Let it flow… raw soldier… sandy.

It's Rob: Girls like their boys washed, here.

a random soldier: Sweaty, yum. LOL Of course, I clean up well. I want to
                  buy an M16 when I get home. The assault weapons ban
                  ran out. Score!

It's Rob: Oh man, there was a huge all student e-mail debate about that.
          Uninformed, opinionated shmucks.

a random soldier: It's great!

It's Rob: Politics tire me out.

a random soldier: A man without weapons is a subject, a man with
                  weapons is a citizen. boyah… fuck you hippie fucks…
                  I need a tek 9 and an M16 and a collapsible stock and
                  AP bullets… for peace of mind and deer hunting…
                  ahem…

It's Rob: Yes! Man, poor deer. Seriously, what an unlucky deer!

a random soldier: If they wouldn't wear bullet proof jackets I wouldn't
                  need this .50 What? They don't wear them? What?

It's Rob: To a .50 there is no such thing as a bullet proof jacket.

a random soldier: Very very very true… I'm going to become a
                  photographer and take photos of a model playing with
                  herself and a .50 round… in black and white… of
                  course. You know it's art… artsy porn.

It's Rob: MMM.

a random soldier: Suggesting something about sexuality and our

a random soldier: generations obsession with violence. I think a canvas
print would be nice. Would go well in my room.

It's Rob: I'm sure your father would approve your meddling in the art
world, too.

a random soldier: *Hello I cannot spell today*... actually no... He'd be
like that's a great scam you got there Chad. Can I get a
cut of that bullshit you're selling? It's all image... we
both know it, you give the people what they want.

It's Rob: Speaking of bull shit...

a random soldier: Yes, yes.

It's Rob: I'm going to a modern art museum on Saturday.

a random soldier: You rang.

It's Rob: To pick out a piece...

a random soldier: I love modern art.

It's Rob: To write a fifteen page term paper on.

a random soldier: OMG... Can I do it for you? NM... you do yours and
submit mine as well to see what grade I get. I really do
have a taste for modern art and fashion. Have you seen
Dolchi's fall line this year? To die for... but art yeah.

It's Rob: Ha-ha-ha!

a random soldier: Sounds like a decent project.

It's Rob: eh... It will be hard but enriching, as I suppose is most of
college.

a random soldier: I love art man. Our lives are art. Life mimics art.

It's Rob: You know, that's very true. We hem our lives off of pre-
established ideas.

a random soldier: It's a performance piece... and it was so tragically close
to perfection. That's why we will make bank if we ever

a random soldier: write a screenplay. It would have to be a collaborative
effort. See me after the war. It was *almost* perfect.

It's Rob: Definitely.

a random soldier: Art BAM. Kick it up a notch Emeril.

It's Rob: Score written by Elliot Smith, resurrected from the grave and Oh
SHIT! It's Good Will Hunting.

a random soldier: Never saw it.

It's Rob: Question, what time is it there? I'm curious.

a random soldier: 1910… We're on daylight savings too… I'm about to go
get some chow.

It's Rob: Mmm… Hey, where the fuck do you type this from? That's
made me curious too.

a random soldier: Um… he-he… a laptop…

It's Rob: But where?

a random soldier: Appropriated from comm.

It's Rob: Like, in a fucking foxhole?

a random soldier: Getting to that… behind a HMMWV… under some
cammie netting… behind some barriers… it's my pad
yo… I'm filming MTV Cribs this weekend.

It's Rob: Where's the humvee?

a random soldier: Outside.

It's Rob: Give me notes fucker…

a random soldier: There's nothing man… I'll send pictures.

It's Rob: Oh, and btw, on your writer's block… You're trying too hard to
get the meaning now… the meaning comes later… just gather
data. Take now what you can't get stateside.

a random soldier: I tried that. It's dull, not progressive. No.

It's Rob: Yeah, so? Patience.

a random soldier: That closeness to perfection, ending in tragic
                separation. That's the angle. The money shot.

It's Rob: Yeah, but we'll save that for later, for now, you take notes on
                your meaningless environment.

a random soldier: Right now.

It's Rob: And I'll take notes on mine.

a random soldier: I would kill for a mountain dew and head. Oh God
                glorious female. I heard a chick on the radio today
                almost busted a nut… Man its bad when it's really bad.
                Called two medivacs in the past two days.

It's Rob: Two medivacs? For what?

a random soldier: Mortars and a squad got chewed up by small arms. Its
                bad man.

It's Rob: Shit!

a random soldier: Its surreal.

It's Rob: That's no good… I heard about that huge raid, only one killed,
                that's not bad.

a random soldier: Which one?

It's Rob: Around 100 or so insurgents dead?

a random soldier: We don't pay attention to the news.

It's Rob: Um, let me check.

a random soldier: Whatever you hear is bull shit. There's an intel stop on
                this province.

It's Rob: Samarra.

a random soldier: Yeah, that's not this province.

It's Rob: Sunni Triangle.

a random soldier: This is the worst place in Iraq.

It's Rob: Yeah, so I hear.

a random soldier: I think we're gonna pay for it during the elections.

It's Rob: The Sunnis are fucking nuts. When are the elections?

a random soldier: January. Maybe they won't fuck with us for Xmas. We
                   will fuck their world up. Anyway, I'm out to chow…
                   Maybe, they'll have cold coke. Maybe. Deuces.

It's Rob: That would be delicious.

a random soldier: Tell Lori I said Hello.

It's Rob: I certainly will… keep your head down, bro… stay safe.

a random soldier signed off at 12:16 PM

Away message from a random soldier:
    The sound of helos in the distance, thumping half as rapidly as my
pulse as I thumb the safety and blow imaginary dust off my sites one more
time… "Three, two, GO!" The door is kicked up and we storm inside,
clearing our areas to the sounds of the mosque reading morning prayer a
block down. The wails of the Imam mingle with the crying prisoner we
have sitting on his knees blindfolded, hands flexi cuffed behind his back.
This was our war.

E-mail Home
10/02/2004 12:20 PM

Hey there,
    Not a lot new today. Heard a rumor from Cpl. Tovar that I and Nelson
(who just picked up Cpl) are being rotated back to Hurricane Point with
the rest of the Comm Marines. I don't think its punishment; I just think
they want to rotate. That kinda sucks cause they PT and do stupid shit
back at HP, but it will be good to see everyone again. Maybe I'll get put
on guard. That would be cool. King got to shoot up a car at the ECP. And
we've been getting mortared pretty bad here at the outpost in the past two

days. They're getting a tad bit ballsy with it. Played with a laser for a little while with Cpt. Welch. He doesn't want me to leave of course, cause I'm his RO by default, being the only TACP trained Marine out here. Maybe I'll get to stay. Doubt it though.

Crypto change over here tonight; it's gonna be a long night. No mail today either, bummer. Prolly get some tomorrow. I'm looking forward to that pack of film before I leave here. Climb up to the roof and take some shots of the mosques and cityscape.

I'm off to try and see what's up with Cpt. Welch's radio and see if I can use the phone in BAS.

Love,
Chad

Instant Message between Chad and Rob
10/02/2004 4:24 PM

a random soldier: Que pasa contigo?

It's Rob: Hey, asshole.

a random soldier: What's up chode?

It's Rob: It's choad and not much, really… a crisp autumn day in
        America's heartland rolling hills and what not.

a random soldier: Yay… hills… rolling that's great. I am going to do so
            many drugs when my contract runs out.

It's Rob: Ha-ha-ha-ha-ha-… try to keep it to a few… You couldn't kill
        yourself before, getting shot at, I'm not going to let you die after.
        But hey, if all else fails we can buy pills from that addict at the
        bar in Dewey.

a random soldier: Yeah, he was strange. I want to kill him like as a
            favor… be like dude… here's a freebie… WHAM.

It's Rob: I'm sure he would appreciate it.

a random soldier: Like robin hood but with more criminal implications.

It's Rob: God, what a sketchy night. Do you remember that bar… just the
        sadness of Dewey in the winter. The drunk married men?

a random soldier: Oh yeah, wow, you remember that night… watched a random soldier: that movie at Kate's.

It's Rob: Oh yeah!

a random soldier: Candi showed up.

It's Rob: Went to the beach.

a random soldier: THAT was sketchy. I was like hello orgy and it was
God, being all like nah. you don't deserve that kind of
luck. I'm really in for it when I die. Hey if you're
gonna go down, go big.

It's Rob: Ha-ha-ha-ha… With God hating you.

a random soldier: Don't hate me cause you're jealous, God. Anyway, did
you pick a piece?

It's Rob: Maybe. A Warhol, "Portrait of Madame Cezanne". The
museum had shit so far as good post '45 art.

a random soldier: I'll look it up in a few.

It's Rob: It's very interesting…

a random soldier: What's it about?

It's Rob: Well, it has the vague outline of a female figure and black lines
dissecting it, cutting it into sections, and arrows possibly
suggesting where to move the pieces. I was able to poke out a
few dimensions of this.

a random soldier: Such as…

It's Rob: 1.) Cubism-by-numbers. It was a popular thing of Pop art to de-
mystify art.

a random soldier: Can you do 15 pages of art critique on that?

It's Rob: Oh yeah, if I try hard enough.

a random soldier: Would it be boring to read?

It's Rob: It's art crit. It might be.

a random soldier: This coming from a guy with the attention span of a
gnat.

It's Rob: Ha-ha-ha… Yeah, dude. Boring as hell. BTW—we're having a
cross-dressing party tonight. You should definitely come.

a random soldier: Wow, I would take it too far and prolly go home with
someone. I'm a really easy lay at this point. LOL…

It's Rob: No kidding.

a random soldier: Ick. I take everything too far. Hello Marine Corps.

It's Rob: People here tend to be pretty hot.

a random soldier: Yeah I miss girls… I heard a chick on the 'net today… a
pilot… she sounded hot…

It's Rob: Nice! What was she doing?

a random soldier: Talking to somebody at division.

It's Rob: Talking dirty, perhaps?

a random soldier: I wish.

It's Rob: You know… I was thinking, last night standing outside of one of
the dorms… How awesome it would be if you were here.

a random soldier: Hmm yeah it would be… but it wouldn't be me.

It's Rob: I know… it was just a thought.

a random soldier: I just pop in and out of everyone's lives randomly… I
think I'm Moriarty.

It's Rob: Ha-ha-ha… Oh, Dean.

a random soldier: Of course… I've been glancing through Desolation
Angels.

It's Rob: Oh good, so you have reading material.

a random soldier: Yes.

It's Rob: What's it about, anyway?

a random soldier: Nothing, as usual, but literally this time. Nothing starts out about his job as a fire watch by himself on this mountain, daringly confronting the void. I know what he means. I run from that void all the time. If I stayed by myself…

It's Rob: The void eventually claimed him.

a random soldier: On a mountain for 45 days I would go fucking nuts. I'd kill myself. I can't be alone that long.

It's Rob: Yeah, see… he got that from Gary Snyder.

a random soldier: Whatever. I like it. It's a great concept which I described back in 8th grade before I knew about Kerouac. I was a screwed up kid.

It's Rob: Nah. Oh man, 8th grade.

a random soldier: Genius baby genius. Ginsberg said it best…

It's Rob: Remember when we almost got in a fight because you called the Marines "grunts" and "cannon fodder?"

a random soldier: …The greatest minds of our generation consumed by insanity. Yes, I do and karma got my ass.

It's Rob: Ha-ha… Or just a really, really proactive irony.

a random soldier: God I'm fucking bored. Yeah.

It's Rob: Anything exciting happen today?

a random soldier: Mortars woke me up at 6… close… I rolled over… went back to sleep fuck the war. I'm tired.

It's Rob: Ha-ha-ha-ha… man.

a random soldier: Check out the pics on my live journal.

It's Rob: So what do you do with your days, anyway?

a random soldier: A lot of nothing. Sometimes posts… mostly nothing.

It's Rob: woah! Dude! The picture!

a random soldier: What?

It's Rob: So you have pics?

a random soldier: Some on there… Uploading more.

It's Rob: Under where?

a random soldier: I dunno… I'm looking at a different page than you.

It's Rob: Well, let me see the pictures!

a random soldier: ? I gave you the address… find it.

It' Rob: Oh, "view more pics".

a random soldier: No fucking shit huh… You're in one of them.

It's Rob: You ever listen to the Dandy Warhols?

a random soldier: No… catchy name.

It's Rob: You'd like them a lot. Do you have a CD player with you?

a random soldier: Yep.

It's Rob: I'll burn one and send it.

a random soldier: Cool… You ever listen to Fall Out Boy?

It's Rob: Never.

a random soldier: Well you should… you'd probably hate them… Post
emo… I like it.

It's Rob: How exactly would you define post emo?

a random soldier: A natural evolution, from whiney and sobbing mellow
rock with catchy hooks to lightly sardonic and self

a random soldier: effacing rock with catchy hooks.

It's Rob: Oh, God save us all. The Dandy Warhols are hedonistic, godless art rock.

a random soldier: Sort of… the I'm not emo cause it was just a phase.

It's Rob: With a sarcastic pop edge.

a random soldier: But I still dream about her at night… but everyone does it… right??? That tone… Emo was all like "I can't live with out you" Post Emo is all like "I'll pretend I can live without you, it just sucks"

It's Rob: PSH… yeah… sad.

a random soldier: Really I know.

It's Rob: So the Dandy Warhols… one of their songs, called "Nietzsche"

a random soldier: !

It's Rob: "I want a god/ who stays dead/ not plays dead"

a random soldier: That's clever.

It's Rob: I do like it.

a random soldier: Do you know any hot gothic chicks? That's my next adventure… first combat

It's Rob: Next, gothic chicks?

a random soldier: …Second; gothic model chick.

It's Rob: There are some in my modern art class.

a random soldier: Definitely, I've started falling in love with every short cute false brunette with too much lipstick and dark mascara that I see… I don't know why.

It's Rob: Ha-ha-ha… You have a lot of those in Ramadi?

a random soldier: No, but there are a lot on the internet… lol.

It's Rob: Woah, what is this?

a random soldier: What is what?

It's Rob: This website?

a random soldier: Blog and etc… all wrapped up… a place to store shit basically and network if you choose? Internet dating isn't cool tho.

It's Rob: Perhaps.

a random soldier: I'm not all about that… I'm still old school.

It's Rob: Yeah… hahaha… a real flowers kinda guy…

a random soldier: Sweet and cuddly and honest… that's me… actually. How WOULD you describe me to a girl?

It's Rob: One sec…

a random soldier: I mean without lying… I guess I think a goth chick would have the actual capability to grasp how fucking brilliant I am. Yeah… lol

It's Rob: 5'9, lean (would mention marines), cynical, witty.

a random soldier: I'm trying to write a description for my blog… fuck it.

It's Rob: Ha-ha-ha!

a random soldier: Pics are enough.

It's Rob: Good pics, too except I look like a fucking clown… hey—I actually have to go get some coffee with some chick from MA.

a random soldier: I'm telling.

It's Rob: A friend… she has big boobs, though. You'd dig her… went to prep school kinda cynical.

a random soldier: I'm not a boob guy.

It's Rob: Me neither, but it's still nice.

a random soldier: I'm a face and "are you evil enough to scare me guy"…
               true… but Rob, you know I only dig chicks I can't
               have… do have fun tho… careful with the coffee.

It's Rob: Well, you'd realize that there are better ways to run a love life.

a random soldier: That's how it starts…

It's Rob: Ha-ha-ha… Right.

a random soldier: Sorry you do your thing. I do mine.

It's Rob: Take it easy, Lance Corporal.

a random soldier: You too bro.

It's Rob: Keep your head down and your helmet on.

a random soldier: Same to you actually… don't get caught…

It's Rob: dude… she's just a friend.

a random soldier: Oh… it's like THAT.

It's Rob: Ha-ha-ha yeah!

a random soldier: You lucky fuck!

It's Rob: God!

a random soldier: LOL!

It's Rob: Jesus!

a random soldier: What… me? Nah.

It's Rob: You thought it was like… that?

a random soldier: Maybe, you guys seem like the progressive couple of
               the 00's… you never know… LOL.

It's Rob: Ha-ha-ha-ha… God, we so are… it's sad… alas.

E-mail Home
10/03/2004 5:11 PM
Subject: Re: Socks

Hey,
That's a negative on receiving socks. No impact, no idea. I do know a mail truck from 2/5 got blown up on Saturday… hit an IED, rolled over, and caught fire. So that sucks. Everyone was just glad no people were in the back and it was just mail. Mail can be lost easier than Marines.
Not much going on out here lately. Bored and wishing I could go outside and play with the Varsity instead of riding bench…
I'm out like a fat kid in dodge ball,
Chad

E-mail Home
10/04/2004 12:11 PM
Subject: packages

Hey,
Guess my shit didn't get blown up. I got all sent mail to date tonight. Film, socks, everything. Cool beans. Gave about four boxes of stuff out to people who needed supplies.
Going back to HP tomorrow, which sort of sucks and sort of doesn't. I'll probably not have internet connection as often now that we aren't going to have a private line run out here. I'll see what's up at the Comm shop and call in the next week. I'm trying to stay positive.
I'll talk to you when I can, much love,
Chad

E-mail to Rob
10/4/2004 10:56 AM
Subject: Real World Iraq

What's up bro?
Prolly won't e-mail as often now, losing my private connection because I'm being recalled to HP. It's not really the rear, but its not Combat Outpost, either. Talk about getting on my Commo's (communications officer) shit list. Maybe I'll get on guard and light someone up a really good and proper.
I've packed my packs and cleaned my rifle. I get to head down MSR Michigan tomorrow en route to HP. That's always a fucking riot. The wild, wild, west. I'm trying to be stoked about it but I never get lucky, nothing happens when I'm ready.
So here it is… I'm looking at the wanted poster of three high value

targets and there, crudely drawn is a box with a snake in it… it's a strangely morbid comment on the latest detainee… our Iraqi interpreter, nicknamed Snake. Found guilty of espionage… I'm surprised he didn't get executed. They fucked him up pretty good though. That's the war, here.

Generation Kill.

Chad

Journal Entry:
Monday October 4, 2004 12:12 AM
Cereal box Religion

Sitting here on radio watch in the dark, using some hijacked Iraqi network for internet, we have a lot of time to ourselves to think…

My thoughts are a jumbled mix of wishing I could go home to Cali or back to SoDel and wishing for an op to come along and go get some action like Nick and Ryan are tonight.

I also pause and have time to wonder what it would be like if I hadn't left… maybe if I had been better looking or said something different or wasn't such a tool, maybe then I could have been good enough for her and happy like everyone else. But maybe she's the reason I ran away so far and so fast. I was out of that town like a bat out of hell as soon as I had a chance. Here's to missing those nights in Dewey with you, out here in the desert morning. I wish things could have been different, but they're not, so we'll never know. The trouble with getting older and getting wiser is that you see where you went wrong. A couple years pass and you move on, but I'm stuck in a place where time stands still. I tried to close my eyes to the pain that's left for me to go. I left too soon with no resolution, no sense of closure, nothing to do. Just sit and think in the dark by myself trying to forget about you.

I hope deep down she sees this and knows how sorry I am, but on the surface I'm so scared to say her name, for fear of rejection again.

…This nostalgia is killing me. This is what happens when you finally lose hope in finding something better and you want what you almost had. That chance at perfection, the way things were… there's something beautiful and tragic about it. It's another case of life imitating art. I'll be alright. There's always a happy ending. Maybe I'll find someone cool who likes the same things I do, who isn't such an evil bitch, and we'll get dressed up on the weekend for dinner and hit some ritzy club in an SLK in SoCal and life will be perfect again. I'll be alright, tonight.

P.S. We just heard an IED (Improvised Explosive Device) go off outside. It's a crazy kind of war. Expecting mortars again, soon. Fuck, they're calling a MEDIVAC… somebody got hurt. Craziness.

Journal Entry
10/04/2004 1:35 PM
Patiently Waiting

So yeah,

Gotta go back to Hurricane Point tomorrow night… I don't want to leave combat outpost. My friends are here, and going to the "rear" seems wrong, even if it's like 4 miles away. It's not the rear, but they don't get shot at as much as we do out here. I can't really explain it. I could run there in like half and hour but is still feels like the rear to me.

There's a really good chance that I'm going to get subbed out for Ross, and come back out here as an RO for Gulf Co. That would be sweet. Hopefully I can get what I want and just come out here. I'm addicted to the rush. It's like a drug, running into a dark house at 2 am and not knowing if you're going to come out alive or if the door is going to explode as soon as it gets kicked in or if someone is going to start putting AK rounds through the wall. You never know. It's the ultimate in extreme sports.

In other news… Still thinking of the girl and wishing I weren't so powerless against free will. I'm so weak sometimes. Here I am with my rifle and ammunition and body armor and war stories… and all I can think about is the way she used to smile and how last time I saw her, my picture was still on the wall… Pathetic, Chad… You're better than that. So I'm told. Same shit different day…

Journal Entry
Tuesday October 5, 2004
Ain't it cool?

Another night the same old shit.

Got back this morning from the Government Center OP. Not much happened. Got into a small firefight early in the night, just after dark. Some bodies hit the floor. We are all okay, no one got hurt on our side. Almost lost Post 3 when and RPG hit right below their bunker. Knocked one of the guys on his ass tho. Ain't it cool?

I'm going to sleep to dream of better days and better parties. This war is stressing me out. I need some rest before I go back on watch later. I feel sick. Ate too much candy, I think. I miss beer, pizza, and girls. Fuck Iraq.

•

Pfc. Andrew Halverson   October 9, 2004
2nd Battalion, 5th Regiment, 1t Marine Division, 1st Expeditionary Force.
Died as a result of enemy action in Al Anbar Province, Iraq.

•

"No one ever goes into battle thinking God is on the other side."
                                                            Terry Goodkind

Chapter 10

Terri's Journal Entry
October 10, 2004

Chad,
         I've been missing you too much to write. Haven't heard from you in several days. Last word from you was that you hated HP and would rather be getting shot at. Would you believe that I can handle the thought of you in harms way, but not be able to deal with your being miserable. I guess a normal Mom would prefer safe and just let you deal with being unhappy. No one has ever accused me of being normal.
         Dad, Ryan and I went to the Maryland Renaissance Festival today. Wish you could have gone with us. I finally have a Celtic cape.
         One month down. Working on the next full moon. Hang in there. I'm with you.
         Love,
         Mom

•

2nd Lt. Paul M. Felsberg   October13, 2004
Company E. 2nd Battalion, 5th Marine Regiment, 1st Marine Division, 1st Marine Expeditionary Force. Died as a result of Enemy Action Al Anbar Province, Iraq

•

Lance Cpl. Victor A. Gonzalez   October13, 2004
2nd Battalion, 5th Regiment, 1st Marine Division, 1st Marine Expeditionary Force. Died as a result of Enemy Action Al Anbar Province, Iraq

•

Journal Entry
October 16, 2004 4:03 AM
Incoming
Same shit, different day...

Sitting here in the shop checking my mail, watching Gangs of New York in the "lounge" area (we've got a TV and an Xbox that plays our DVDs). Just got back from the Gov't Center. Got mortared over there and some shrapnel from some 155mm arty shells rigged to blow up on a convoy. Small arms fire, etc. Good times...

Also got mortared while chillin in the shop. That's just annoying, having to watch a movie in body armor and a helmet.
I just thought I'd update this. Not much goin' on right now. Radio watch tomorrow, I guess, don't know when I'll go out again.
Chad

E-mail Home
10/17/2004 12:55 AM
Subject: Good Morning Vietnam

Just thought I'd say hi. Love you guys.

Chad

•

Sgt. Douglas E. Bascom   October 20, 2004
Individual Ready Reservist assigned to Weapons Company 2nd Battalion, 5th Marine Regiment, 1st Marine Division, 1st Marine Expeditionary Force. Died as a result of enemy action Al Anbar Province, Iraq

•

Journal Entry
October 20, 2004 7:29 AM
I have to pee

I just drank a large bottle of Gatorade. It's dark out. I have to pee. I'm scared to pee in the dark. There are spiders in the porta potties... I'm not scared of bullets or RPGs or mortars, but man... spiders... ICK! I think I'll go pee on a Bush. I mean, bush. Ah, bush... What am I thinking...? RANDOMNESS IS VOGUE. Byatch. (I learned that word from Lindsay Lohan... byatch.)
Going to the gym. lata.

Journal Entry
October 23, 2004 9:50 PM
Empty Iraqi Nights

Que Pasa,
	Got off of radio watch a little while ago. Still hyper from the soda I had at dinner (we don't drink a lot of caffeine here, last time I had a Mountain Dew was like six weeks ago).
	Update to the previous journals… Fuck the girl. I can't wait to get back to Cali…
	In other news, I'm going out again in a couple days. Wish me luck. They're trying to level the Observation Post like its fucking cool.
	Send me some love. I'm off to the gym again (trying to get bigger for all my fans… lol)
	I'm out like a blind kid in paintball,
	Chad

Journal Entry
October 25, 2004 4:42 AM
Good Morning Vietnam… I mean, Iraq…
Good Morniiiiiiiinnnnnnnnnnnngggggggggggg Ramadi!

Another beautiful night, here under the starry Iraqi canopy above… one more day closer to home sweet fucking home… and all that that entails. It got kinda chilly tonight, down around 70 or so… we're freezing our asses off. I'm supposed to be watching the phone here at the comm. shop but no one is paying attention to me and it's 02:45 in the morning, so I'm just gonna update the old journal and shoot the shit by myself playing solitaire… exciting day, huh?
I've been looking at tattoos to find one to cover up the dragon that's on my back at the base of my neck… it came out way too small and I got it back in comm. school… My first tat, didn't want it too big… def not big enough. So I think I'm getting it covered up with intertwined Celtic knot work dogs (i.e. devil dogs, it's a light USMC reference without getting the whole motto Eagle, Globe, Anchor, as well as to my heritage). Nick and I have this agreement to get one dog tag of ours on our ribs, and one for the other one if either of us gets killed out here. It's groovy. We're all a little morbid, I think, but it's the thought that counts, right? I'm trying to find a good Odinist tat paying tribute to the Piper but I can't find anything my style. Everything is like super Viking bullshit. I may settle on some runes in a band around my left ankle. SO passé but I do want one or two, so that when I get old I can look back and be like yeah, I was fucking cool too, I got the most out of it all… And then I'll listen to my Marshall Mathers LP in the basement and the grandkids will talk about how weird old people

are.

I'm out, I have to go finish this watch and then I'm gonna rack out.

Terri's Journal Entry
October 25, 2004

Chad,

Hey. Still missing you quite a bit. Wish you had been here for Ry's birthday dinner. Bet you do too. Mexican and a corona would probably be a chunk of heaven for you right now.

The election is finally getting here. I'm so sick of the whole thing.
Love you so much,
Mom

•

1st Lt. Matthew D. Lynch   October 31, 2004
Weapons Company 2nd Battalion, 5th Marine Regiment, 1st Marine Division, 1st Marine Expeditionary Force. Died as a result of enemy action in Al Anbar Province, Iraq

•

Terri's Journal Entry
October 31, 2004

Happy Halloween. Hope you got the candy we sent. We carved a couple pumpkins. Mine was a basic slant-eyed demon. Ryan carved an ode to Halo 2.

One year ago today we picked you up at boot and took you to Charleston Place. So today is your first Marine Birthday. I hope you're getting what you needed. I hope you always do.
Love,
Mom

Journal Entry
November 2, 2004 3:24 PM
Anti- Iraqi Forces? Looks Iraqi to me…

I'm mad fucking tired.

Firefight at the Government Center the other day… took a lot out of me actually. All that adrenaline shocks your system I guess. Plus we got hella mortars really close to the shop last night. I've got some shrapnel from it hitting the roof. Blew huge chunks of stone about the size of your head sixty yards. Wicked good times.

In other news, got some mail today. I'm about to go play some PS2 and maybe upload a couple new pics. I'm out like a blind kid in a gun fight.

Terri's Journal Entry:
November 3, 2004

The election is over and Bush won. I'm disappointed, but not surprised. It's not like the options were outstanding. People are sheep. No one cares about this war. It's not as important as preventing gay marriage.

All I care about is you coming home safely. I've spent a large part of my life trying to make the world a better place. Good intentions only go so far. Let someone else do it for awhile.

I love you,
Mom

•

Lance Cpl. Jared P. Hubbard   November 4, 2004
Weapons Company 2nd Battalion, 5th Marine Regiment, 1st Marine Division, 1st Marine Expeditionary Force. Died due to injuries received as a result of enemy action Al Anbar Province, Iraq

•

Corporal Jeremiah A Baro   November 4, 2004
Weapons Company 2nd Battalion, 5th Marine Regiment, 1st Marine Division, 1st Marine Expeditionary Force. Died due to injuries received as a result of enemy action Al Anbar Province, Iraq

•

Lance Cpl. Sean M. Langley   November 7, 2004
Weapons Company 2nd Battalion, 5th Marine Regiment, 1st Marine Division, 1st Marine Expeditionary Force. Died due injuries received as a result of enemy action Al Anbar Province

•

Journal Entry
November 7, 2004 8:31 AM

Another day closer to coming home,

Haven't bothered to add an entry in awhile, the internet has been really shitty for the past week or so and it won't let me upload new images now. Bummer, eh?

And my e-mail refuses to load the text box in compose, so I'm kinda fucked for sending mail. Guess I'll have to start writing letters. Booo snail mail. Oh, how I loathe your sluggishness…

I've been working out a lot lately, nothing else to do around here anymore. Gained 5 lbs! I'll never have the strong chin and jaw line of some Abercrombie model, but I can damn sure kick his ass and steal his girlfriend with tales of my exploits in raghead land and then be all sorry and emo about it and mention something about the duality of my existence. Maybe I'd write a poem and send it to her one night when I got drunk and lonely. Ah... those are the days...

I can't wait to get home. I want to 1) hug my family. 2) Drink myself stupid with my bros in Cali. 3) Drink myself silly with my friends back in DE 4) go surfing 5) get my skydiving license 6) Use the license to base jump the grand canyon... I haven't planned much farther than that.
I'm out to take a shower and hit the rack. Send me some love.

Terri's Journal Entry
November 10, 2004

I have kittens! They're only about a week old. Their momma gave up on them. I'm not ready for more cats, but the only option was to let them die. Dad thinks it will be good to have something to care for. I guess he thinks I need the distraction. It's not like I'm getting much sleep anyway.

Mailed your Halo 2 today. Ry is playing hookie from school so he can play. Mailed a big box of assorted stuff too. Christmas garland to soup mix.

Love, Mom

E-mail to Rob
11/11/2004 4:10 PM
Subject: I see a red door...

Que Pasa,

With all this drama in the Ramadi, its kinda hard bein' USMC, but somehow someway, we comin up with funky ass shit like every single day. Rollin down the street smokin' hadjis, sippin' on Camelbacks. Word.

So what's up bro? Afraid to e-mail me or what? Internet here sucks, granted, but still I get to check my shit every once in a while. Anyway, it's starting to hit the fan here, I just thought I'd check in and let you know that I still cry myself to sleep listening to Dashboard Confessional and dreaming sweet emo dreams. But I'm a killer and it's all business when the sun is up. Mwuah.

I want to get laid and drunk and HIGH AS A MOTHERFUCKER. It's our Vietnam. I rolled in from a three hour firefight last week feeling pretty giggly and pleased with myself, and not two hours later I was listening to Vietnam rock and playing Monopoly with my bros. What the fuck is the world coming too? I love it like I can't describe. But it still blows. I miss DE and the Cali Dream.

I'm out.

Instant Message Conversation between Chad and Rob
11/11/2004 11:45 PM

a random soldier: Fuck you.

It's Rob: Holy shit!

a random soldier: I know right… internet just got IM over here.

It's Rob: And you just got internet?… Back from the rear or something?

a random soldier: Ha-ha… rear… I don't know why I was bitching. About
                  a week after I got here, the old firm base was taken
                  down cause we couldn't defend it. This is the only one.

It's Rob: Waaait, wait wait…

a random soldier: Hello frontline.

It's Rob: Where the fuck are you?

a random soldier: Ramadi… Hurricane Point.

It's Rob: Didn't you go back to the rear?

a random soldier: We no longer own combat outpost. What I call the rear
                  was on the other side of town.

It's Rob: Oh.

a random soldier: I was just bitching.

It's Rob: Okay… aaah, I get it.

a random soldier: Cause I hadn't really killed anyone and I was pissy.

It's Rob: You were in a firefight? What the hell was that like?

a random soldier: Several, but it's awesome. It's like God shining down
                  and touching you and you are hyper aware and then
                  it's shockingly scary and somebody dies. A guy I knew
                  lost an arm and a leg two days ago… Fucking SUCKS!

It's Rob: What! How? Don't talk to anyone else, I'm so much more

It's Rob: important…

a random soldier: Sorry, like literally 8 windows.

It's Rob: Ha-ha-ha-ha… Understood no worries.

a random soldier: I can't keep track… I got my bitches on one hand… homies on the other.

It's Rob: What's a man to do?

a random soldier: And my pimp game ain't been the same lately.

It's Rob: Yeah… sand in your crotch doesn't do it for the ladies much.

a random soldier: Some.

It's Rob: But what the fuck happened to your friend?

a random soldier: He got hit by an RPG. I wasn't there thank God. But Show…

It's Rob: Holy shit!

a random soldier: One of my best friends, he saw it… said it was fucking horrible, I can only imagine. I've never seen Show that upset. I almost fucking cried for him that he had to see that shit.

It's Rob: Is the guy okay? The one who got hit by an RPG, I mean.

a random soldier: Yeah he'll live.

It's Rob: How are you?

a random soldier: I'm fine. How are you?

It's Rob? Oh, I'm fine. I'm not in a combat zone. It's cold here.

a random soldier: So, at night sometimes we put on a movie and get a can of duster and get fucked up until we almost die.

It's Rob: So very Platoon.

a random soldier: I know, it's why we do it. A very good sense of poetic
            justice here.

It's Rob: You said Ramadi was heating up? I've read shit in the news.
            Sixteen guys got hit in a car bomb or something?

a random soldier: That was some Army dudes… We call it a VBIED not a
            car bomb.

It's Rob: VBIED?

a random soldier: Vehicle Borne Improvised Explosive Devise. We were
            watching Ecks Vs. Servers the other day and in the
            beginning they use a VBIED. Yeah, we shut off the
            fucking movie. Some things… too close to home.

It's Rob: No shit… Jesus, I'm very glad to hear that you're okay. What do
            they have you doing these days?

a random soldier: Radio watch or go to an OP for a day or so. Watch.
            Shoot. Watch. Come back. Sleep. Eat. Play Xbox.

It's Rob: OP? Xbox?

a random soldier: Observation Post/Point.

It's Rob: You guys get Halo 2 yet?

a random soldier: It's coming in the mail via my lil' bro.

It's Rob: Amazing. It's fucking awesome. So why is Army in Ramadi?

a random soldier: They are the boss, our battalion works for them, sort of,
            they stay out of our area.

It's Rob: figures… Lori says hi!

a random soldier: Hi Lori… Wow, Jill just burned me. That was
            surprising.

It's Rob: Did she? Well, she's dating someone.

a random soldier: Not like that.

It's Rob: Oh ha-ha-ha-ha!

a random soldier: I was talking about watching fashion TV.

It's Rob: As you are known to do.

a random soldier: Hey I love fashion.

a random soldier: J: Usually war turns boys to men… not to women…
                        OUCH!

J: Ha-ha… love you!

a random soldier: I told her she wasn't allowed to be sarcastic or witty
                        anymore. It's shocking.

It's Rob: Ha-ha-ha-ha… However crude, the wit develops in college I
                        guess… Jennifer Mason died.

a random soldier: No way… how?

It's Rob: Hit by a car when crossing Route One across from Taco Bell.
                        Medivaced to Christiana… where she died.

a random soldier: Wow. That's so random.

It's Rob: Yeah.

a random soldier: I mean damn. Of all the ways to go. That blows.

It's Rob: And the first thing I remember about her? Or one of the first
                        things, anyway? Her tits. Conclusive evidence that I'm a rotten
                        person, and/or we're all doomed to near-Neanderthal tendencies.

a random soldier: I don't even really remember her except I think I
                        thought she was mildly attractive… I can't remember…
                        face to name. I've seen a lot of death.

It's Rob: That's about right, anyway.

a random soldier: It's not so surprising anymore.

It's Rob: How did last week's firefight happen?

a random soldier: I already said, I'm not telling you anything until we get
home.

It's Rob: Eh… It's your story, so I guess it's on your terms… fucker.

a random soldier: Jill always asks if I've killed anyone… I'm like, you are
a morbid little girl.

It's Rob: Yeah, that's not a nice question to ask. Well…

a random soldier: So I'm trying to hit it with her friend Brooke like its
cool.

It's Rob: Have you met Brooke?

a random soldier: Many a time, though often drunk… last time I talked
to her she asked me for drugs. I was like girl, if I had
any, you'd be the first to get them. Lol… good times,
DE.

It's Rob: I'm going back in a week. I'll tell it you say hi.

a random soldier: Ha-ha!

It's Rob: You know, Delaware is good in small doses… stay for three
weeks, a month go away again. Any more than a month and
you feel yourself going stale.

a random soldier: Yeah, so you should send me pictures in the e-mail.

It's Rob: You know, it is time to send a letter and spend my tuition on
postage.

a random soldier: LOL… so I was an idiot… I've been thinking that.
What a dumb ass idea.

It's Rob: What? Go to Iraq, or hit on Jill when you're in said sandpit and
she has a boyfriend?

a random soldier: OK… a) joining the Marines was dumb. I'm an artist
and this is a waste of my creative effort.

It's Rob: Aaaaaha-ha-ha-ha-ha-ha-ha… I don't mean that in a mocking
sense at all. I just love hearing you say that.

a random soldier: b) Brooke is way hotter… and I am so an artist. It's performance art. My life is my palate. Fuck you.

It's Rob: Actually, I'm studying your kind now in art history.

a random soldier: My kind? I have a kind? Oh alas, I am a cliché… I should eat a grenade.

It's Rob: We call you conceptual artists. You do shit like fluxus and happenings. You make fake clothes out of plaster and fake steaks and fake cake and try and sell them at a fake store in downtown Greenwich. Hahahahah! That just made my night . BY THE WAY… interesting bit… my writing professor is a literary hot shot; somewhat. Back in '90 he interviewed Ginsberg… He let me borrow the tapes. Three hours of Allen Ginsberg talking about random shit.

a random soldier: So I had quit Kerouac right, and the other day I picked up Desolation Angels again and realized I was writing shit like Kerouac when I was eleven. The random sounds.

It's Rob: Ha-ha-ha!

a random soldier: It's like static in your head.

It's Rob: Beep! Bop! Boooow!

a random soldier: You put it on paper.

It's Rob: Yeah, Kerouac kinda sucked in his later days. It's like HEY, this doesn't work anymore.

a random soldier: You get weird punctuation followed by one brilliant line and then more static… exactly… He so faded. It's tragic.

It's Rob: Now Ginsberg…

a random soldier: I have an audio file of Ginsberg someplace reading poetry.

It's Rob: He was a fucking literary success, but I guess Kerouac really epitomized beat, joyous and spontaneous, yet at the same time

It's Rob: tired, walked on and pathetically self-absorbed.

a random soldier: He was insane.

It's Rob: You know.

a random soldier: Lonely and manic.

It's Rob: If I write one decent thing in my life it will be you and I, like
          Kerouac wrote himself and Neal Cassidy.

a random soldier: I have a short story in my notebook… it's decent…
          about 80 pages.

It's Rob: You've been working! Good.

a random soldier: In bursts… Duster frees my mind like alcohol… It
          starts off on the beach in the rain (of course) with the
          main characters suicide in front of his naked pregnant
          girlfriend. She freezes to death holding him. It's tragic
          but she was having his best friend's baby… Wild, eh?

It's Rob: Wow, that's really uplifting.

a random soldier: Sounds far fetched but I like it…

It's Rob: No, it sounds good.

a random soldier: It's not so soap opera when you read it.

It's Rob: It actually sounds quite good. I keep thinking about this
          summer and the party you threw and you know on the boat
          over, I wrote… I have to be attentive. I have to be a really good
          fucking student now, because this could be the most important
          night of my life.

a random soldier: Why?

It's Rob: It's the intersection of everything… all of our sad, pathetic little
          lives which we cherish, and protect, and elevate in importance
          intersected around your pool that night.

a random soldier: Very true.

It's Rob: I haven't seen you since pulling out of your driveway and going back to Jersey. It was the most important day of my summer and, I should say, probably the best.

a random soldier: Yeah, it was pretty good.

It's Rob: You know, you would enjoy Jean Paul Sartre.

a random soldier: I would enjoy a rum and coke more though.

It's Rob: The two might go well together. You like that sad drinking shit.

a random soldier: My brother is getting published soon... Won something with a poem about suicide... I was like, wow. And he did an art project for school entitled God is Dead. I have corrupted the boy.

It's Rob: Ha-ha-ha-ha-ha-ha-ha-ha-! At Cape! They must have loved that.

a random soldier: Yes, everyone apparently knows he's my brother.

It's Rob: Just think...

a random soldier: He's got the same problem the Anderson brothers did.

It's Rob: ...He could be a good little litnerd, studying his Blake and Whitman...

a random soldier: Reputation precedes him.

It's Rob: ...and you've turned him to Nietzche!

a random soldier: He's more of a programmer than a litnerd. I just want him to be able to keep up with me when he's old enough. I like your profile. You all seem a bit naive.

It's Rob: Dude, whatever, I waited nine hours and forty minutes to vote.

a random soldier: It's true that in a fair world one vote might count, 500 make a difference, and 5000 a change, but not if something as important as global stability rested in the hands of the American Public... fucking kidding me. Democracy is a farce. There is no election for the people.

It's Rob: But voting is the only way to participate in democracy.

a random soldier: We are duped into thinking our opinions matter. Or not. But what a grand scheme it would be.

It's Rob: Well, be cynical.

a random soldier: College of the… Finish my sentence… College of…

It's Rob: Ramadi? Hard Knocks?

a random soldier: Elec…

It's Rob: Electoral college.

a random soldier: There you go.

It's Rob: Safeguard against total democracy, yadda yadda… but tell me…

a random soldier: Yadda yadda?

It's Rob: …If I don't vote, what kind of state do I live in?

a random soldier: I'm not saying you shouldn't vote… It's just that this vigor that these KIDS have for voting… it's like playing adults.

It's Rob: Well, we are adults.

a random soldier: Suddenly concerned with the state of affairs… that is part of the system.

It's Rob: Well, adult enough to vote.

a random soldier: That they support and foster them. It's so ridiculous and full of self import.

It's Rob: Well, I'm just saying. Fuck yeah, I waited in line… I'm hardcore. I knew Bush would win.

a random soldier: My computer is about to crash, sir… I'm watching the bar tick away…

It's Rob: Well, I'm glad you have internet access. Will this be a semi-

It's Rob: regular thing?

a random soldier: Sort of… I'll be on later tonight.

It's Rob: As regular as before?

a random soldier: No… be right back… actually no… I'm leaving… bye!

It's Rob: Take it easy… talk to you soon, hopefully…

§

"Have you killed anyone? Only girls ask that question. That's just rude. Gruesome little girls."

Chad made that comment in a phone call about a month before he was killed. He told me guys never asked.

Most of us will never know what it's like to drop a bomb or pull the trigger. As a society we tend to forget what it is we ask these young men to do. Dying for their country is only part of the whole. My favorite quote from this war was from an anonymous Marine in Al Anbar Province who said, "America doesn't realize what they're asking us to do when we take a city. Marines don't shoot rainbows out of their asses. We fucking kill people."

Chad never told me and I never asked. There would be time later wouldn't there? "Some things I'm going to have to be a lot older and a lot drunker to tell you, Momma."

§

E-mail Home
11/12/2004 3:04 AM
Subject: Que Pasa?

Howdy y'all…

I've spent most of my day so far at this new internet café we've just got set up in the CP. It rocks my socks. I'm sure they'll find some way to fuck it up but for now its fun and relieves some stress.

I'm going to try to upload some photos later… hopefully I can find and borrow a USB memory stick from someone to swap them off the other laptop since I wiped my SD card to take more pics. They're stuck on the other drive right now. No matter, I know all the computer guys in the Battalion and it shouldn't be too hard.

I'm off to surf the web I've been brutally cut off from the last couple months.

E-mail Home
11/13/2004 9:55 AM
Subject: Re: Welcome to the web

Howdy,
I'm chillin here in the internet café for about twenty minutes… thought I'd say what's up. Got a package from you today with Gobstoppers and Mountain Dew and stuff. Loved it!
I can't think of anything else to write so I'm out.

Journal Entry
November 13, 2004 7:14 PM
Insert Creative Title Here

One more day closer to home,
And someplace I can roll down the street without getting shot at or car bombed or mortared. Woot. I can't wait.
Iraq has definitely gotten old. I want to come home. Seriously. Like, now.
Not much going on today. Got to sleep in this morning cause I had a 24hr post yesterday. They've got this new internet area here so it's cool, I should be logged on again pretty often, except when someone gets killed, then they disable all outside connections. Morbid, huh? I found out a couple days ago that a guy I knew got an arm and a leg blown off by an RPG. I am definitely sick of being here.
What a fucked up war. I'm landing a bird tonight to dust off some guys who get to go on R&R to Qutar (spelling?) for some time off. I'm thinking about just jumping on with them.
Heres to the nights…

E-mail Home
11/15/2004 5:44 AM

Howdy,
Not a lot new but things have gotten much better since we got reliable internet. Now we just pray it doesn't get "secured," which is the Marine Corps way of saying that someone high up gets a hair up his ass and decides for some reason we don't rate to have good internet. And that person probably wouldn't make it out of here alive, but, alas, such is life.
Not much new here. Don't know why the links didn't work off my e-mail. Kinda weird, but I'd be much obliged if you could work on that music for me, along with Eminems new CD Encore. Not to sound needy

or anything, right? Lol.

Journal Entry
November 15, 2004 3:49 PM
Rockets and Mortars AHOY!

So we've been wearing our ballistic vests and kevlars (helmets) around for the past two weeks inside the base, right. Well we haven't been hit bad for several days and we're told we can walk around without them again. So like an hour after we get that word, what happens? BOOM... Rocket. It's a beautiful war. WTF!

•

Captain Patrick Marc M. Rapicault   November 15, 2004
Weapons Company 2nd Battalion 5th Regiment 1st Marine Division, 1st Marine Expeditionary force. Died as a result of enemy action in Al Anbar Province, Iraq

•

Corporal Marc T. Ryan   November 15, 2004
2nd Battalion 5th Marine Regiment, 1st Marine Division, 1st Marine Expeditionary Force. Died as a result of enemy action in Al Anbar Province, Iraq

•

Corporal Lance M. Thompson   November 15, 2004
Weapons Company 2nd Battalion, 5th Marine Regiment, 1st Marine Division, 1st Marine Expeditionary Force. Died as a result of enemy action Al Anbar Province, Iraq

•

"Be convinced that to be happy means to be free and that to be free means to be brave. Therefore do not take lightly the perils of war."
Thucydides

Chapter 11

It was cold for a November morning but sunny. I was sitting on the deck feeding the kittens when Rich brought me the phone. "He's moving to a Weapons Company," he said as he handed it to me.

"Hey!" I said, taking the phone.

"Hey, Momma. How are ya?"

"I'm good. What's this about going to weapons?"

"Yeah, I told Dad. I have to move to a weapons company. Remember I told you about Cpl. Thompson from training?"

"Yeah."

"He was an RO for weapons. He was killed and they need a new RO. I'm it."

"Oh God, Chad! I'm sorry! What happened?"

"He and a couple other guys were killed by a VBIED, suicide car bomber, who attacked their convoy. It was bad."

I was silent. It was too much at once.

"So I have to go."

"Okay… where will you be?"

"Oh, well, my new barracks will be practically across the road from the ones I have now. But I won't be at the Comm. Shop anymore. I'll be going out on ops with Whiskey 3. My address changes though. I'll call you tomorrow with the new one."

"Okay, so…?"

"I've got to go now, but I'll call."

"I love you."

"I love you too, and Mom, thanks for not crying."

When he called the next day to give me his new address. I confronted him.

"Define "I had to go", Chad."

"I have to, Momma. I can't let someone else fight this war for me. I can't stay where it's safe and watch other guys die. I can't."

Terri's Journal Entry
November 16, 2004

So you're going to a weapons company. I have to let that sink in for a few days.

KIA

We heard on the radio that was in our hooch... two KIAs.

Everyone listened attentively. One HMMWV hit by a VBIED. Two KIA. Totally unrecognizable.

It hurt, as usual. Everyone shook their heads and said it was a bullshit kind of thing. Fucking Iraq.

I brushed it off and we went to go to the cake cutting ceremony for the Marine Corps 229th birthday. When we got there it was cancelled. Slightly relieved that we didn't have to attend, we ate dinner and griped about the war.

Three of us were walking back from dinner when one of the other Marines from our platoon crossed the road and stopped us.

"Hey." He said

"What's up?"

"Before you hear it from anyone else..." He spoke quietly, hesitating.

We waited.

"It was Cpl. Thompson and Cpt. Rapicault."

It didn't make sense; I had just been talking to him in our shop this morning.

"Our..."

"Yes, ours."

We walked away, devastated. I felt tears spring to my eyes. I held them back. It wouldn't do any good.

At the shop, no one could meet anyone else's eyes. Too much pain reflects back.

Bullshit fucking war.

Terri's Journal Entry
November 18, 2004

You know when you thanked me for not crying about your going to a Weapons Co? Would you be ashamed of me if you knew I cried my eyes out when I hung up the phone?

Here it is flat out: I don't believe you and I will ever see each other again. I feel it deep inside, in a place I can't argue with. One of us won't make it through this war. So what do I say to you here, should you come home and I am gone? You know I love you beyond words. Beyond Worlds. I won't tell you to look out for

Ryan. That's a given. Dad, too.

I guess first of all don't be sorry. You had to go. We both know that.

Secondly, don't ever think that I "gave up" anything to be a full-time Mom to you and Ryan. It was a choice I made willingly and I've never regretted it. So what if I never won prize for literature, or saw the world? I had every minute possible with the two of you. Long walks on the beach and in our woods, playing in the snow, dancing in the rain. Bonfires and parties. Traveling to art shows. Endless summer days by the ocean and diving for pirate coins in the pool. It couldn't have been better. To be able to honestly say that I fell in love with my husband more every day and that my sons were my very best friends and greatest joy, is my definition of a very successful life.

So if I'm not here when you get back, it's okay. Don't change who you are. Don't hesitate to live.

My love is always with you.

E-mail Home
11/19/2004 7:00 AM
Subject: Re: Yo

Hey Guys,

I know I called last night but I just got off post and saw your e-mail, so I thought I'd drop a line or two and say hello.
Hello.

An so there it is. Got up last night in the middle of the night for several hours... hadn't planned on that. I had forgotten it was crypto changeover and Pokorny (the other RO) came and woke me up and was like "Dude, crypto." So we changed a buttload of radios and it took like and hour and a half but then Ssgt Garcia told me to go practice night driving with NVGs and I was up until like 0600 doin' that. It was good practice but this Ssgt is going to be "daddy" for the rest of my time here, and I've heard some rumors that he's really controlling of the drivers. Like, screaming conflicting directions no matter what you do... Yeah, it should be a fuckin' blast. I start driving on Sunday.

Hmm... not much else to report. I'm out like a blind kid in laser tag.

Journal Entry
11/19/2004 2:35 PM
Moved on up...

So...

Some VERY bad shit happened the other day and to get straight to the point... I'm the new RO for WPNS W3... I wish it didn't have to be this way, but I like the new platoon. I'll be going out about everyday or so, depending on the opsched and everything. I wish it were under better circumstances.

Everyone was hit pretty hard by the news. I'll recover when I'm stateside again. Now I just have to survive this fucking war. Its gonna be a lot harder than I'm used to, I guess. Wish me luck.

Journal Entry
11/19/2004 5:05 PM
Whiskey, women, and machine guns...

2/5 Gangstas true old skool... Rollin down the street smokin' hadji's, sippin on Camelbacks, laid back, with my mind on my money and my money on my mind...

Just got off post on one of the bridges. I have to get issued new NVGs. I don't want to go. I want to be irresponsible and call in sick to work (yeah, right) and just go to sleep and wake up when I feel like it. You know, get out of the Corps, go to college, maybe travel for a little while with some girl I'll no doubt fall for (I'm not a player, I just crush a lot) and get her to marry me and settle down someplace warm. Or I can continue doing this for a few years. It's in the air. You never know... CAUSE I'M GROOVY BABY, YEAH.

Well now that I've added a completely random and somewhat pointless journal entry, and made you read it, I'm going to go try to accomplish shit. I'm out like that dude that got shot in Building two. Word!

Boys Like Me
Death walks all around
He follows boys like me
Protects us from ourselves
Not from kindness, but necessity
Boys like me
We're soldiers, criminals or worse
We keep death rich
Put souls into his purse
So make me pull this trigger
Make me pull a gun
I'm not afraid to die
It's my time in the desert sun

E-mail Home
11/21/2004 11:56 AM
Subject: Re: They're letting you drive?

Hey,
      YES, they're letting me drive. I think the other guys in my vehicle

were paranoid as fuck about letting me drive today at first, but even Rios and Cpl. Sebena were like, hey, we thought we were going to die today but you're pretty good. Well damn straight, I AM good. Mission short, only about four hours. It was cool. None of us got hit by IED's or anything.

A funny note, slightly morbid, but funny if you were there; we were pulling security on a back street for the raid (it was a cordon & search, a nice form of the Vietnam tactic of search & destroy) that was going on, and one of the vehicles from the another whiskey element left, so we had to cover our own ass on the south side. So I was standing there in between the doors, next to the driver's seat, and the gunner says we have a car behind us. Not the first time that's happened, so pop off a couple warning shots. Homeboy in the car is still hauling ass and is now like thirty meters from us. It was game on. We could see they weren't aiming anything at us but you don't have to aim a car bomb really, so my gunner tore up the radiator with a 240 medium machine gun we had just mounted on top. He was still coming towards us (this is like a split second later, but we're just fast) so I'm like, fuck this dude, and I shot out his front right tire.

CRUNCH. Tire goes down, dude loses control and hits a wall, vehicle smoking. We're sitting around laughing cause it was just hilarious after all that tension. Two dudes get up out of the car with their hands up, looking PISSED. But they're lucky we didn't shoot them straight up, so fuck 'em.

Spent the rest of the day in the rack, woke up for chow just now, and came here to check my mail. Stay tuned for tomorrow's adventures…

Journal Entry
11/22/2004

The barrel of my rifle is cold as I rest my cheek on the front post and close my eyes.

My mind is a medley of gunshots and love songs. There are twelve jack-in-the boxes in my head, six are writing poetry while three are cleaning their M16s and the other three are sleeping.

This is foolish, I tell myself, even as I realize how natural and necessary it is. I want to focus on the war, to live day by day, but no one can. You'd go nuts. So we segment our minds. Stress turns into indifference and desire for sleep. Boredom on posts turns into conversations about home and who we used to be, or fantasies about killing a random civilian out in front of us. Bloodlust isn't the worst thing I've ever felt. Even when we're together, even close as brothers, we all walk alone.

Bullets and mortars startle you. Bombs can kill you. RPGs are horrible. It's the loneliness that I hate the most though.

So I think about her. Idolize her. Objectify her. I would die to rest my head on her chest and listen to her breathing, simply because she might be the only one capable of being still, not saying a word, and still understand me. This nameless pain fades in the light of her acceptance. I am not so vile when she looks at me, kisses me like she means it. She knows and doesn't judge. In my head anyway.

She doesn't exist, not really, a personality in my mind to keep me from losing hope. A life based on a familiar face, on something that might have been, but I came here. On something we all know will never happen. Maybe I'll go home and we'll fuck, but it's nothing. It will never be right. We are doomed from the start.

E-mail Home
11/23/2004 10:43 AM
Subject: RE: Good talking to ya

Hey Momma,

It was good talking to you too! I am acclimating pretty well, faster than I thought. I'm already starting to make some pretty good friends. Ssgt yelled at me today (former Drill Instructor, tends to spaz out a tad bit) for having one hand on the steering wheel (we were sitting still, geeez...) and said I had to fill forty sandbags. Some of the other guys offered to help me. I'm just not going to fill sandbags unless someone brings it up again. I'm hoping Ssgt Garcia forgets. I am the eternal slacker, fearless in my ability to shirk any and all responsibility. Hoo-fucking-rah. Lol.

Anyway, got a few packages last night. Two little Christmas trees (rather cool) and a package of hygiene gear and a nice throw for my bed. The more blankets out here the better, it's like hell frozen over with this icy wind. We're surrounded on two sides by a river so you can imagine its like ten degrees colder than the rest of the city, especially at night.

Went to Junction City around breakfast today for a logistics run (a perk of being in Weapons Co. and on Day Task) and got to eat at their chow hall. It was bangin'. And I bought a couple of techno compilation CDs and a little boombox CD player and a rug. The rug was about 3' by 5' and it was only $8 so I got it. No more cold feet getting out of the rack to take a leak at night! Woot! It's the little things you know.

GREAT NEWS: Official word is that our flight date back to CONUS is mid-March, which means we should be out of the shit and over at JC somewhere in the middle of February and definitely the beginning of March, if not sooner, depending on the turnover with 1/5. They're the unit rumored to be replacing us. It sucks, cause they just got back when we left. Better them than us. Everybody is stoked at the news cause we didn't expect to be leaving until April. And rumor has it that decompression time may start as early as Feb because of the huge amounts of combat stress. This deployment has been far rougher than the actual war was.

Um, that's all folks. Don't do anything I wouldn't do!

Journal Entry
November 24, 2004 10:14 PM
Vacant

Feeling pretty vacant, empty minded… lots of lyrics coming to my head right now… can't stop thinking at the same time… Thanksgiving is tomorrow. It's morbid cause you always worry about dying on the holidays… it's a day of thanks tho:
I'm thankful for my family.
I'm thankful for my rifle.
I'm thankful for my HMMWV.
I'm thankful for my friends.
I'm thankful for music.
I'm just glad I'm not dead.

See? It has a rhyme scheme. I can't stop the music. Woot!
Here's to another holiday away from home

Terri's Journal Entry
November 25, 2004

Happy Thanksgiving, kiddo. We kept it quiet here. Hope they at least fed you decently.
Blessed be.

Journal Entry
November 26, 2004 10:34 PM
Operation Turkey Shoot

Happy belated Turkey Day,
Went on a big op and found a ton of weapons caches. Things have been otherwise quiet.
Can't wait to get my Christmas packages.
I'm going to bed, going out tomorrow morning.

E-mail from home
Date: 11/28/2004
Subject: Watcha doin?

Hi Chad,
Just sayin' hello. Not much new here. Waiting for the new automatic timers to turn on the Christmas lights. Yup, Dad and Ryan actually got the lights hooked up last night and today after a trip to Lowes we have power towers and extension cords and red, white, and blue floodlights in honor

of out favorite Marine (that would be you…) we miss you and love you so much. If it weren't for the damned curvature of the earth thing you could probably see the glow. (Provided of course the breakers don't kick when it comes on.) Let it glow, let it glow, let it glow!
Love, Mom

E-mail Home
Date: 11/28/2004 10:58 AM
Subject: Re: Watcha doin?

Howdy,
Finally worked up the energy and time to come wait in line to use the internet. We switched to Day QRF today so we can't go anywhere except around the hooch during the day. Next week we go to night task. I'm not looking forward to it but we only have to do it two more times and we'll be out of this hole.
I really like it in WPNS. I'm doing well here and I'm making some friends pretty quickly. I've adapted well. It's stressful sometimes but most days we go out and then come back, do a little maintenance on the trucks (it would suck to break down in town…) and then play Madden 2005 like it's a form of religion. We held a tourney today before we got called out. I lost two rounds and I don't usually lose. Sometimes, but never like that. You can imagine I took the losses pretty hard. I'm not speaking to Alarid right now. Lol.
P.S. Be glad about the curvature of the Earth thing. We've got some pretty long range guns. Oh and I have a scope on my rifle now, I'll send pictures. It looks totally badass.

Terri's Journal Entry
November 28, 2004

Put up the tree in the living room today. And yes, I've had Christmas music playing non-stop. There's a song by Amy Grant called A Christmas to Remember that reminds me of last Christmas and the great time we had. I'm so glad you got to come home. Miss you as always… Love.
Mom

Instant Message Conversation between Chad and Rob
November 30, 2004 12:36 PM

a random soldier: Eh muchacho!

It's Rob: Hey Bro.

a random soldier: What's up?

It's Rob: I'm actually getting ready to go to class.

a random soldier: Lovely.

It's Rob: How's the desert today?

a random soldier: I'm getting ready to do Comm checks and go to bed…
op tomorrow.

It's Rob: op where?

a random soldier: In Ramadi… Internet is not secure, can't pass you
specifics… opsec, you understand.

It's Rob: Absolutely.

a random soldier: So what's up next in class?

It's Rob: Actually, you know what I was thinking about in the shower for
some god knows what reason… Erin.

a random soldier: LOL!

It's Rob: What a great fucking story.

a random soldier: Yeah, but I just read Angels and Demons, the prequel
to The Da Vinci Code… Totally does what I meant to
do… but better.

It's Rob: Nah, Erin is untouchable.

a random soldier: True and that's the reason it sucks… you can't relate to
him. I wrote a new story.

It's Rob: The death on the beach one?

a random soldier: It starts out with a suicide of a boy on a beach, in the
cold December rain, next to his pregnant naked
girlfriend… yeah, I like it better… Then it backtracks…
You can actually emote with this guy… My style has
matured since Erin.

It's Rob: You mean he's a little softie like you?

a random soldier: Pretty much. He finds out his fiancé is pregnant with his best friend's baby… offs himself… she dies next to him, self induced hypothermia The story is the reasons why.

It's Rob: When you get married, I'm going to screw your wife… all your stories demand that I do so.

a random soldier: It's tragic but a nice exercise… If you fucked my wife you wouldn't live to read them. I would rip you apart with my bare hands and then I'd write about it.

It's Rob: Ha-ha-ha-ha, but not until after I fucked your wife… Alright, bro… off to lunch. Sleep well, and keep your head down in the op.

a random soldier: As always… don't do anything I wouldn't do and for God Sakes… write me an email. Kate shows me more love than you do.

It's Rob: I was going to this afternoon!

a random soldier: Nyah writes me, Candi does, you don't.

It's Rob: I do so!

a random soldier: Some best pal you are… gah.

It's Rob: And my emails are so much better.

a random soldier: Yes they are except, Kate wants it finally… how ironic.

DECEMBER RAIN

The End

"Einie, meini…"

"Oh God, please don't…" Kate's voice was a soft pleading whimper, barely audible over the patter of rain on sand.

"Mieni, Mo…" Sean flicked the barrel of the pistol in his hand with each syllable back and forth rhythmically. Kate's temple, his forehead, Kate's temple…

"Catch a tiger by her toe…"

"Please, Sean!" Kate's cries fell on closed ears.

Her long blonde hair was soaked and stuck to her face and breasts. She pleaded with him, terrified as he looked down on her nude body, caked with wet sand. Her clothes lay nearby. "You don't…"

"If she hollers, let her go…" Sean elevated his voice to a mild yell, giving her a pained gaze in the dark. Short black hair that he usually kept spiked and gelled now lay flat over his eyes. His features, some would describe as good looking, but flawed by a weak chin and eyes that turned down at the corners giving him a look of permanent sadness, or maybe deep thought, now had a strange, absent look. He was someone else tonight. "Einie, meini, mieni …"

The shot split the darkness and echoed for miles under the low cloud coverage. Kate's parents probably heard it from their house.

Sean's body did not fall immediately. The bullet snapped his head back with ferocious force, exiting somewhere in his lower back as it bounced down his spinal column, impacting one knee as his body twisted around, landing face up on the beach, tears in his eyes as he fell.

Kate screamed for what felt like hours. She didn't know how long it had been when she stopped and began to cry softly, the tears mingling with the December rain on her high, unblemished cheekbones. She crawled over to him and closed his eyes.

The park rangers found her the next morning. She was curled up next to his body, clutching him with both arms wrapped around the black and white motorcycle jacket he wore, 9mm still in the palm of one extended arm. Her blue eyes were closed and she was resting her head on his chest, bare legs wrapped around one of his. They would have looked like sleeping lovers if it weren't for the small bullet hole in Sean's skull or the unnatural blue tinge of hypothermia on Kate's flesh pale skin.

Wind and sleet had erased the footprints of the night before. With the presence of heroin and MDMA in his system and hers, and the half empty bottle of vodka in Sean's car, they would officially rule it a drug related double suicide. That was only half of it.

-KATE
  -Dialogue w/ James
    -flirt(?) who w/ ,who(?) reciprocated(?)
    -Her to school
    -concern for relationship
  -Dialogue w/ Cara
    -Sean, looking for you
    -Sean calls cell, K does not answer
  -DLG w/ Ben
    -Art school that fall
    -summer job
-SEAN
  -Racing his car w/ friend (celica)(neon)

-party at Matt's, calls K's Cell
-shows up at party late, asks for K, finds out she went back to her house with someone
-rides by house to check. Worried
-sees Ben's car
- Ben and K making out drunk
-Sean busts window with lax stick, pulls Ben out, nearly kills him
3.Aftermath
-At work with James, coffee shop
-details fight w/K. Its over
-brings up leaving town
 4. Back in Town
-Sean finds James
-Sean discharged after war
-wounded shoulder still bandaged
-agree to meet up at old coffee shop with the old crew, back from college
5. Reintroductions
-James DLG Kate
- compliment
- Sean still has feelings (wants to pick up things)
- Kate brings up failed R-ships in college after Ben, still loves Sean
- Attraction to wild side
-Kate and Sean Dialogue
- Greetings
- Flirt (she's still toying with him)
- *must show Sean's weakness to her*
- *Emphasize tamed beast theme*
- Sean asks her out for dinner
6. College again (Nov. next year)
-Sean and James at state w/ friends
-Sean writing on napkin about missing K
- Talk of marriage, *emphasize devotion*
- brings up plans for New Years party
(Intends to ask K to marry Him)
7. Back to the future
- New Years Party at Beach House
- Everyone present
- asks to marry (everyone expects yes)
- K says no, runs out crying
- Sean excuses himself from party, embarrassed
- Follows K's car to beach parking lot, chases her down She's been drinking
- K admits pregnancy
- Sean is relieved, says he hopes it's a boy, gets happy
-K tells him it belongs to James

- S is devastated calls James
- James wants to explain, meets him at lot
- S says he forgives J, loves him like a bro, pulls a picture and a gun from
  dash…
- pic is of S holding a birthday card standing next to J when they were 12
- Beats J to the edge of his life, says he doesn't blame him, he
  blames K
- S leaves with K in tow

DECEMBER RAIN-CHAPTER 2
THE BEGINNING

May 16, 2003

Loud hip hop music throbbed from Cara's parent's surround sound system in their living room, now packed with drinking high school grads, full of that youthful determination to look cool, but most would find themselves puking on the lawn in several hours. Where the lights cast shadows, couples made out, oblivious to the party.

"WOOOOO! OH THREE!" James yelled out to no one in particular, pushing the stylish wire framed glasses back up on his nose. They were fake; Sean would tell you he only wore them to maintain his air of the academic, uber-smart-misunderstood-emo-rock-guy of the group. Friends gathered around chatting about colleges and reminiscing about good times and inside jokes.

"YEAH!" Matt slapped James hard on the back, almost knocking the beer away that James was squeamishly sipping at.

"So, Cara, who are you rooming with up at state?"

"You know Julia Jameswell, the field hockey captain?" Cara was pretty, short blonde hair pulled into a pony tail, she's known for being a bit on the airy side of smart.

"What a sweet piece of ass!" Kyle pushed some brown hair out of his eyes and wiped spilled beer off his lacrosse jersey, "Sorry."

"Anyway… ", Cara cast Kyle a scornful glance. " I will be rooming with her over at Patton."

"Sweet," Matt nodded with enthusiasm. A huge bulk of a guy, he was looking forward to his share of frat parties in the near future. "I hear those are like party dorms over there. It's at the edge of campus, right?"

"I know. I hope it's not too distracting from school." Cara didn't have the natural gift of academics that most people in their clique did. She had to work at it. In a way, they had all been brought together by scheduling of "advanced" classes as an experiment in middle school. Since then, the same group had become the poster children for district wide standardized tests… Parents active in school as well, they could get away with anything. Untouchable. Now their world had just changed, dramatically.

"You'll be fine!" Kate adjusted the short skirt and bathing suit top she was wearing. A beautiful girl, she was arguably also one of the most gifted artists in the area. "I'll have the real trouble. It's a whole new state! I've never even been to Philly!'

"Shut up! You always do fine, K," Cara squealed as someone walking by grabbed her butt.

"Has anyone seen Sean?" James asked.

Matt looked at his watch. "He said he'd be here by 10, its 11 now." As if on cue Kate's ring tone began blaring its version of some rock song. It was Sean.

"Who's that?"

"Sean."

"You going to answer that?"

Kate looked at Cara and Chelsey. "Girls?"

"Hell no." Chels was one of Sean's ex-flames.

"Let him sweat, girl." Cara wrote it off. Sean was always doing something stupid and being late.

"Pull in that leash some more." Cara laughed.

"Hey, Kevin!" Matt yelled across the room. "Call Sean, find out what he's doing!"

Kevin gave him a thumbs up, looking for his cell phone.

"I hate it when he does this!" Kate looked angry now, chugging a Mike's Hard Cranberry.

Kevin hung up the phone. "He said he's racing Ryan's Celica and Drew in the Neon. They're racing past the state police station. He said give him ten minutes," Kevin threw back a shot of rum from the bottle, "I told him your battery was low."

"Thanks Kev." Kate thought for a moment. She kissed him on the cheek. "You are such a good guy friend, Kev. Can you drive me home? I don't want to be this drunk when Sean gets here."

Kevin was a decent looking guy but new to the group, a former boyfriend of Cara's. Matt and Cara exchanged glances. Was Kate trying to snub Cara or what? Kate was prettier but Cara's adventures with guys were more notorious. Maybe she was jealous and wanted to play around.

"Yeah, sure, K let me find my keys." Matt and Kyle both shot warning glances his direction.

"How much have you had to drink?"

"Couple of shots." Kev walked a straight line, mimicking a field sobriety test. "I'm good."

"Right, well, be careful." James handed Kev. the keys and hugged Kate goodnight. "Hey, Kate, call me tomorrow?"

"Sure, Jimmy. Tell Sean I said I'm pissed."

"Okay, deuces, girl." He threw up a peace sign as she grabbed her purse and walked off with Kevin.

Sean walked in about 20 minutes later and grabbed a plastic cup, heading to the keg.

"Hey, Jimmy, you seen Kate?"

"She went home," James and the guys were playing some drinking card game. People were starting to pass out or leave.

"She didn't drive again, did she?" Sean hated when she drank and would have told her mother if she had driven. Matt threw down a card. Everyone took a shot of beer.

"No man, she went home. Kev dropped her off."

"Oh, cool," Sean drifted off in thought, "So was she mad?"

"What? Hold on" Matt looked distracted, put down another card. "James, take a shot. You're goin' down son. No, dude, she was just drunk."

"Alright, well I'm gonna drop by her house." Sean glanced at his watch. A little before midnight. "I'll see you gents tomorrow." The party was dying out anyway.

Sean flew down the highway at about 100mph with the sun roof open on his Eclipse. The warm summer night felt good, made him feel more alive than ever. *(more)*

Then he almost dropped dead.

Pulling onto the road to Kate's development was Kevin's car, pulled off to the side of the road. Two people were moving around in the back. It hit him instantly. Kate had never cheated before, not that he knew, he figured someone would have told him. They love giving bad news. In three years, never cheated, why now?

Sean kept rolling down the street without slowing down. He pulled into the cul de sac at the end of the road and tried to convince himself he was wrong. "What the fuck?" He muttered to himself as he felt his heart breaking. Anger or sadness, Sean was starting to feel sick. The door opened and Sean popped out, interior light dinging as he fumbled around in the backseat, moving as if suddenly inspired, or perhaps well rehearsed, smooth and confident. Sean closed the door, wrapping a yellow and blue jersey around his left fist, a titanium three foot offensive lacrosse stick grasped in his right. The walk to Kevin's car was a blur. He felt so violent it made him gag. The left fist impacted Kevin's left passenger side window at the same time as a boot impacted the side panel. The window shattered into a thousand tiny pieces inside the car.

Kate had her shirt off and was going down on Kevin. He turned around as the glass was smashed. His back had been turned to the window. Now he was being pulled through broken glass with his pants down.

"Fuck you!" The titanium shaft landed with a sickening thud as it impacted Kevin's rib cage under the heart. Kate put her shirt on and Sean heard the door open. "Stay away. Slut!"

Snap. Sean felt the vibration of Kevin's forearm breaking through his weapon, smiling with satisfaction. He hit him again. And again. And again. The blows rained down. Face, legs, ribs, neck... Sean was using bare fists now on Kev's face, causing serious damage, Kevin now unconscious.

Finally, after what seemed to Kate like forever, she thought to get between them. She'd been paralyzed by the violence which Sean had displayed. It was out of character. Sean was always calm unless he was looking for a thrill, usually racing or on drugs.

"Sean! Sean! Sean!' she screamed his name. "I'm sorry!"

"You did this." The wild look was gone from Sean's eyes. "I would never hurt you. You did this to him. I love you so much."

"That's sick, Sean." She used a much gentler tone, walking to him. He didn't push her away but he looked off into the dark, ignoring Kevin's moans on the ground. "I was drunk, you weren't here…"

"Shut up."

"What?"

"I said, Shut Up," Sean began to cry a little. "Why did you ruin it? So selfish! It was PERFECT KATE!" he finished the last part screaming at her.

"Kate." She held him, looking down at Kevin's broken body. He was coming to. "You were robbed by a masked man. Do you understand that?"

She nodded. Sean could go to jail for what he just did. A masked man.

Sean kissed her. "It's over now. You ruined it." He walked away and left her with the mess she created. He could already hear the sirens in the distance…

DECEMBER RAIN-CHAPTER 3,
AFTERMATH

"I'm leaving next week."

James blew gently at his latte, leaning back against the counter. "Where?"

"Boot camp."

"What?" James had always heard Sean talk about it, but always the officer route, after college. Never enlistment. It seemed a waste. "You're Nuts!"

"Got in a fight last night." Sean sipped iced chai, stirring it idly and looking at customers perusing books at the other end of the shop.

"So I heard, everyone knows it was you."

"That got out fast."

"E-mail. IMs. Cell Phones. You know how it goes."

"Whatever. It's over now anyway."

James looked up at his friend over his drink. "You look like an ignorant ass. You know, you could have killed him. I'm surprised you didn't."

Sean smirked, obviously amused at the thought. "Maybe I should have."

"Why? You're a disappointment."

"James," Sean was making himself another chai, "If you had only one thing that kept you here, in this world with your family and friends, and your future, and someone tried to take it all away, to cut that line… you wouldn't let them would you?"

"She's only a girl, Sean. You're better than that."

"You have no idea what it's like, Jimmy."

"Imagine what it's like to have your mind spin in a thousand conflicting directions and it rips you to fucking pieces, brings you to tears when you are alone with this void…" Sean drifted off. "You chase it away with pills and adrenaline and fake smiles… but that's not when it wants you. The evil is private. It takes you in bed, watching TV. When you're checking your e-mail in the dark. When you close your eyes to rest. It's always there… waiting."

James waited for him to finish. Sometimes he knew Sean was brilliant, less of a voice and more of a prophet for their generation. And sometimes he was a babbling lunatic. At the flip of a coin.

"She gets rid of it, brings out my better side always. When she whispers in the dark, my demons fade away and we are all that's there. She catches my eyes and traps all the wrongness in me and reflects it in hers so that I may see. I need her."

James, for once, was temporarily at a loss. Sean had never told him why he was so devoted to her. James had thought it was sex. This was much worse, somehow. "Wow. Did you tell her?"

"Fuck, no. She'd think I was out of my mind."

"Aren't you?"

"Does it matter?"

"I suppose not."

"I told her it was over. I have to leave, Jim. This town reeks of her. So I'll embrace what I run from. The Corps will know what to do with me."

"Don't go, man. There's a fucking war on!" James was genuinely angry now. "Not for her."

"No. Not for her. For me. This place will kill me with her gone." Sean was watching the ocean out the window somberly. "You and I both know."

"Do what you wish, Sean. You were always the brave one, if not misguided."

"I know what I'm doing, Jim."

DECEMBER RAIN-CHAPTER 4
2 YEARS LATER
-BACK IN TOWN-

The cell phone call had taken only minutes; the drive had taken not much more.

The two friends met up in the parking lot and exchanged hugs in the place they had last seen each other. One was shaven headed and had his arm in a blue sling under a white and blue leather jacket. The other wore Dickies and a tee shirt, his long hair swept back off his face.

"James."

"Sean."

They grinned like children; both happy Sean was back home for good. The bullet he had taken in Iraq had destroyed his left shoulder. The medical papers cleared in just months. Sean was back.

"So are you going to start college this fall?" James ordered a coffee as he thumbed through a book on the tabletop.

"Yeah, I have nothing else to do. Sit around and drink beer and watch TV? The void would destroy me." Sean now spoke of the void as an entity, James noticed. Sean laughed it off.

"You really would have gotten along with Kerouac, Sean."

"He could learn a couple things from me."

"Have you solved how to beat the void?"

"No."

"Neither did he. He's dead."

"Fair enough."

Sean doodled on a napkin.

"How is she?"

"Who?" James looked at him, fearing the answer.

"Kate."

"She's good. Still in college, doing well."

"Good." Sean waited expectantly.

"I don't know if she's with anyone. After all this time, Sean? She doesn't speak to me now, anyway."

"Why not?"

"Not after that night with Kevin. You're dead to her."

Sean took the last words hard, almost with physical impact. "I don't know..."

"What's that mean, Sean?"

"Before I left for the war last year... she let me in to talk. My picture was still up on her wall."

"You're getting yourself worked up over nothing." Jim shook his head.

"Now you sound like him."

"Who?"

"The kid in the mirror every night."

"Sean."

"You know I'm alright."

"You need help."

"I need her."

"Stop objectifying Kate. She obviously doesn't want you." James hated hurting Sean but he was driven by concern. Shock therapy maybe.

"You don't know how it is. Two things bring me peace, Jim. I've been around the world to find them."

"What are those things?"

"Proximity to my own death and Kate."

"Do you keep a journal?"

"Volumes, why?"

"So that when they put you in an institution I can show them your writings and they can sedate you for the next sixty years."

"Fuck you, Jim."

"Its good to have you home, Sean."

-REINTRODUCTION-

Matt's wedding had been a splendid event, paid for by his parents. The bride, pregnant with his child, had looked stunning in the white dress, but deceived no one. There had been no time for a bachelor party.

"He still misses you, Kate." James leaned across the glitter strewn white tablecloth and whispered conspiratorially. "A lot."

"Does he?" Kate looked over at Sean standing by the spiked punch bowl and then seemed lost in thought. "He's barely noticed me."

"He's terrified of you. Please don't hurt him."

"I never did."

"Bullshit, K, you know that. But he's my friend. Our friend. Be gentle."

"I will, Jim, don't worry."

"You look great by the way."

"Thanks. So do you. Doing anything Friday?"

"What – no – I mean, you can't."

"SShh!" she giggled. "I was just kidding."

"Oh."

Sean approached with three glasses of punch, beaming. Without a word, he handed them out to Jim and Kate. Whipping out a pen, he wrote something on a napkin and passed it to Kate. She laughed and smiled at him.

"Its been a while, Sean."

"So it has, K." Sean sat down as James excused himself, mumbling something about cake.

"So what did you learn, warrior?" Kate always asked patronizing questions in such a serious manner it often was impossible to determine if she really wanted an answer.

"I cannot run from myself."

"That's wise. Perhaps you should try drinking it all away?" What an acid little girl; Sean thought.

"I have, princess. There's not enough liquor in the world to drown the pain of unrequited love."

"So I hear."

"What would you know about that?"

"Emo lyrics and stories of silly boys who only want the things they can't have."

"Touche."

§

Journal Entry
November 30, 2004 10:33 PM
Though I walk through the valley...

I love you
when you're not here,
but I'm never here
to love you.

I adore you
when I'm wasted
but I'm wasted
on adoration.
The sex is better when I'm high,
fucked up with lust that keeps you tied.
I try everything to demean you,
I hold you down and objectify.
I love you so much I hate you.

So yeah, another day in the ghetto gone by. Got a lot of mail today so that was a serious pick me up. The poem is strange cause I just got inspired/depressed for a moment. I don't know why. There's got to be something wrong in my head. I need some medication or something. My moods spike way too fast and too often. Maybe the government can compensate me when I get out. I could use the extra meds/cash.
I want to be a civilian when I grow up.

"If you're born to hang, you'll never drown." – Put that on my headstone.

"The more sand that has escaped from the hourglass of our life, the clearer we should see through it."

Machiavelli

CHAPTER 12

Terri's Journal Entry
December 1, 2004

Another month down. Hope you're holding on. When we talk on the phone I can hear in your voice that you're trying to protect me, and since you tell me about the IED's and mortars and guys you know who've been hurt or killed, it must be that you're holding back what this is costing you inside. So I ramble on as if I don't hear it and tell you mundane stories of home. I hope and pray I'm not failing you Chad.

Love,
Mom

E-mail Home
12/1/2004 11:59 AM
Subject: Re: Notebook

I got Halo 2 and a Christmas package from you guys last night! Love it all! Gracie, gracie. I'll try to call tomorrow night or sometime thereafter. Right now I'm going to bed, we were out late today.

And yes, I'm really in Iraq! How cool is that?

E-mail to Rob
12/01/2004 11:48 AM

We just got hit by an IED. Woot!

Madden got knocked out of the vehicle and lost a tooth. Their vehicle has splintered glass up front. Mine has two chunks of bulletproof glass taken out about even with were my heart is when I'm driving. Seeing it all happening through NVGs was a helluva rush/nightmare. Apparently it was a 155mm artillery shell on or under the road. MY NVGs were "whited out" like a motherfucka and I was virtually blind for about three minutes whipping down the highway at like 45 mph. To say my life is exciting would be an overstatement, but damn when it rains it fucking pours.

Glad to hear from you again, man. It's been awhile. And don't let yourself get down or feeling trivial. We're exploring in our own ways on the paths meant for us. If you were walking my path, you would learn nothing. Same goes if I were mistakenly following yours. It's simple, sometimes, the parallels in our lives. I am discovering what darkness really lies in the hearts of men. It's sort of Lord of the Flies out here at times. And you are discovering introspection and self loathing and feelings of comparable insignificance at its finest and most poignant. Besides that, we're working up one HELLUVA story. Where the beat generation strayed off, we have a chance of making it better. The greatest minds of our generation and what not. Historically all the truly influential writers of their respective times have known each other. I like to fantasize that the same applies.

And I happen to love art, especially obscure photographs on canvas. And nudes of gorgeous girls. But hey, wifey might not like that right so I'll have to keep it to a minimum if and when I ever settle down.

Trust me Rob; you wouldn't be happy if you were here right now. Grass is always greener on the other side. I think it just clicks with my personality. Like Kerouac on his damn firewatch mountain, I have found a way to confront the "void." And I think I'm winning. Or I'll self-destruct. You never really can tell. Maybe I like it too much and everything I do in life will pale in comparison. I worry about that. And being alone. That's what scares me most, you know. Not bullets. Not bombs, or heights, or high speed. Being utterly alone until I die, or being with someone who doesn't understand what it's like to go insane in the dark by yourself and throw out wild words and stanzas and you read them the next day and you are a different person. Having no one know what that's like is as bad as not having anyone at all. How nuts is that?

I've ranted long enough for a while. Your thoughts, bro? What are you afraid of, really?

Chad

"He who seeks to slay the dragon should take care not to become him."
-you know who

Journal Entry
December 2, 2004 9:27 PM
Bullet Holes in the Cemetery Wall

Been listening to some Johnny Cash today. Developed a new respect for his lyrics and that gritty soulful voice. Probably not good music to listen to out here but sometimes I get sick of techno and metal. I have to hear something different now and then.

Gotta get up for a Comm changeover in the middle of the night. That's depressing since I'll probably end up changing most of the gear by myself cause one of the RO's isn't here. Bummer. I really like to sleep a lot.

E-mail from home
Date: 12/3/2004
Subject: 'lo

Hullo Chad,

How's life? Normal here, which is to say, show in one week kind of normal. Dad and I have to do the big DU banquet thing tonight and hand deliver some invitations. Tomorrow night Lisa Says No plays at Smithers. I'll dance one for you.

Decorated the tree in your room last night. Ry refused to put the star on 'cause that's your job. After discussing it (put it on the damn tree Ryan…) he unceremoniously stuffed it on. It's crooked, but I'm not to touch it.

Orphans are doing well. They appear to be going to live so they now have names; Little Dude, Cami, and Bootleg. No one seemed to like my more literary choices for names, but we did avoid naming them after video games.
Hope you are well. We miss you.
  Love,
  Mom

E-mail Home
12/3/2004 12:46 PM
Subject: Re: 'lo

Hey,

I'm doin' good, glad to hear that everything is "normal." Insurgent activity is probably going to pick up again soon once they get organized, so we're just kind of standing by. Such is life.

Not much new here. Still always tired. But that's got to be some kind of reaction to being here. Just helps to pass the time if I'm asleep. We're down to about three months of action and then we're gonna' blow this pita stand. WOOT!

Tell Ryan not to get defensive about the star. Unless he really wants too. In which case I can do nothing about it, but hey, whatever floats your boat. He never listens to me anyway. He still misguidedly believes he'll magically be able to whoop me at Halo. HAHA
  Love,
  Chad

Journal Entry
December 3, 2004 9:27 PM
The Freedom Fighters Died Up on the Hill

So I'm totally sore right now.

Just burned out in the gym (with Hanz and Hoss, my name is Franz) and decided it would be a good idea to box for a while. It was not. I am pooped, and I have truck watch at 0200-0300 and then wake up again at 0530 and clean up the house, move the trucks to the QRF spot, eat some chow hopefully we don't go out again and then we've got to do radio shit at 1300… it's not gonna be a fun day tomorrow… Not that anyone cares but me.

So I started writing a gothic novelette today. So far I've managed to set the scene in duh… Los Angeles. I know it's trite, but that's the point. A cathedral bought out by a dotcom p2p corporation and turned into a Hollywood hangout, playing as the central meeting place for the screwed up characters inside. Not your typical vampire novel. Less vampire in the literal sense, more like those who have so lost faith in everything about the American dream that the counter culture can create personalities less than human. The story is that of one individual who loses his humanity all together, and how he feels about it. So far, anyway. All I've got is a stellar scene, but no filler yet.

So the IED the other night cracked my windshield, and that's getting replaced I think. Two chunks/holes right like where my heart is positioned when I'm driving in the glass. WOO DAMN, I love bulletproof glass!
I'm going to bed.

In the Valley
A Gothic Short

Authors Intent: This short is intended as an exercise in atmosphere and bringing reality to the genre of gothic fantasy, an attempt at personalizing the stereotypical antihero and turning the mysterious character into something recognizable, if not entirely human. The story, while admittedly lacking plot, will itself be a foray into a world of runaways, freaks, intellectuals, bored children, geeks, sociopaths, and other creatures that walk the streets of the darkest perceived city in the world. It's the story of men and women who have lost their humanity. It is the story of the underbelly of a civilization whose culture is so intent on searching for enlightenment and prosperity, and at the same time incredibly educated and cynical, that the fusion has caused the creation of a trendy dark side. You can't always smile. Sometimes, it's cooler to cry.

Setting: Los Angeles, St. Vaince, an abandoned church bought out by the fashion savvy owner of a dot com corporation for a Y2K bash, now a trendy Hollywood night spot playing host to celebs and whoever the management thought added to the purposely shadowed atmosphere.

Introductions

Dark wave trance pulsed loud enough through the house sound system that it covered the sounds of conversation but did not totally impede it. The acoustics of the former church of St. Viance, converted into L.A.'s newest gothic spot for celebs, posers and assorted freaks, was one of it's awe inspiring features. It had been purchased by a wealthy young executive of a P2P file sharing company for it's Y2K bash five years before. It had been restored, the altar housing an array of DJ equipment and a visual display synced with audio on the wall behind. The pews had been removed in favor of a dance floor of a black faux marble. To the wings sat several bars selling expensive, vampire-themed drinks to the club goers as they left the dance floor and headed to the dark alcoves recessed into the wall and furnished with art house furniture and heretical religious icons.

A popular mix of the old techno favorite "God is a DJ" pounded its heavy bass and euro-trash vocals at the moment.

In one of the alcoves, Adrian Moriarty poured himself another glass of black polish vodka from a decanter in an ice bucket on the glass table, one Prada boot propped up beside it. The vodka tasted the same, but it looked more imposing. In L.A., looks counted more than reality. To that end, there was a semi-legal weapons check next to the coat check. Private Security guards for those important enough to have them, were forced to wait outside while their bosses partied upstairs in the VIP section overlooking the dance floor.

"Take care that if you stare to long into the void…"

"That the void does not also gaze into you," Adrian finished, smiling at the young twenty something in gothic-tinged school girl garb, showing fangs as she approached, twirling her blonde hair around one finger. "Sit down; you're the first one here." Adrian stood up and received a kiss on the cheek from the girl, eyeing her small breasts that were pushed up and together by the miracles of modern lingerie, protruding seductively above a white button down that was tied off at the stomach. The short black and gray skirt and black pumps completed the look. Tasty, Adrian thought.

The two made small talk while they waited for more members to arrive. Her name was actually Sara, but she went by Sky in most circles.

Morianty grinned and made witty comments, and tried to make eye contact through her wire thin glasses. "Sky, huh? Sounds like a stripper I once met in Yuma."

"Who said I wasn't a stripper?"

Well, he thought, that would explain a lot. In any case, she was making him all hot and bothered, and he quickly stood up to greet the next member of the group. A dark goth…

E-mail from Rob
12/05/2004

So I think I'll put on socks. Be right back. There. Much better. The Ohio winter is starting to bear its sharp, nasty teeth. Funny too, because a week before Thanksgiving, it was 60 and windy here, which was sweet. The cold blows. Especially when it's blowing, and it's even colder, and then it blows exponentially more. So I'll stop wasting your time, now. Life is busy. I just *almost* finished the organization and exhibition of an art competition. I set up the gallery space in the library Atrium yesterday, which took a decent three hours seeing as my help bailed on me. We got some really good submissions; the theme was Gender Violence, for the 16 Days of Activism against Gender Violence. First place was taken by some tall goofball who rides a sweetass Vespa around campus. Yesterday, today, and for the rest of the week he has/will be striking himself 226 times a day, one for each unreported rape that occurs each day. Plays with idea of demo graph identity, what being a "man" means, and all that fun shit. The beatings are done in private, with a text plaque and photo-filled binder as the sole evidence of anything having happened. He got 75 bucks for this. Yeah, finals time is approaching. I know that the sooner I start my research paper, I'll feel better. But I would rather write to you, listen to U2 and hear Shawn tell me about his partycapades last night at Syracuse.

I appreciated your comment about the beat generation. If only it were that easy, dude. We live in a society dominated by dolts like Anne Coutler, Bill O'Reily, and Rush Limbaugh. Who the hell would ever listen to what we have to say? Who would care? I mean, it's certainly worth a shot, and it needs to be done. But when I read that, I thought of our days in Fred's class, reading Kerouac and not caring. God, how easy it was! If it could ever be that easy again! Either way, come home. The complacency and ultra mundane await you with steepled fingers in Delaware. I miss you.
    Be Safe.
    Rob

E-mail to Rob
12/05/2004 12:50 AM
Subject: Re: My feet are so cold.

So,
    Maybe I wasn't suggesting so much as a beat revival, but the art in writing seems to be dying to the science of it. Anyone can create a fiction novel based on the same old dragon riding heroes facing off against some unstoppable darkness, or a space opera with some rehashed plot, or the umpteenth installment of NetForce or some exceedingly mundane "thriller." Not many publishers bring out the art form anymore.

What happened to experimentation that actually made sense, and wasn't just hipster ramblings set to the cadence of a post Shatner drum, as cliché as another Radiohead set... There's this enormous subculture with no voice, lurking around, splintered into a thousand fragments. You have the raver kids, clinging to PULS and doing E to block out whatever they don't want to think about. It's denial at its finest, of something everyone feels. Religion used to be the opiate of the people, but now we're too smart for it, Catholicism is at its end of days because all the dirty secrets and hidden gospels are out, and science is the new god, because science is still alive. Drugs are better than religion anyway. God can't touch your mind (unless you're one of those uber Christian kids who are no better than the druggies) but heroin damn well can. Our generation uses drugs not for fun like previous generations; we use them as fucking medication.

You have all the emo boys and the screamo girls and we're all just angry because we've been robbed of something, but we don't know what it is. The gamers and geeks and literati delve into pleasures of the mind and we're all guilty of fantasies about a virtual life... its evident in the popularity of today's fiction, in the internet, and "reality" TV. It's easy when we're so plugged in, and sippin a latte while you play Everquest on a wi-fi connection at Starbucks and talk to a fantasy girl on IM. Anything to kill the mundane or anything that forces everyone to, on some level at least, look at who they really are.

On the other side of the spectrum you have things just as bad... the hip hop giants and stick up kids, glorifying the animal nature of violence and materialism, something they don't even realize is evident of the times, not just their chosen lifestyle. You have the vampires and the Goths and the industrials and the cyber fetishers and a thousand perversions of your choice and delusion. Its all different sides of a thousand sided die. The youth is splintered because our generation has no identity. Gen X had what they wanted, created the X Games, the internet as we know it, eBay and all else. Gen Y as they call us... nothing more than the spoiled, over-educated, plugged in and nihilistic children of the X'ers. There is no voice. Think about it. Any group we have is a reaction to some other original idea. The Young Republicans, struggling to defend the dying value system of our parents, justified on their own terms. Same for the up and comers of the Democratic Party as well. The intellectuals who know they are. Just like us, who think we're not part of it, but damn if we're not the cause of it. Just because you can see the sickness doesn't mean you're not infected. I'm searching consciously, but everyone else is searching too, they're just unaware. What's the CAUSE though? WHY is it so fragmented? I believe there is a reason. I just have to define it. It's nothing simple, like darkness, but it's something along the lines of hopelessness, and the reaction to it... That will be the mark of a generation.

So I need a thesis statement. And a degree. Oh well, I've got my M16.

You're thoughts? Oh, and the art show sounds cool by the way. Wish I could be there.

It's very cold here, too. I am freezing my balls off on watch at night. We're on night task now so we have to go out at night (obviously) and it freezes on the hummers. It's a bitch.

I wish it would snow,
Chad

Terri's Journal Entry
December 5, 2004

The band played tonight. I guess it's really the 6th; oh well. I haven't been to sleep yet so if today is really tomorrow it means nothing to me.

I had an interesting conversation with a political Science major from Wesley College tonight all about the election and the War. He was a bit drunk, but I don't think sobriety would have made much difference. He basically said he disagreed with Bush's stance on the war and wasn't confident on National Security but voted against Kerry because Heinz imports its tomatoes. Ah, the benefits of a fine American education. Patti was there with me and proceeded to tell him I had a son in Iraq, and she had one in Kuwait and another training to go, so he wasn't going to impress us with his political astuteness, and basically was he just a hypocrite or was he a coward as well? He staggered off into the night. No doubt back to the dorm Mommy and Daddy pay for to sleep it off and wake to remorseless apathy. I saw a bumper sticker the other day that said "My son is fighting in Iraq so yours can party in college." It's sadly true.

I hope you're safe tonight.
Love,
Mom

Journal Entry
December 7, 2004 4:35 AM
Lie to me.

Less than a 100 days left in hell, gents and ladies… My life for the month after I get back to Cali is going to be a massive waste of time and oxygen. Party, party, party, sleep, sleep, sleep, party, party, party. That's all I'm thinking about today, because it gets me through.

Urgh. Mission soon, I think, breaking the relative peace and quiet of the last week. I'm about to go to the gym, work out a little bit, go back and stuff my face with candy and cookies from the box under my bed, and then rack out until it's time to tempt fate one more time.

Do ray me fah so la ti doe… Nothing else to write. At least I'm happy today. And damn, it's a Monday, even!

E-mail to Rob
12/08/2004 5:17
Subject: Mad Road Driving

Glad you liked the pictures. I bet you can't guess my rifles name... (hint; it has nothing to do with your mother, seriously)

I'm a big fan of the Aviators right now... so sue me. Goose might be dead but golly those are swell looking sunglasses when you're rockin' em with cammies and an M16. Couldn't pull it off in the real world but fashion is irrelevant out here. I've been wearing the same set of cammies for like two weeks. I smell really pretty.

Eh, not much new here. Still doin' the same things we always do. Killin' people or killin' time. Heard there's going to be a new adaptation of Alice in Wonderland (speakin of killing time; mad hatter and etc) this year. I'm all about the drugged out Alice. I want to do a stage play of the entire book except in bondage gear and drag. But then, no one here pays me for my artistic qualities, so I can only dream quietly.

I had this vision the other night of an art project when I get home. Get a suitable model, put her on a gothic style crucifix, naked, and shoot the picture in b&w film but here's the cool part; you do it so that the prints come out on five separate canvases in pieces, arranged or mismatched on the wall. For body, vertically, and the other two horizontal (making a cross) where her arms are. Obviously the center canvas would make up the trunk of her body/cross. Duh. The point would be a comment on the divinity of the Goddess in ancient religion being killed off by the Catholic Church. Goddess worship literally being crucified. I'm a pretty good photographer when I'm not taking shots with a 2 in x 2 in digital camera, and I'm sure I could pull it off. I've lived in the art world since I was three, no doubt I could find a suitable dealer. I think it would sell. I've developed a great eye for art over the years, and I know what will sell at shows. You're selling an image, not a product. That is the key thing to selling art (one of the most important things I've learned from watching my father make a career out of a niche category of art). Really considering my options in that field. My momma was a photographer, I've picked up a lot of tricks from her, but it's not something I ever took seriously. I wish I could draw, but I can't, so photography might be my medium... Your thoughts?

So I've ranted long enough about my hopes and dreams after the shit hole I'm in. You still going to major in English? I'm glad your semester is going/went well. I worry about you, you know.

Toodles,

Chad

E-mail Home
12/10/2004 4:22 AM

Hey,
Sorry 'bout the lack of correspondence, we've been busy as all hell. I've gotten called up like every single time I come over to the internet center. Not much new though I'll write later when I've got more time. Tell Dad I said Happy Birthday.
Love,
Chad

Journal Entry
December 10, 2004 2:37 PM
Remember That One Time?

Errrr....
So I'm sitting here chillin' in the internet center trying to remember what I came here to do... Just got done a "Health & Comfort" inspection, which means people of higher rank come by and go through all your stuff, which you have dumped on the floor or your rack, cause they feel like it. We DEFINITELY don't get paid enough...
So yeah, I'm totally bummed out right now for no reason. Tired as fuck cause every time I've gone to sleep in the past two days we've had to "stand up" which means get in the trucks with all your shit on and go out or wait for the word to go out. Normally, I wouldn't complain, I mean that is my job and everything. But this morning we stood up 15 minutes before our shift was over. Argh!
I'm California Dreamin' like it's still cool. I live in the OC for cryin' out loud. I wanna' go back! Two and a half months left, right? Something like that. Word is we're going to Japan next year too... Will I ever just get to par-tay? Census says... Yes, but only briefly. At least in Japan you don't have to be 21. I won't even be 20 til' July. I'm a youngin, I know, but I've seen more than most people my age, too.
Same shit, different day...

Terri's Journal Entry
December 12, 2004

Missed you at the show. Took pictures to send you and that almost made it worse. I'm missing you so much lately. Everyone says it's just the season, but its not. I know so little of what life is like for you there but I feel the change in you. I have no idea how to help. But my heart is with you.
Love,
Mom

E-mail Home
12/13/2004 6:17 AM
Subject: Re: Survived the show

Woot!
Sounds like a pretty good show. Wish I had been there to hit up the vodka punch and everyone's wives… By the time I get home for another show I'll be like 21 or 22 anyway.
The dreams finally started last night. I didn't think that was going to happen to me. I though it was along the lines of the same myth that everyone who goes to war feels bad about killing people and pisses themselves their first time in combat. Apparently you just can't stay here that long without getting a dream you think is real, cause all the details are so vibrant in your mind when you're under fire that they still come through in the dream.
It's wild.
Anyway, I'm doing good, got some sleep this morning. Night QRF and all that, you know.
Chad

Smoke it All

…fill this page with empty thought, still burdened even in their hollow sounds, weighted down as if my mind was the armor that pulls my body, shoulders and soul aching for release. I want to kill to break the time. Fuck all this retention snap away with a shot in the cold dry air; send someone to the grave because I am sick with the vision of myself. No guilt resides here, only aggression and hate and misplaced affection coming like the tide, swelling up before it dissipates into the dirty sand and the stench of this city. Everyone deals with this war differently the war doesn't bother me, really. It's just this lack of anything substantial. There's the void again, compelling me to divulge its mysteries, to unlock the answers in my own head. The best thing is when I escape thought at all, to stop searching and take things at face value. She used to validate everything I was asking for but since I had it things get worse day by day I can't look myself in the mirror. I don't know who I was, but I'm not him now never had this problem before there seemed like a point back then. Something to say I stood for, someone I wanted. Now all my dreams are meaningless and far away. I wonder if death would bring peace or just regret for something I should have done. Another cigarette burns away. I could burn this entire world. Smoke it all.

E-mail from home
Date: 12/14/2004
Subject: Monday

Hello,

Just a Monday here. Not much new. Gearing up for that whole Christmas shopping thing. Wanna go to the Mall? Shopping has always been more fun with you.

Dad took my workout with Rick this morning. I think I ate too much party food. Actually, I know I did. No common sense where food's involved.

It's getting ready to turn nasty cold here. Highs in the 30's. It needs to snow or there's just no point. (The orphans don't have a clue. They should be fun in the snow. Usually kittens are much older by this time.)
Well, I can't avoid it any longer. Time to shop. I love you.

Mom

E-mail Home
12/14/2004 4:52 AM
Subject: Re: Monday

It's about 12:45 on a Tuesday afternoon, I'm sitting in my beanbag chair naked eating cheetos… Not really… just watching too much of that Ron White guy off Blue Collar Comedy Tour, I guess… lol.

Spent all of last night at OP VA on standby to go kick some ass… four hours later, we didn't go anywhere else and I've had like five hours of sleep since then so I'm up and kickin' trying to get some stuff done before I go back to sleep. The usual tasks, you know… Clean my rifle, ease the springs on my magazines, clean them out, add some tracers, eat some food, check my mail, put fuel in the truck, check the fluids, blah, blah, blah… four more days on NQRF, damnit… I can't wait to get on guard task next week.

Sorry to keep bitching, I guess it's a grunt thing.

Wish I could go to the mall with you, but I'm doing this Iraq thing right now and I really think it's working out… lol. I do miss Christmas shopping. And New Years with the crew getting shitfaced just for kicks. I've missed all my favorite holidays this year. Such is life. Next year will probably be Japan, but after that, I'll be non-deployable (two pump chump) and get out of the grunts to a Pogue Unit for my remaining months.

Thinking about getting a new car, not sure now. Maybe just a bike, and spend the rest of my cash on video games and booze! Not really… I'm checking out the new Mustang, actually.

Same Shit, DD,

Chad

E-mail Home
12/16/2004 5:17 AM

Hey,

Not much new here. Rumor has it that we're getting two beers and a shot of rum tonight. I am skeptical, but it's the best rumor I've heard in a long long time. The one about Lindsey Lohan being in the back part of playboy last month was a good rumor and that turned out to be true, so I have hope for the beer.

It's cold as the seventh gate of Nordic Hell, here. Standing watch requires at least a couple cups of hot chocolate to keep us from freezing to the concrete. I put on my helmet this morning and was rewarded with a frozen skull. It's cloudy and windy, too. No idea about what the temp actually is, but because we are surrounded by water like 400m to the south side and like 30m to the north the wind chill is fucking brutal, not just brutal either. Fucking Brutal.

Typical grunt bitching from me, as per the usual. I'm learning to be a mortar-man during my "sleep time." So yeah, I'm stoked to go on guard next week. Finally we should get more than a couple of hours uninterrupted sleep. I don't think I ever went so long at this weird of a sleep schedule before. Everyone is suffering. Keep getting horrendous nightmares now, I think because of the schedule. Indirect fire in real life isn't that bad, because we know the chances of getting hit are pretty slim, but when you don't know you're dreaming and shit starts cracking off around you its stressful, you know. You wake up and are all disoriented cause you were asleep but now you've got adrenaline pumping out of nowhere. Once we get on a normal pattern I should be good to go.

Love,
Chad

"Take care that if you seek to slay the dragon, that you do not become him."-N

Journal Entry
December 16, 2004 3:27 PM
My Life is a Monument to You

I like coming up with really hipster sounding titles to my journal entries. I think it makes me look sensitive and sincere. Girls like that, right?

Not much new, as per usual. War is 95% waiting for something to happen, and 5% actual fighting. Boredom is the bane of my existence. Oh, and mortars. They suck too, but it's been quite peaceful recently. The news was reporting eight Marines dead in Ramadi but that's wrong, in case you were wondering. No Marines have been killed here in about a month. I would know, cause we're the only ones here. And no we didn't drop any bombs either. Reporters just suck.

Finally growing my hair out. It's been shaved since August (I have a REALLY ugly head, didn't really notice until I had no hair and then I was like whoa can't go out in public like this…) so it helps to combat the cold. It's freezing here, we've got hella wind chill off the water that surrounds this base, and the bridges we're guarding next week should succeed in freezing my skinny ass the rest of the way off.

Rumors of beer and shots tonight to ward off the mad crazy combat stress around here. The lack of action is actually making us all more tense, like the quiet before the storm…

I'm going to go play guitar rather badly (I know like two songs, lol) and try to catch some Z's…

Terri's Journal Entry
December 17, 2004

Still not ready for Christmas. Got you a few things you really don't need in Iraq so I just wrapped them and put them under your side of the tree.

I wish you could be here but understand why you aren't. So instead I'll wish you dozens of future Christmases full of joy and cheer and people you love.

That's what I wish for you the most you know… someone to love and love you back your whole life through.

When you find her, treat her well. Be kind and honest and once you're sure, give her your whole heart. The best of this world, the greatest gift we are ever given, is love. Someone will be very lucky to have you Chad. You're a true romantic. Don't settle for getting less than you give. If that's the case, she isn't the one. Love can be work, but its not cruel and it doesn't play games. True love is a kind of salvation. It can even save us from ourselves.

So I wish you love,
Mom

Journal Entry
December 18, 2004 1:54 PM
Emily is Addicted

Thought maybe I'd add an entry so here it goes;
Drank two beers and a shot of rum the other night, our holiday present from the Corps, and boy was it worth it. I was buzzin a wee bit, I'll admit. Poke fun all you want but hell, I've been here a while damnit and I'm all detoxed out. I'll make up for seven months of lost time when I get back. My liver is going to beg for mercy.

Finally getting off night QRF, thankfully. One more night of this shit.

I'm a hurting pup; I haven't slept more than three hours straight in a while. Starting to mess with my head. Going on guard now, which is like our rest period. One more cycle around and we should be on our way home. Elections coming up here, it could be a bad one.

Wrote a song last night, my buddy who can actually play guitar is writing the music for it. We're so talented. The song is typically emotive and it goes like:
(Excuse the spelling, I am an idiot)

As I write this requiem
for remembrance
I remember innocence
and the look of rejection in baby blue eyes
and how desperation looks on a wounded boy
the lights are on in your room as I drive by,
two guilty silhouettes on a Saturday night,
and I'm wasted.
I waste all my time,
writing about how rejection looks in baby blue eyes
and how it wears on a heartbroken boy...

I write this requiem
in remembrance
and I remember indifference
begging for death on the wet pavement
and not slowing down at the city limit sign
confusing the stars with bright street lights
and I didn't look back 'til I hit the coast
watched a California sunset that wasn't my own...
And I'm wasted.
I waste all my time,
trying to die on a rainy back road,
and now I'm taking the same way, the same way home...

I wrote an end to that but I don't like it, so until I fix it, it won't go on here. Critiques, comments appreciated. And of course anyone who knows me from home can see right through it, but she never reads this profile anyway, so I don't give a fuck. I'm kind of hoping she does and maybe she'll know it's about her and she'll ask me if it is, or maybe I'm just that inconsequential and she just won't understand or maybe just not care at all.

§

The following version was found among Chad's belongings when they were returned from Iraq. There's no way of knowing which was his preferred draft.

Requiem II

As I write this
Requiem in remembrance
You're the only thing I try to forget
I remember- Saturday nights on a moonlit high
Lights off in your house
As I drove by
I never really had a chance
and I
Write this requiem for innocence

I used to wander the streets in my car
Looking for reason among street lights and bright stars
I spent all my emotion to define this
Scribbling on napkins
Trying to capture rejection and how it looks in your eyes
As they reflect the innocence of my intent
And the wounding of a boy

I recall running away to the Orange County line
If distance is denial than I'm doing fine
I watch the sun set on the pacific coast
I guess its not much better than my own
Time doesn't heal the deepest wounds,
Threw away a hundred unaddressed letters written to you
Afraid to speak out your name because it means I never really left
So I wrote this requiem for innocence

E-mail Home
12/19/2004 1:47 PM
Subject: Re: Beer Buzz

Que Pasa?
    I just got done eating some spaghetti from the chow hall (miracles of a microwave) and coming off post. I had the 1700-2100 shift tonight. I've got it again at 0900 so I'm going to finish up online and go get a haircut and

rack out. Wish I didn't have to get a hair cut but regulations are regulations, and it's my duty as a combat Marine to uphold them even in time of war.

Oohrah.

Sorry about the one liners, I've been busy/tired as usual. And nothing has really happened, so there's not a lot to tell.

Any who, I'm off to do other stuff, mainly... sleep. G'night and G'morning, depending.

E-mail Home
12/20/2004 5:52 AM
Subject: Re: It's Snowing

Have fun in the snow!

It's not snowing here, but we've been seeing some WEIRD things on post. There's these two UFO's that are green and do all these insane, impossible antics in the air, and a red one that pulls the same shit but usually just in circles... and then last night me and Rinn saw the weirdest thing we've ever seen in our entire lives. We were on the south bridge, looking around and trying not to freeze to death despite the amount of layers we had on, and we see a flash. Naturally we get behind cover quick as hell cause flashes around here only mean one thing, and usually involve someone trying to kill you. After a split second we looked up (this all happened extremely fast but your brain registers things quickly once you know what to expect) and saw about three klicks away an IMMENSE strobe light lighting up the entire sky. We were like what the fuck... it must be something electrical exploding, right? But then north post saw it again later someplace else for a second. So we report it in, and everyone was making jokes but that was really weird and it's not anything the military knows about. Well, our military on the ground, anyway. It was too big to be anything we have, strobe wise. It was bright like lightening, but directed the opposite way. I was joking around that this would not be a good place for ET to try and make peaceful contact.

That's pretty much all that's new. Here's to missing a white Christmas...

Love,
Chad

Journal Entry
December 20, 2004 4:06 PM

She always tells me no

I want to be in a rock band and reach out to young girls
screaming my name.

I want to be in a nu jazz ensemble and smoke with urban
 hipsters and activists while drinking Jack D from a glass
(Marines do it from the bottle)
I want to be in a punk band and bang high school chicks who
hate their dads.
I want to be in a goth band and have self involved and
sensitive friends.
I want to be in an emo group and have girls cry as they sing
my lyrics and try to console me (hey it works for everyone else, what am I doing
wrong?)
I want to be in a band.

Not really. But it would be nice to see girls again. Iraq is growing old.
Infantry units = No females. I have a one track mind right now. I am
useless. This post is useless. I will get no kudos.
Ninja Vanish!

E-mail Home
12/21/2004 2:30 PM
Subject: Re: nine below zero

Howdy,
    I was all stoked cause I was going to call you tonight but the phone
center is down. Damn.
    Glad to hear someone else is suffering from the cold besides us. Makes
me feel better. Lol. The lights are still an unexplained occurrence, and it's
not desert-y enough for a weird light show.
    I haven't gotten a package in a week or so, and no card as of yet,
probably get mail tomorrow. I've been sleeping as much as possible,
about seven hours in the past two days… lol. Just when I thought I would
get to rest, too. Damned working parties. Every time I go to sleep, I get
woken up for something just goddamn stupid like an hour and a half
later. It's predictable and annoying. And if you bitch about it, it only get
worse, because then the world just TRIES to screw with you, because
you mentioned something about getting screwed with. Oh, I LOVE THE
MARINE CORPS. Dreams have effectively ceased because I never hit REM
entirely… ha-ha my life is a shithole and I love it so.
    Miss you guys too,
    Chad

Terri's Journal Entry
December 21, 2004

Happy Solstice. We we're going to bonfire but it's seriously cold! I'll just have to make due with candles and hot spiced wine.

Baked cookies today. It's just not the same without you stealing the dough or burning your fingers stealing them off the pan.

Wishing you would call. Hearing your voice is so much better than e-mail.

Love,

Mom

Journal Entry
December 22, 2004 4:12 PM
All I Want for Christmas Is To Forget

I already mailed this one out to a couple people, but if you haven't gotten it yet… We've been making up Iraq themed Xmas songs for the past couple days. So there's a sick sense of humor in the Corps, we know… Anyway, our best one is:
50 Cal Rock

50 cal, 50 cal, 50 cal rock
Over Ramadi, shots always ring
Lock and load it and waste some hadjis,
In the frosty air…
That's the 50 cal, that's the 50 cal
That's the 50 cal rock…
It's a bright time
In the night time
When I'm driving with NVG's*
It's a fine time
It's about time
To find another IED*
That's the 50 cal, that's the 50 cal
That's the 50 cal rock…

*NVG's are our PVS7B's, our night vision goggles, and IED stands for Improvised Explosive Device, the roadside bombs they try to and sometimes succeed in killing us with. Hadji is the frowned upon slang we use for Iraqis. 50 Cal is our heaviest machine gun. That should decrypt the whole song for you non-hard dogs out there. Lol.

E-mail Home
12/23/2004 5:39 AM
Subject: Re: Hey

Hey Ma,

It's almost Christmas and I'm sitting here before post writing you an e-mail, thinking that I'll try to call tonight. I bought a card for the other kind of phone center we've got here (runs over the internet lines) because every time I've tried to call our ATT center has been either down or closed. I feel bad cause I haven't called in a while, but don't take it personally, it's just a matter of conflicted schedule (choose between sleep, e-mail, and food) and a screwed up phone center that has been out of commission for about a week now. Not a good time for that to happen. You'd think it would be a priority at this point.

Ryan's "blue tower of death" computer sounds pretty cool. I've been talking to him through e-mail pretty often. Everyone is sounding like they're being good. You guys have to be somewhat adjusted to me not being around by now, so it could be a lot harder if this was my first year in the Corps. I can be thankful for that, at least. I'm so used to not being home now it's not even a huge deal. Of course I miss you all and the Holidays make it worse by far, but I'm still doing really well, I think. Hope you are too.

Heres to a Christmas we'll all be spending on post and a willing sacrifice at that if people are warm and safe at home.

Love,
Chad

Journal Entry
December 24, 2004 12:14 PM
Somewhere Over the Rainbow

...Somewhere over the Rainbow/ The Emerald City...

This town at night is a perversion, tinged green by my optics like a filth laden Emerald City. This yellow brick road is paved with shit and rubble and roadside bombs. The gutters run with waste and blood.

My mind rejects this version of Oz as I scan the darkened streets for a target, listening always for the thump of a mortar round or the deeper horror of an RPG, screaming like a banshee overhead, howling someone's name. The halting silence here is punctuated by anonymous gunshots and hissing radio traffic.

No one came out to greet us when we killed the wicked witch. I want to kill all the munchkins in this place. They are seeded with the evil that is the other half of my soul. Everything they are is ugly, just like everything I reject when I squeeze the trigger, and take another life through the looking glass that is my scope. I am killing myself over and over and over again. I have died many deaths in 4X zoom. I will die a few more times before I wake up.
I click my boots together in vain.
There's no place like home.

Terri's Journal Entry
December 25, 2004

Merry Christmas, Chad. It isn't the same without you here. Ryan doesn't have anyone to play the new video games with and Dad doesn't have a hunting partner. Your presents are still wrapped. I've been fighting tears all day. I'm so afraid we'll never have another holiday together. Walked outside tonight to look at the stars and make wishes.
Love,
Mom

E-mail Home
12/26/2004 10:58 AM
Subject: Re: Christmas Cheer

Hey,
Would have had a decent chow last night but I was on post again so I had some warmed up turkey. WOOHOO! lol.
Whatever. Next year I'll be in Japan, drinkin' saki and eating someplace expensive. I'd rather be home, though, that's for damn sure. But you get used to a lot of things in the Corps; I guess holidays that aren't holidays are one of them.
Did you read my latest blogs? One of them is a story/ journal entry I wrote the other day; I thought it was down right publishable. It's kinda a concept piece, to see what I can do with this material.
We're back on day task now, waiting for shit to cook off like a bunch of fat dudes at a bbq competition... Such is life. I'd be lying if I said I wasn't looking forward to it, someplace not so far below the surface. On one shoulder you've got sanity and reason, telling me that I should stop wanting to do this anymore, and bitching about being timed and wanting to go home and not see anyone else get hurt, and on the other shoulder is a wild eyed kid in cammies who you wouldn't recognize, wearing boots with a rifle in the ecstasy of combat. I have always struggled with duality, and this is its latest incarnation.
"...The greatest minds of my generation..."–Ginsberg

Enough rambling for me.
Love you guys, hope all is well and Christmas was happy,
Chad

Journal Entry
December 26, 2004 8:31 PM
Come On Just Shut Up

I fucking hate Iraq.
(How much more eloquent can I be?)

December 26, 2004
I remember getting out of the shower and walking over to my bed. I'm putting on sweatpants when we hear it.

A hollow acceleration sound screams over our roof, but it doesn't process. I'm looking up from the floor. Everyone else is there in various positions of oh-holy-shit. We're laughing because there was no explosion and we're not dead. Woooo.

For about three minutes there's nervous laughter and everyone tries to justify why they hit the ground. Eventually we walk outside and look at the hole the rocket made about twenty yards away.

We can't find the rocket. It's probably buried under the concrete. It might go off so we go back. It's cold outside.

The garden of my mind is in winter
Dead leaves crunch under dirty snow
Frozen here are all the places
I would like to go
You talk like someone who hasn't changed
Your static American dream stays the same
My countless hours spent questioning
Are fruitless in the effort to find out what it means

E-mail Home
12/27/2004 11:49 AM

Hey,
Still no mail or pics from home, don't know what Ryan's doing wrong to send it (dude, make sure you're uploading the attachment) but it's probably something I would make fun of him for not knowing. Lol.

We just got mortars again. I'm okay. Will mail you tomorrow but I'm dog tired from driving all day today.
Love you,
Chad

E-mail Home
12/29/2004 7:31 AM

Hey Momma,

Thanks for the socks; you know how I can't ever hold onto them. Somewhere in the world is a secret sock stealing society (that's alliteration!) plotting in dryers and on clotheslines and under beds everywhere. Guard your socks; lock your drawers.

We just got back from an op today that we sat at an Out Post for the entire time. Went to JC yesterday and bought some stuff and ate chow there. Not a ton new here, as usual. Not surprisingly, the hadjis are trying to pick up the ball where they left off, but I think they've been severely crippled by the loss of Fallujah and our constant raids. We'll see by the end of the month how much ball they want to play.

Did I mention I got a new truck? This one is heavier armor and has better suspension and acceleration, even if top speed suffers by about 10mph. Big deal, I like it a lot. I'll try to get pics up again in the next week.

Love you all,
Chad

E-mail Home
12/30/2004 10:59 AM

What crackin?

Same ol' some old, here. Maybe its not, but I can't think of anything significant to report right now. Mundane military stuff you wouldn't care about. You know how it is.

Couple days left before we go on day QRF. Cleaned my weapon today. Sat at VA Center for like six hours waiting to do a fifteen minute screen (kind of a patrol in conjunction with another unit) it sucked. Probably do the same thing tomorrow that we've done the past three damned days. Mortars and rocket attacks have picked back up after a long lag in accurate direct fire. You should see us scatter or hit the deck. It's gotten gradually worse as time has gone by. It used to be everyone tried to act all not scared, but we're so close to making it out of here. It's all about survival. I went diving into a truck today when I heard a rocket scream over like it was hip. That is so totally wounded.

That's my new word. Hipster slang is cool. Like, my coffee was cold and had no sugar, it was totally wounded. Word.

I'm going to go play Madden 2005 or something equally non-productive.

Love love,
Chad

Terri's Journal Entry
December 31, 2004

New Years Eve. Not much in the party mood. It was good to talk to you the other day. I'm glad you have some good friends there with you. Maybe one day we could have them over for one of our summer parties. Here's to the future...
    Love,
    Mom

"War is an ugly thing, but not the ugliest of things. The decayed and degraded state of moral and patriotic feeling which thinks that nothing is worth war is much worse."

John Stuart Mill

CHAPTER 13

E-mail Home
1/1/2005 9:57 AM
Subject: Re: Auld Lang sine

Hey,

Sorry I've been a bit absent, I've been trying to find the energy, both physical and mental, to drag my ass over to the internet center and all that it entails. To say I'm exhausted is beating a dead horse with a stick, I know, but shit... I'll come home and I'm going to sleep, uninterrupted for three days, except to piss and eat. And maybe not even then.

Been running some ops, quick little insignificant raids and what not. Keeping busy. Everyone is all spazzed out over the lack of direct contact we've been expecting. It's like that scary music in a horror movie that keeps building up to a climax but then it's just a cat or something stupid that crawls out from the shadow... anti-climax sort of, but keeping with our paranoia.

I'd stopped going to the gym for a while and I lost weight, I went back tonight and I've really digressed, so I'm a little pissed off at myself for being so lazy and losing all that time on getting bigger. I guess I finally have a New Years resolution. I asked one of my buddies what his resolution was. He said to kill one more dude before we leave. Don't think he was joking.

Missing you,
Chad

E-mail from Home
1/1/2005

Happy New Year Chad,
     Should be NY's eve for you right now. Hard to believe 2004 is almost history. I think this has been the longest year of my life.
     We're just cooking and staying in tonight. Wish you were here to steal the cookies off the hot pan as soon as I open the oven. I wish a lot of things. Mostly that you come home safe. I can't imagine what you've seen and experienced over there, so I also wish you the luxury of time to sort thru it when you get home. And by home I really mean anywhere you aren't coming under fire. I also hope you know how much I love you and genuinely enjoy who you are.
     Mom

Journal Entry
January 2, 2005 7:01 AM
It's Been Awhile

     Been awhile since the last time I wrote anything of actual meaning, and I don't expect another one soon...
     Running a lot of Ops I can't tell you about (I'm so secret squirrel!) and some inside jokes popped into existence that you just wouldn't understand, so I'm trying to think of something of consequence to write about...
     I wish there were a way to explain all of this but there isn't a good analogy. Boredom and stress and frustration and adrenaline and the ultimate contrast of a vast array of emotions mixed up and shaken around in your head and the only people that possibly have a chance of sharing the same knowledge are around you 24/7 and they are just as bad as you are. My reality is not like your version anymore. I fail to explain properly. I'm sorry. I'm a writer, I feel like I should do better.
     Like they said in Vietnam... "It don't mean shiiiiiiiiiiiiiiiiiiit.

Journal Entry
January 2, 2005 10:07 PM
55 mph In the Wrong Lane

     So I was bumpin' down the MSR right (2/5 slang for main supply route Michigan)...
     Long story short I got stuck in some alley ways like hella far behind my platoon and I pretty much figured I was fuckin' dead, but somehow through the grace of my awesome skill, we survived to get to the highway and back with our unit... but on the south side of the highway, heading against traffic on a one way lane at 55 mph in a five ton armored hummer

like a bat out of hell... it was like some Grand Theft Auto shit right there...

You can't get a rush like that back in the states. Sometimes it's not that bad. Until it's really bad.

B & C

Clyde's eyes, usually brown and droopy at the corners, had turned a wild green in the light of the pacific coast sunrise. His whole face had taken on a feral tone. The smirk on his face one of total satisfaction.

Surf pounded at the bottom of the cliff he had parked his car on, and a slight mist hung in the air. There was a chilly breeze coming in off the ocean, messing his short black hair and cutting through the bloody wife beater shirt he wore.

Clyde threw back his head and let out a rebel yell, gripping the 9mm in his right hand, and almost empty fifth of ten dollar vodka in his left.

Still grinning to himself, the youth turned around and took a hit off the bottle, then poured some across the cut on his muscled chest where the knife had grazed him last night. A girl with short blonde hair sat passed out in the passenger seat wearing his blue leather racing jacket, sleeping peacefully. The little silver Z4 he had stolen was probably reported by now, he mused, they should get rid of it today.

"Bonnie..." He whispered, tucking the pistol into his drab cargo shorts and opening the door. "Hey, wake up."

Bonnie yawned and rubbed at her light blue eyes as Clyde watched her, hypnotized by the light hitting her highlights. She is angelic, he thought, a fallen angel sent to me.

Clyde walked around to the drivers side and pulled out a little backpack from behind the seat. He pulled a thick hoodie over his head, flashed a crooked grin at Bonnie. "Do you still love me?"

"Mmmm..." She stretched out and walked over to him, wrapping her arms around his middle, putting her head in his chest. "Yes."

"We should get a hotel room this morning and clean up. I have a friend at SDSU who makes college I.D.s. We'll get them tonight and head south.

"Ick, I need a shower." She looked down, scowling at his dried blood on her hands. "So do you."

"It's a date."

At the same time, in police stations and highway patrol cars all across the west coast, the modern version of an all point bulletin fixed and emailed photos of Clyde Warren and Bonnie Suthers, wanted for a shooting at an L.A. club and the death of seventeen gang members. They had escaped with approximately six million in US cash. Police officers were baffled.

Bonnie was sipping a bottle of water and painting her nails when Clyde opened the hotel room door with their new IDs and a set of BMW keys.

"Call room service, I'm starving."

Bonnie just laughed and picked up the phone.

Agent Asa Reeves crouched over the bullet casings on the street outside the Cheetahs in LA, completely stunned. Seventeen members of the Santos Familia had spent their last moments on earth fighting outside this club… killed by what police could only describe a military discipline. Their main suspects had reached a new record with this latest shoot out, having bottled up both exits to the strip club with at least four shooters, all apparently using assault rifles except one, who had been shown on video inside the club getting in a knife fight over a blonde stripper but producing a handgun and killing three bouncers before running with the girl out the front entrance of the building where pursuers were met with devastatingly accurate rifle fire from over watch position buildings across the street. Gang members had fired blindly in an arc across the street, but to no avail. When the police arrived there were no survivors except club employees who had not tried to pursue. Reeves studied a bullet pried from the door. NATO standard 5.56, a common military round used by infantry all over the world. Reeves knew he was dealing with professionals. Probably ex-Marines. This area of Cali was crawling with them. It was only a matter of time before someone figured out that their "useless skills" gained in their multiple tours in Iraq, primarily urban combat, actually did have an application.

The EDA was freaking out, of course. They had lost four agents in similar hits in the past two weeks up and down the coast. Every major deal that had been set up had been turned into a blood bath. Whoever these guys were they were well connected.

Terri's Journal Entry
January 3, 2005

Hey. Had nightmares last night. I'm no good at being helpless, and there's not a damn thing I can do. I can't keep you safe. I can't take away the pain of experiences I can't even understand. I need to look you in the eyes. Will that ever happen again?
   Love,
   Mom

E-mail to Rob
Date: 1/5/2005 11:24 AM
Subject: Doir and Dolce

Rob,

You know, I want to lead a revolution. I want to deal art and do cocaine off the line between a naked hipster's clit and her belly button. I want to be photographed smoking a cigarette and drinking Jack from a bottle. I want it all.

And not really just to be cool. Just cause its performance art. You know what I mean? I want to be a visionary, not a burnout. Too bad it's all been done before.

Wrote a long poem today, probably my best ever, entitled Wail. It's a small grin to Ginsberg's Howl, referenced in a one liner. It's a three pager, roaming over this fantasy of walking into a crowded room and opening fire on the complacent people and the loss of our voiceless generation. Life is annoying like the buzz of static from a television on full blast. I want to shut it all off and find some silence in the chaos. It's written from the point of view that yes, I might be out of my mind, or I just think I'm out of my mind because the world would reject the idea that it would be beautiful. But it's possibly the best thing I've ever written, not from a technical standpoint, but I finally captured the desperation I've been mulling over. That's why it's called Wail. Because the whole poem is an ode to the lack of faith in anything our generation experiences, medicated and plugged into the net like drugs and information are the new religion. I'll type it up tomorrow. Its sounds heady and conceptual until you read it. But I think you'd understand. It's not dark in the way like, emo dark; it's more just terrifying because I finally got that demon out of my head without sounding forced or trite. I need a xanax. I chain smoked until my head pounded.

In other news, I'm just thinking about girls and guns and coming back to CA and the SoDel scene or what's lacking thereof. I want to buy a new Mustang with my blood money. And a 9mm. I'll probably get the 9mm first.

I miss the girl and I miss the way you look at me when I say "I miss the girl."

I'm still a wreck. How about you? You never say what you really mean, now. What do you want from life? We're getting older; better figure it out.

-An older version of iago, machi, Chad

WAIL

This is a message in noir
A cigarette hanging from thin lips
This fractured thought
Like views of myself in a shattered crystal ball
Duality becoming a generation's choice

Destroying to create
Performance art... Fuck
Eyes are wild beneath closed lids

Burning through bruised skin
Wear dark sunglasses so this stays tucked in
Blood rushing lusting like E in my head
Desperately grappling to wrap words around misplaced sanity
Scrambling frantically

These weapons in outstretched arms
Feels like Christ
I hang in the balance
On my mental crucifix
And I am resurrected
Having walked through the valley in the shadow of the dead
I know what I've seen
Let loose inhibition and show you the dream
Suddenly primal in my psychosis
Bullets fly like seraphim
I watch the world burn as bodies fall around my flames
Like Lucifer from heaven

It's so rock star
This giddy slaughter
A real horror show
Watch myself from the outside in
Sipping synthetic moloko
Violence becomes symphonic
Ginsburg's need to howl
All twisted around
Some ranting opus obscene and neurotic

Red stain on white tile is a sieve
To leech away the noise of our lives
Grating and ugly as fuzz of static TV
Shut it off

The wail is ripping up and down my spine
My soul tries to tear itself away at this frequency
Then self awareness kicks in with the introspection it brings
How do you define genius in a deviant mind
The pinnacle of perfection
A living breathing real thing
The random derivative far from the norm
An accident of unholy vision and unwavering nerve
American killers in paradise back from your crusades
My delusion becomes yours as the dark muse plays

Communion is taken from a dirty needle
Administered by ministers preaching chemical sacrament
The real opiate of the people, music and internet
Medicate our kids and log us in
Grown up in the empty presence of a dead god
We turn to a xanax oxycontin
Cocktail religion

The youth are strung out
Nothing to say anymore
It's the end of our wailing
A generation is lost walking in the footsteps of those before us
All these killers in paradise
Who have nothing to say
Desperation is the cost
Of American Faustian deals
As the sun sets on the holy land
The sun sets in Hollywood

No one ever says anything that matters its just more letters forming gibberish in a billion voices surrounding me with oral fetish lingo slanguage it's vocal porn to fill my eyes with a billion visions of realities that never come to pass and this empire of violence that revelation by the Dali Lama that all life is pain and joy is only the relief this inspires me because the way the cold night air burns my lungs refreshingly taking refuge in the silence I delude myself I lie with habit that something better exists back home in your arms it's a vicious cycle of delusion because you're not really there its just a muse to keep me occupied in the meantime before I die mortality presses and my pen shakes with sickness my own hand isn't steady wracked with despair no matter what I do I can't escape the wail... I'm drowning in my own remorse I am doomed to private hell wishing you could share this with me.

Journal Entry
January 9, 2005 5:19 PM
Sick of This

Just realized how pissed off I was that I write about Iraq all the damn time. It gets a bit old. So annoying, isn't it? I'm sure everyone else out in internet land is bored with hearing it too.

Guess I've been letting this shit define me. Well I won't do that anymore cause I'm starting to forget who I used to be. Looked in the mirror today and didn't recognize the guy staring back at me. Who the fuck are you, I said. Who the fuck do you think you are?

The only answer I got was a cammie blouse with a nametape. That's my name but this isn't me. This is a side of me but it was never dominant before. I want to go back to being Chad. I want to go to a concert and rock out. I want to hear a loud bang and not flinch reflexively. I want to talk to a girl and charm her with dry wit alone. I want to have long hair and dye it some color, any color, other than black. I don't want the dark circles under my eyes to be permanent. I want to go back to being artsy and cool. I don't want to be this new kid forever. I don't want everyone to look and me and patronize me and think I'm doing something awesome and self sacrificing for my country. I don't give a fuck. Half of us are here essentially as mercenaries. Big shock, world… We're not complete tools. Not everyone in the Corps is a brainwashed super American idiot. I hate this image.

Sorry to be such a bore. I'll try harder next time.

What I want to be when I grow up

I guess I want to see the world without being behind the sights of a rifle for once. Everyone says they want to travel but they never do because they're afraid. I don't have fear anymore. I've been away from home so long that I don't belong there anymore. Home is still a great memory and a nice place to visit, but I can't live there.

How to travel is the question. You've got to do something for money. It's a Catch 22. You have to have money to leave, but you can't leave your job to travel.

So what now? My love of music calls for me to be involved in production, no real interest in trying to DJ for the rest of my life… But that's pretty much a set job, nothing remarkable for the memoirs. I'd get complacent pretty quick in that lifestyle. Complacency kills.

I want to pearl dive in India and spearfish in the Caribbean. Live like a monk for a couple of years, writing the entire time, learning what I can from some time alone, doing what I want to do, even if it means (or especially if it means) leaving behind any materialism. Photograph everything.

I never understood Kerouac's rambling until I got older, why he would leave everything and just start off on some grand, ill fated journey to nowhere in particular. I assumed it was a means to further his career as a writer/visionary.

Now I understand.

Somewhere out there is happiness, because the only thing inside is the void. Maybe it's a girl, maybe it's a place. I don't know, but its not here. It's not in my American dream.

I could lose myself in the opiate that is clubs and music and drugs and women and sex and money and fast cars and murder and fashion… A part of me is drawn to that life. I'm just smart enough to be good at it.

The other half of me says it would be a waste, I would not find what I am looking for. It would be a waste of this life to indulge myself in that forever. It's too easy, and when I grow old, if I grow old, who will care if I fucked a model on the back of my sports car, because she's old and saggy now anyway, just like me. Age is tragic only when you have done nothing remarkable in your lifetime. Complacency kills. You get trapped in the same routines and patterns and pretty soon you've got kids to take to the Homecoming dance and you're telling them not to get drunk like you did, because they're underage. They grow up and for a lot of people that's all they experience. Simply aging in the same spot.

I don't want to die thinking I should have done things differently. I could die tonight in a firefight perfectly happy because up to this point I have lived my life with a passion and the only thing I have to regret is that I didn't have time to tell anyone the things I've learned. I never expected to live to see 21 anyway. You can't be concerned with things like that, because they cause you to be complacent when you get somewhere safe.

Journal Entry:
Date Unavailable
What a long week…

We've been so bored at the lull in action we had a battalion wide Halo II tournament last night. My partner and I made it to the finals but got taken out before the last game. That's the most action we've seen in a while. Shit should get fun again at least for the end of the month.

Spent a lot of time writing last week, developing some better material. I need to get home before I can finish anything though, I have a few unresolved issues I should fix back home with certain people that I fucked up in high school, and then, you know, I left so fast it was like whoa.

Been listening to some cool music lately. The demo CD that came with the new Fatboy Slim is better than the FS CD itself. Got the new CD by The Music, called Welcome to the North, and its growing on me despite the pretentious title. I really hate their band name but the CD is catchier every time I put it on. I'm also rocking out to the new Eminem CD, Encore. A lot of people come down on Em but he's more the voice of the generation than a lot of stars you probably think are more talented. Where angst was with Kobain in the 90's, anger is with Em now. It's not as breakthrough as it was hyped to be, but whatever. It's still Em.

Fav singles as of right now…
Kings of Convenience- I'd Rather Dance
Radio 4 – Absolute Affirmation
VHS or Beta – Night of Fire

E-mail Home
1/10/2005 4:58 AM

Hey,

Don't worry about me. Wouldn't say that I'm any more stressed out than normal. Night task affords us a lot of sleep (I got almost seven straight hours today… feeling pretty good) which is key. I'm pretty good on supplies, I got Uncle Bobs package last night, that was cool.

I can't ever do justice to the mental hell I've been through, far more than the physical. I am my own worst enemy, in that respect. It's not as easy as just being able to vent to someone, so don't be offended if I don't seem like I want to be more than vague. Right now I'm doing fine. We'll see when I get back to the states if I revert to who I was, or if this current incarnation of me is permanent. It may just be that I'm growing up. All the changes are probably unnoticeable to anyone except me. I have a lot of decisions to make about the direction my life will take, so a lot of it will be decided on the fly and probably within the next two years. Sorry to be so mysterious, I don't really understand why I do what I do anymore. You wake up one day and you're not the same guy in the mirror. It's not even what you've done or why, it's just like suddenly I woke up and went to brush my teeth, and I'm like, who the fuck are you? Thought I had it all figured out. Guess not.

Been chillin' all day with my friends. We're all really eager to get back into the fight or go home. One of my buddies gave me a 256 card so I'm collecting video. There's a badass "moto" video montage running around the unit with two versions… There's the 2/5 version, which starts out with some dude in a vehicle loading a 9mm and saying "We're gonna kill some mother fuckers today…" and then some classified carnage, and then there's the toned down version with no blood or anything. They're both cool, but I'm going to make a badass one with everyone's footage.

Incidentally, our Halo II tournament might be on 60 Minutes along with some guys being interviewed from the unit. Dan Rather was here. Almost got in a fight with the camera guy though. Didn't realize I was being filmed and I was like "Get that camera out of my face." He got all but hurt. Probably thinks he's hard cause he's out here "with the troops." Bullshit. He has no god damn concept. I hate reporters.
Any who, I'm out. Say hello to everyone.

Love,
Chad
P.S. Ryan, I still own you at Halo, it's not that much different.

Journal Entry
January 10, 2005 3:03 PM
Sandbag Empire
Writing this on the fly...

Postcard from the war
Wish you could be here
Wish you could see this
Empire of sandbags
A million identical boot prints marring
Dirty sand
Littered with the remnants
Or our lives
And chain smoked cigarettes
Wish you could be here

...Okay so it's not great but it's my first attempt at capturing a chunk of this place for future reference when I'm old and forgetful. I just like the image of the million boot prints this occupation leaves behind. It's symbolic.

Heard from an old friend the other day, she still loves it where she's at, but the boys don't thrill her, so I'm totally thrilled. One day I'm going to go back there, to that little deserted resort town, and then I'm going to finish what I started way back when. One day when I'm older. If I only knew then what I know now... things would have gone much smoother.

First thing I'm going to do when I get back to Cali... Twelve pack of Bud with my name on it. I might make it to six... he-he... our tolerances are all shot to hell. It should be good times.
Not a damn thing new in paradise

<u>Em Said</u>
Em said,
There's something about surviving a shot
But there's nothing like surviving a bomb
Still standin after the explosion
The nightmare unfoldin
Smoke in my eyes
Steel rains from the sky
And I
Love the smell of fuel burning
Lets me know I'm alive
The adrenaline high
Sets me off on this trip

I'm still enthralled
They ain't killed me yet...
Junkie

Shots ring out and the blood starts to rise
Combat junkie get his fix, gets his high
Take stock of my rifle, take stock of my mind
Revel in the fact that I'm still alive

The closer the explosion, the better the rush
The thrill of mortality is all I have left
Suck in the concussion, feel the impact on my chest
No fear for the future, no regret
They can't stop the kid, they ain't killed me yet

E-mail to Rob
Date: 1/11/2005 5:20 AM
Subject: DCFC

Hey bro,

Got your gifts yesterday! Thanks a million send Lori my love. I've been rocking out to lonely boy rock since I got it last night. You know what... I've seen people get blown away by .50s, shot by M16s, and bodies charred by grenades... but it took Death Cab for Cutie to almost make me shed a tear.

So I'm counting down the weeks until I return to the places I should be. This is not one of them, but if I had something to prove before I left then I guess I proved it now. Maybe I had to believe that I wasn't all talk and I had the balls, or maybe I just wanted to die. Either way, I think I made the best kind of mistake. Still can't wait to get back to SoCal... and who are you calling a puss??? In case you forgot, on one of the song lists for a mix you put... "To help you with your SoCal dreaming... you little pussy". You'll pay for that when I get home, mister-chads-too-far-away-to-do-anything-about-this guy.

So these days pass with the quickness that is mediocrity, waiting for the right explosion or the right street to go down. Was reading a book today (started on the Borges) and something blew up and rattled everything and everyone. I think I'll skip the 4th of July this year, maybe go someplace quiet.

Here's to the nights,
Chad

Here I sit/ between sandbag walls/ I've seen bodies burned from a mark 19/ heard the wails of women/ men wounded by M16's/ and never shed a tear/ but the mix

CD you sent to me/ makes me cry/ Death Cab for Cutie makes me cry/ wasted and worked my entire youth to get away and be where I am/ now I'm here and I remember/ how it was perfect for a little while longer/ I'm so homesick I could die/ and here I sit between sandbag walls/ wishing I were back home where I belong/ guess the grass is really greener on the other side/ she means everything/ he means everything/ to me/ lost myself in the chaos/ found it all again and wept/ for the time/ for the life/ for the things I'd forgotten/ all these wasted nights spent trying to remember/ and there it is/ right there in front of me/ Death Cab for Cutie made me cry…

E-mail to Rob
1/12/2005 5:36 AM
Subject: Acronym Fetish

Sorry to be so unhip, DCFC, M67, PVS7B, M24OG… The list goes on.

Kate's art illustrations are decent, though I can't see that anime style really going anywhere, at least not in watercolor. It's a bit high school art class, but I should really see her realism pieces. She could sell a lot of art if she knew what angle to work… But I struggle not to care. Let other people screw up as they will, right?

I wish I could go to a Gatsby themed party… Geesh, culture would be nice. All my friends are murderers. And frankly, that gets a bit tiresome. I DO love pirates though. That's my ideal job. Pirate.

Woo, gotta run. Love love.

Chad

<u>Love Letter</u>
I pencil in this love letter
Anonymous
Rewritten a thousand times over
Chain smoked cigarettes get it right
A mix cd plays the soundtrack
Through ten dollar speakers of
My solitary introspection
 In the dirty sand of a war torn country with
A hundred boot prints moving
Remnants of calm and echoing the occupations
This started as a lover letter
To someone I don't know
These empty days leave so much time for thought
Hours unbroken by mediocrity
With nothing else to do
But wish I was somewhere else
With you

There's nothing on my mind
So I fill it with fantasies
Chain smoked cigarettes get it right
I can't even relate to myself these days
Guess I forgot who I'm supposed to be
Guess I forgot who she is
But I remember our last kiss
And my picture still taped to your bedroom wall

E-mail Home
1/13/2005 11:03 AM
Subject: 10 Questions

Found this in last months issue of GQ, answer and get back to me, or pass it around as annoying chain mail!!! Woot! Figured I'd start it with two people whose answers I would actually read.

1)What would people say you are best at?
    C- Writing? Or Halo 2 depending on whom you ask.
2)What are you most proud of?
    C- Everything that's taken me to this point, being in the Corps.
3)What job would you do for free?
    C- Working on a boat some place tropical
4)Who do you most admire?
    C-Any two people completely in love
5)Imagine yourself as very old. What would you tell your grandchildren
   is the most important thing in life?
    C- Fear no god, and find love, because it will be the only thing to
    make you stop searching
6)What were you doing when you last lost track of time?
    C- Writing another story no one will ever read
7)How do you want to be remembered?
    C- As a great thinker
8)What excites you most?
    C- Combat.
9)What do you hate?
    C- Complacent people
10)What can you do about both?
    C- Not a damn thing.

E-mail Home
1/16/2005 2:14 AM

Hey Ma,

What's crackin? We've been doing a buttload of Ops the past couple days but no contact. I guess Hadji doesn't want to play with us anymore... We were really looking forward to kicking some ass too. You should have seen us. Everyone was all hyped up to go out again and we were cleaning machine guns and loading extra magazines full of 5.65mm putting more MK 19 grenades in the gun trucks and checking gear... and then... nothing... boring!

Guess I can't complain too much though. No one gets killed when we're not in contact, right?

Good news but don't spread it around too much. Our advance party leaves Iraq in February. The main body leaves about a week later. This is much earlier than we had expected. So within a month we should at least be at JC hitting on Army chicks and eating their food. Sweet.

Take it easy, love love,
Chad

E-mail to Rob
1/16/2005 2:29 AM

So dude,
I'm so fucking tired; I'm going to make this brief. I'm still motion sick from my NVGs.

Just wanted to say hello and you should listen to VHS or Beta "Night on Fire" cause it's a cool song and you'd vibe on it, I think. What's new in the world of Kenyon? Hey, our dates changed by the way. I should be out of here by the end of February! Sweet huh?

Keep it real,
Chad

E-mail from home:
1/18/2005

Are you okay?
Love,
Mom

E-mail Home
1/18/2005 6:27 AM

Hey,
I'm fine. We've been really busy. Going out a lot.
You okay?
Love,
Chad

§

Not long after we received that e-mail, Chad called. I could hear the irritation in his voice, as if it were silly to be worried.

"We just hadn't heard from you in a couple of days," Rich told him.

"Don't worry, Dad. If anything happens the Marines will let you know quick. You won't have to wait," said Chad.

Yeah, that made us feel so much better.

§

Terri's Journal Entry
January 19, 2005

Haven't written in this for awhile. I don't seem to know the words to fit the feelings.

When I talk to you and hear how tired you are I worry. Then you'll laugh and I start to believe we'll make it through all this.

I live and die to turn on the computer and see an e-mail from you. It all seems to be getting harder. Maybe I'm just tired too.

Instant Message Conversation between Chad and Rob
1/18/2005

It's Rob: Jarhead!

a random soldier: Bitch! What's up?

It's Rob: Nothing, another frigid day in Gambier… classes and what not, the occasional cigarette… You?

a random soldier: Many cigarettes and it's only 7 am.

It's Rob: How was your day?

a random soldier: Just starting… yours?

It's Rob: Pretty routine. I meant your yesterday.

a random soldier: Routine actually.

It's Rob I can only imagine what 'routine' entails.

a random soldier: Same shit different day… so when's your next break?

It's Rob: March… Does this fall within your leave?

a random soldier: Hopefully.

It's Rob: It had fucking better, if not Lori and I had a splendid idea… you should come up to Kenyon for a few days.

a random soldier: How far of a drive is that?

It's Rob: Pretty far, I'd suggest flying.

a random soldier: I'll probably be road tripping a new stang to Cali, I might be able to drop by for a day or so.

It's Rob: A new stang?

a random soldier: 05 Mustang.

It's Rob: Holy shit… apparently those things are amazing.

a random soldier: Yeah, like me.

It's Rob: Buying it with you salary? Or whatever it is…

a random soldier: Yeah, I've made some cash out here.

It's Rob: How much?

a random soldier: 14K… so far.

It's Rob: That's 13, 500 more than I have… prick.

a random soldier: Ha-ha. I work for a living bro.

It's Rob: Oh yeah? Well I… read books, and… shit.

a random soldier: Ha-ha!

It's Rob: So, how are things, pre-election? I heard a bunch of shit about borders being closed and that Archbishop captured, and released without ransom (!) I immediately blamed you.

a random soldier: Fuck 'em… We're killing people 'nuff said?

It's Rob: But what about the Archbishop? I mean that was you, right?

a random soldier: Shhhhh… I don't know what you're talking about…

It's Rob: Was that your money making scheme?

a random soldier: No, that's simpler, but no.

It's Rob: I would definitely credit you with ransoming high clerical figures.

a random soldier: I've done worse… so what's up man? How's the collegiate life? good bad ugly?

It's Rob: It's fucking dull. I like school but I'm seized by brief moments of feeling insignificant, pointless, etc… Maybe it's the winter… Also, I'm discovering slowly that I don't like a lot of the people in my major, and they likewise may not like me because I wear polo shirts.

a random soldier: You know what I'd do?

It's Rob: I can only guess.

a random soldier: I'd get one of those spiky bracelets from hot topic and wear it with the polos… just to be like fuck you, art whore.

It's Rob: I find the contradiction more cogent simply as an English major wearing Abercrombie.

a random soldier: Hmm true… I didn't realize that was just a Cape thing.

It's Rob: There's this guy in my Shakespeare class… brb, I need to kill a bug for Lori.

a random soldier: OK

It's Rob: Done and done… it was teeny… she's a wuss.

a random soldier: So am I… I'm afraid of spiders.

It's Rob: Speaking of spiders is it fact, or just stateside gossip about camel
      spiders?

a random soldier: They're huge… I've only seen one… I peed.

It's Rob: I saw a picture, it looked absolutely hideous.

a random soldier: Yeah.

It's Rob: Leave it to Allah to create something like that for his people…
      God makes deer, cod, bison… Allah makes flesh eating camel
      spiders.

a random soldier: They're both desert religions. Worship Allah or some
      nailed God it's really the same. Everyone dies the same
      way.

It's Rob: But some lives aren't populated with camel spiders… please
      bring me home one.

a random soldier: Ha-ha-ha-ha!

It's Rob: Live, if you'd please. I'll tame it, teach it to write Sanskrit… what
      a great party trick.

a random soldier: I'm too scared.

It's Rob: Chad!

a random soldier: I'd shoot it.

It's Rob: You drive a humvee and get shot at… take jar, capture spider…
      you'll warm up in time.

a random soldier: Nope… rather get shot at.

It's Rob: Some friend you are.

a random soldier: I know… I'm a puss. I'm tired as fuck bro… I'm going
      to bed.

It's Rob: At seven in the morning? They're cruel.

a random soldier: Doing what? What do you want from me… standing a random soldier: by on QRF.

It's Rob: Quick response?

a random soldier: Waiting to go play… yeah.

It's Rob: Shit… how often do you get calls.

a random soldier: Randomly. You should see us when someone starts
                  shooting… everyone runs round… someone plays "My
                  Sherona"… it's our song.

It's Rob: Are you serious? That's demented.

a random soldier: Deadly.

It's Rob: But so fucking cool.

a random soldier: I know right… time of our lives… really tho I'm
                  leaving goodnight.

It's Rob: Yeah, yeah… sleep… night dude.

E-mail Home
1/20/2005 7:53 AM

Hey,
    Not much new as usual. Woke up to a not-so-normal indirect fire
attack. Not so normal cause there was more than a couple rounds and
they were like, hitting shit. Fun times.
    We're still on night QRF, switching over to guard for ten days starting
on Sunday. I'm on with one of my friends so it should be less boring than
usual. Planning on shooting someone off of south bridge again. That
should liven things up a bit. Nothing like a good burst from a machine
gun to start the week off right.
    You can tell everyone not to send any more packages. Right now word
has it that advance party is leaving in February, full changeover will be
done and then we're out of here around the beginning of March. Sweet
deal.
    Send everyone my regards,
    Chad

Blood soaked dreams/ blood soaked dreams/ I'm so sick with the American
dream/ blood soaked dreams/ all my fantasies/ who am I to question you/ but

you'd question me/ we are the problem/ don't need a solution/ all I need is a magazine/ rounds in the chamber of my M16/ blood soaked/ fucking dreams/ the world burns/ a women screams/ I'm in love with my M16/ condition one/ the war is on/ sandbags and cigarettes/ ammo cans like my conscience/ spent and empty/ you should see my blood soaked dreams

Rape pillage kill in my blood soaked dreams/ all my darkest thoughts are clean/ the smoke of explosion brings purity/ in the aftermath of the orgasmic war/ we stop to count/ the casualties/ the world burns/ a women screams/ red sunrise and the morning brings/ fear of the youth with their M16s

Instant Message Conversation Between Rob and Chad
1/21/2005 8:55 AM

It's Rob: Good morning, LCpl.

a random soldier: Evenin' compadre.

It's Rob: How are you?

a random soldier: Good. Just got off post (why am I only talking to you when I'm on guard week? Weird)… last cycle went pretty fast. How's things?

It's Rob: Cold… but good, I'm finally taking lit classes.

a random soldier: Cool.

It's Rob: Yeah, the reading load is intense but, Lori's is worse. She's taking romanticism, modern novel, and us civ through lit… all upper level English courses.

a random soldier: Ouch!

It's Rob: If you saw her bookshelf, you'd wince.

a random soldier: Don't you love useless majors?

It's Rob: Hey!

a random soldier: LOL!

It's Rob: I'd like to think an English degree from Kenyon matters somewhat.

a random soldier: Hah… ok… joking dude, just a joke… it's actually an
    accomplishment. I just poke fun at English majors.

It's Rob: Oh, me too… especially the pricks in my major… thrift-wearing
    bearded pseudo intellects love to reference obscure 17th century
    British literature and quote Middlemarch.

a random soldier: I maintain my counterculture fetish for prep clothes
    and pop culture. It's so punk nowadays.

It's Rob: See, that's what I say… when the collar is popped, irony and
    highbrow satire unfurl like a flag.

a random soldier: I concur.

It's Rob: And now: I hustle off to class…

a random soldier: Have a blast.

It's Rob: I shall write you an e-mail today.

a random soldier: Yay! I'll send you pics tomorrow.

It's Rob:!!! Exciting… well, take it easy… eagerly anticipating your return
    stateside.

a random soldier: Ditto.

It's Rob: Adios compadre.

a random soldier: Adios.

Journal Entry
January 22, 2005 3:37 PM
It's Raining, It's Pouring…

Counting the weeks…
    Not a damn thing new around here, just waiting around for
something to happen, writing and dreaming about home as usual. Oh
yeah and girls. I miss y'all.
Blah!
    I'm going to play air guitar.

Terri's Journal
January 22, 2005

> *Snow! Made you a snow angel. And Ryan nailed me with a snowball.*
> *Miss you.*
> *Love, Mom*

E-mail Home
1/23/2005 2:17 AM

Hey,

Glad you guys got to see some snow. It's true, I'm not a big fan of the white powdery stuff (unless it includes snowboarder chicks) and definitely not ice, but I'm glad you guys got some this winter. Makes it seem like home.

It rained buckets here and knocked all our cammie netting down and turned what is usually granular sand into silt and deep mud. Fortunately it stayed dry for post this morning. It would have been a pretty sunrise if there weren't so many damned Iraqis. I'm on post with one of my buddies though, so it's going pretty quick. Nineteen four hour posts left before next cycle, our final cycle.

Sorry if I've seemed out of touch. Nothing going on here as usual. Just that mundane thing we do that no one else would consider mundane, but you get used to your environment I guess.

Stay safe you guys, Love you.

Chad

Instant Message Conversation between Chad and Mom
Date Unavailable

Momma: Zat you?

a random soldier: Yep, what's crackin?

Momma: Morning, what's new?

a random soldier: Not a lot… went out for about 10 minutes today… that was fun, if brief. Not much new… writing some e-mail.

Momma: Not a very long recess.

a random soldier: He-he no there was nothing to play with… we were ambushing a boat that never showed up.

Momma: I'll assume on the river… I'm having my first cup of coffee.

a random soldier: Sounds good.

Momma: Tried to sleep all day but the phone rang.

a random soldier: We're all about the instant coffee here.

Momma: Whatever works.

a random soldier: Sleeping all day sounds like a plan… I'm going to sleep for like 3 days when I get back.

Momma: I'm in a funk and I quit, not that it does me any good. No one notices… good coffee tho.

a random soldier: What do you mean? I'm a prince of depression, I understand.

Momma: Thanks. Kinda like that.

a random soldier: Ever write something that was so honestly true but so poignantly fucked up that it can never be published?

Momma: Yes… rather a stopper.

a random soldier: I wrote something like that today, they'd kick me out if I ever published it. It's a waste but it feels better. I finally captured what I've been trying to say this entire war. I'll let you read it when I get back.

Momma: I'd be honored… sorry to be a bummer today.

a random soldier: I'm a bummer all the time… it's okay lol.

Momma: The phone line is being skittish. Could lose you.

a random soldier: It's okay.

Momma: Well, I try to save it for those who help create it… my Dr wants me to take drugs.

a random soldier: Try some liquor, It's better for you.

Momma: My body just won't go there anymore.

a random soldier: I rue the day that ever happens to me.

Momma: So sad, so very sad.

a random soldier: If Ryan weren't still in school I would suggest some green leaf but he'd be traumatized at that age. Hold out for a couple years. (I can't believe I just told my mom she needed a bong hit) LOL!

Momma: He already wonders what I keep in those jars and baggies in the cabinet.

a random soldier: LOL… I still do. Hippie. Just stay strong for me mom. You don't have to be a superhero. I know you're stressing and this can't be a great time for you but Dad and Ry really need ya' til they grow up. You should take a vacation once things calm down… go to someplace not Delaware.

Momma: Charleston next month should help and you already have. Don't worry about me I'll hang in there. I just might not do the dishes for a week.

a random soldier: I try. I understand mind numbing and indescribable pain better than anyone I've ever met, silent and sometimes screaming. I feel it way down in my spine sometimes and then it shivers up and the world looks like shadows. Trust me, I'm there with you, but then suddenly it's okay again. You never know, right? Poor momma. I love you! Wish it was just a phase… it's my muse though. I take it as a gift now, not everyone sees the world like us. It would suck to be blinded by light all the time, right?

Momma: That's why some people write hallmark cards for a living.

a random soldier: I agree… the one thing I've learned with age is how to control it.

Momma: You made my day Chad. You have always been that one other that gets it and is still willing to go on.

a random soldier: I'm going to be a visionary for my generation. We're voiceless. Gen X had a voice, mine does not. We're shattered kids… no vision No generation has been this split and so plugged in.

Momma: But it has a techno soundtrack…

a random soldier: Hipsters, Goths, Christians, rockers, ravers, Wall Street pirates, and junkies and a million subcultures with nothing to say

Momma: Latte, no whip.

a random soldier: I think if we can capture that, Rob and I will be bigger than Kerouac and Ginsberg. Not a beat revival, really, just a couple kids who fucking get it. Wrap words around that split, that lack of faith in a goody two shoe world… gold.

Momma: As you have since you opened your eyes. I've always told you that you were special, that's what I meant. Then I had to try to prepare you for the weight of it.

a random soldier: I'm glad I came here… I had to be sure.

Momma: I know… back before I was fluff there were dark places inside I had to visit.

a random soldier: I know. I don't want to get too metaphorical but I don't have a kid, so I don't have to give it up. I'm strong enough it won't consume me… go read "Desolation Angels" by Kerouac… seriously get a copy. It's all about his confrontation with the void, it helped me understand why ultimately he lost but he spawned an art form. Some of it rambles, a true scream written out on paper, but the parts where he finds that… something… it's brilliant. You should read it I think it would help you whenever you feel insignificant or depressed. It helped me anyway.

Momma: I'll check it out.

a random soldier: Coolness… love you Mom.

Momma: Love you Chad.

a random soldier: The only other two people who get it are Rob and K…
Robs in love with me… I've got it bad for K… lol… so
goes the joke.

Momma: That was funny. And true.

a random soldier: Yeah it's a work in progress. Rob's trying to find an
indie film maker while we're young enough to play
ourselves… Take Sundance by storm.

Momma: Michael Moore is giving grants.

a random soldier: He's an idiot… I'd just as soon put a round in his
pompous ass as take a grant… He's as much of an idiot
as Bush… just on the other side of the spectrum… I've
got to run, Momma, Ewton is waiting to walk back. I
love you, be safe and try to find one thing you enjoy
today, even if it's small. Bye bye.

Journal Entry
January 24, 2005 12:36 AM
Thought about it

I was on post this morning with Ben and basically we were talking
about why the fuck we are here, besides you know, having fun and being
bored all the time and people trying to kill us. All this was while aiming
weapons at traffic (its necessary when you have a scoped rifle, and you
need to use the scope, don't judge me!)
I realized, we're in Iraq because it doesn't matter about freeing Iraqis.
They will piss away their freedoms and become corrupt but subtle about it.
It's their culture. But at least all these foreign fighters and extremists now
have a battlefield. A place to stick it to us Americans. And that's fine with
me. I'd rather fight them here than have my family killed in a bombing or
snipers gun down an innocent in the street. So basically, we're here to be
like… fucking bring it. Its better here then home, you know?
Pick your battles.

<u>Mister</u>
He's standing in the dark
He's standing by himself
Staring at a mirror
Doesn't know who he sees

Dark hair, dark eyes, the boy looks like me

He's trying to figure out
What other people see

Do they see the ruins
Of what used to be his heart
Do they notice the times he's failed
Does it show through the dark
What do they say
When he's walking away
What will they remember
When he's gone

E-mail Home
1/25/2005 2:45 AM

Hey Momma,

Just got the package with the water toy (tell Ryan I got all the rings, with water) and other coolness. Thanks much. Love it how you know me so well. We're going to play with the paratroopers later. We had a competition with the balsa wood planes last week.

Generally we're on post anywhere between three and a half and four and a half hours, depending on if they change it up or post and relief goes late or something. I've been sleeping, playing a lot of Halo 2, and watching movies. It's pretty good right now. Guard schedule is sometimes cool, sometimes not.

Love love,
Chad

E-mail to Rob
1/25/2005 3:01AM
Subject: RE: I like Steve Reich, Phillip Glass, and pretentious minimalist music

Sup broski,

I'm a minimalist writer, not really a minimalist music guy. My brain is all shot to hell and ADD like it's a fashion (oh it is) so I dunno. But if you like it, I might. Shouldn't send another package though, our mail should be cutting off soon.

Sled ride sounds fun. Spent all day today up on post with Ben looking for some excuse to kill someone. It's harder than it sounds actually. Coming up with a reason, I mean. Basic conversations and such help to pass the time, but you see something fishy (we've got like a weird sixth sense from

staring at one area for days on end) and it goes like this;
"Dude, you hear that/see that?"
"Yep."
"Call it in?"
"Nah. Wait."
"If he walks 20 yards closer to that hole I'm going to roll him."
"Okay. I'll get the camera."
"That's a bag in his hand."
Looking through scopes/nvgs/thermals
"Yeah. If he drops it, fuck him up."
"I've got a bead on his head. Man it would be awesome."
"Fuck yeah, bro. Shoot two shots so we can say the first shot was a warning
and he didn't run."
"Alright."
"Aw shit. He's leaving."
"Fuck."

It pretty much goes like that all day. Or just get stoned on post. But you
didn't hear that from me.

I'll see how I react to people when I get back, but I shouldn't have a
problem with audio. I've got my share of stories, I guess. I'll never be able
to explain it, but I'll give it a shot. It's an alien mindset, and you lose it
partly when you get back to the states, and it changes your perspective on
what you've done. So I'll see.

Have fun in class for me,
Chad

E-mail Home
1/27/2005 5:44 PM

Hey Momma,

Not a lot new. Another day, another really big boom and I'm still here.
What's up with you? Snow melt yet?

Tell Dad I said to get a Harley. I know I'm a bad influence on him. It's
my job as eldest son to induce mid-life crisis on the father. It's in the guy
handbook, I swear.

Love you, Chad

Instant Message Conversation between Chad and Mom
1/27/2005

Momma: Hey.

a random soldier: Howdy.

Momma: What big boom?

a random soldier: Ha-ha… a really big one. Had me and Ben shaking for the past hour.

Momma: Do tell.

a random soldier: Scared two grown ass killers bad enough we don't remember functioning or anything. We just did like a robot and moved with the program… We had to hug afterwards.

Momma: Bonding is good. You ok? Ben?

a random soldier: I'm alright… he's alright but it was a weird one… We're pretty jaded when it comes to things blowing up. This one was so unexpected.

Momma: On post?

a random soldier: Yep, we were paying attention and everything but that kinda made it worse. Cause it still was like whoa. I can't explain it properly in text.

Momma: Ok. At least you're ok if shaken.

a random soldier: Like a martini.

Momma: Humor. That was actually funny… glad you are fine… glad he's fine. Would like to hear the story when you call…

a random soldier: I'll tell you when I get home.

Momma: OK… Love you. Shaken is better than stirred.

a random soldier: Love you too.

Instant Message Conversation between Chad and Rob
1/27/2005 5:55 pm

a random soldier: Boom. Really big boom.

It's Rob: What's this? I know my presence in your life is explosive.

a random soldier: Dude, I can't even explain.

It's Rob: What happened?

a random soldier: Ben and I were on the bridge, right?

It's Rob: Okay.

a random soldier: End of our post… chillin… talking… smoking…
watching our sectors. Now we are pretty seasoned
marines, right? Ben was in OIF 1 as well. Seen lots of
shit.

It's Rob: Yes.

a random soldier: Shot lots of shit. Etc etc… so with that in mind…
something exploded (don't know what) close enough
to scare the living fuck out of both of us… that doesn't
do it justice though… we're jaded.

It's Rob: Shit!

a random soldier: Like whoa… but damn this one got to us… We were
shaking so bad we had to hug… you will never bond
with anyone else like that.

It's Rob: Christ… What was it?

a random soldier: Because there's no way to explain… Don't fucking
know. That's what makes it weird… within the time it
took for the blast/concussion. We were both armed and
freaking out… which is odd… because we don't
usually do that.

It's Rob: Was this the Christmas Eve bridge?

a random soldier: Same bridge. It's like fear/anger/adrenaline/confusion
and it hits you in less than a second.

It's Rob: I can't even imagine.

a random soldier: Next thing you know your rifle is in hand and you
don't know what the fuck happened.

It's Rob: Was it at the end of post?

a random soldier: Yeah, about 10 mins before we got off… scared the piss out of two grown fucking killers.

It's Rob: Ha-ha-ha, so what the fuck did you do for the rest of post?

a random soldier: I've been hit directly before and it didn't catch me like that one. I have combat stress out the ying yang.

It's Rob: Wait, you've been hit? You didn't tell me this!

a random soldier: We talked about it and hugged and tried to make peace with the explosion… no purple heart.

It's Rob: Ha-ha, cave men vs. cave bear… hit with what?

a random soldier: My vehicle has been hit before… I chipped a tooth.

It's Rob: Oh yeah, that's right.

a random soldier: From the concussion… but yeah, that shit sucks. This was somehow worse I don't know why.

It's Rob: You weren't expecting it… its totally capricious.

a random soldier: Hell no. Neither of us remembers what the fuck we were doing 20 mins before. It's like your entire body tenses up so bad it hurts and you don't know if you're dead but you're going to kill someone and then you're left alone to think about it.

It's Rob: But you're alive. You're alive.

a random soldier: I keep telling myself that… So does Ben.

It's Rob: Was he the one with you in the picture? The cigar picture?

a random soldier: Nah that's Mikey… Ben is on my web page… go to my address… he's on my friend list.

It's Rob: Yeah, I'm looking at it.

a random soldier: I'm still wigging out.

It's Rob: Well Christ, Chad… something blew up near you.

a random soldier: That's never happened before I'm like, no shit.

It's Rob: Just keep telling yourself that you're alive.

a random soldier: But it's never bothered me before and that, in fact,
                bothers me.

It's Rob: Is it because you're so close to getting out?

a random soldier: No idea… just had to tell someone from home and you
                had the best chance of comprehending. It takes a lot to
                rattle my cage you know.

It's Rob: I know, Christ, I can't even imagine what I would do… it's sad,
        you know. You've totally ruined my world view here.

a random soldier: I'm sorry.

It's Rob: Nah, it's a good thing. It's so easy to be complacent here. I shit
        you not, I take less for granted knowing you.

a random soldier: And I you.

It's Rob: And I feel so stupid because you tell me these things and I just
        feel so inadequate because Christ, what can I say?

a random soldier: You shouldn't. It's got a heavy price.

It's Rob: We grew up together.

a random soldier: Dude, as much as I love in some ways having this
                knowledge it all sucks when you have a nightmare
                about your buddy getting blown away. The price is not
                worth the knowledge.

It's Rob: I'm so sorry… God, I'm so sorry Chad. I should be there with
        you. No matter how little I belong there.

a random soldier: No you definitely shouldn't be here. I just told you it's
                not fucking worth it. I mean it's cool cause I'm so much
                older now… wiser… more confident and I have cool
                stories. But man when it's bad it's fucking horrible.

It's Rob: But you know some people here they sit back and make snide references to the war and they don't even fucking know… they have absolutely no clue and god, I hate it so much, this protected nest of academia.

a random soldier: I was talking to Ben about it last night, cause it was like that the first time he came home. A lot of people get in fights. That's why I'm going to stay away from the topic when I get home because I'm so high strung right now I could kill someone with my bare hands and quickly. So, no party when I get home.

It's Rob: Ha-ha-ha… yeah…

a random soldier: Because I don't know how I'll deal with people yet… seriously though. It's so not cool. I don't want to be that guy.

It's Rob: Did you hear about that guy… a Marine who went nuts and killed cops back home? He was stationed at Pendleton and he didn't want to go back.

a random soldier: Yeah, King knows him from 2/4.

It's Rob: No shit!

a random soldier: They lived with us before the war… we replaced them here… cool guys… we turned into them… when we got here, everyone was like , damn these guys are depressed. They shoot at everything… we won't do that. Here we are now. If it moves, it dies. We are so those guys…

It's Rob: Listen, just for the record there are no politics between us. No matter how I feel about the war, or whatever, it has no place between us.

a random soldier: I know that. I really do.

It's Rob: And the first hippie to say anything to you, I'll fucking kill.

a random soldier: You probably won't have the chance.

It's Rob: You'd be wiser to let me. I'd go to county… you'd go to

It's Rob: Levenworth…

a random soldier: Only if he died… Marine fights are short and brutal. You should see it. Not a lot of punches get thrown… lots of knees and takedowns. We know what we're doing. That one guy WANTED to kill those cops. It's not like Nam in that respect… pride… we have a lot of pride. I realized that just now… talking about how good we are at hurting people. It's fucked up isn't it?

It's Rob: Ha-ha-ha… Yes, but it's not your fault and it's not my place to judge.

a random soldier: As if no one in the world is better than us… part of the programming I guess… I'm a fucking tool but its okay… cause a self aware tool is more acceptable.

It's Rob: Yeah, we're swelling in ranks… it's chic.

a random soldier: So it is.

It's Rob: So do you know anything about your next deployment? Like, for sure?

a random soldier: Nope, maybe Iraq again depends… it's a MEU… they go anywhere.

It's Rob: Yeah, this is true.

a random soldier: Schedule changes.

It's Rob: And holy shit, what are you doing for the election?

a random soldier: Hiding… hahaha no, shooting people probably from off the bridge.

It's Rob: I liked your first answer better.

a random soldier: They extended our guard week for it.

It's Rob: Jesus! Any idea about the turnout in Ramadi? CNN's saying shit like "promise of democracy in Iraq!" though it now says "violence picks up in Iraq" but Jesus, it sounds like the Iraqi cops are getting slaughtered, like, by the 10's.

a random soldier: You want to know what the turnout is? Hah these
people piss us off… piss away their freedom
expecting 10% of Ramadi.

It's Rob: Jesus, fear. Wow. Yeah. Actually I have to go now. So, listen be
careful.

a random soldier: As I can be.

It's Rob: February is the shortest month of the year.

a random soldier: Or the longest… depends on your point of view.

It's Rob: Twenty eight days. Time is not relative. Twenty eight days or
less, and you're out. Now be careful, and write the old man once
in a while, huh? Though I think I need to e-mail you back.

a random soldier: It's your turn.

It's Rob: True. Tonight, then… Take it easy Chad… be safe.

Journal Entry
January 28, 2005 4:01 am
Boom. Really Big Boom.

So imagine you're in Iraq, and you're standing on post. You're a veteran
of some shitty situations and a lot of explosions, to the point where you're
so jaded that usually you go look to see what is exploding outside. You're
with a friend who is the same way. Adrenaline junkies, maybe.

So finally, after IEDs and mortars and all the normal shit, you're
watching your post, minding your own damn business, and you are
hit by such a confusing mix of shockwave/boom/adrenaline/anger/fear/
delight that you don't remember anything before of after. All of a sudden
you're aiming a rifle at the dark and you're shaking like a leaf. All of this
confuses you more, because you've been in worse explosions. So what do
you do? Chain smoke cigarettes and try to make peace with the explosion.
That's what I'm doing now. Just have to cope with it. I don't know why it
was that particular boom that did it, but man I guess you had to be there.
Helps to write it all down someplace. Just so I can remember, not that you
can forget something like that.

Terri's Journal Entry
January 28, 2005

Okay, so I didn't like the big boom. I couldn't help thinking about you dying. I've tried to keep my mind from going there, but sometimes I can't control it. You're in a freakin' WAR. It's all too surreal. I can't do this. Don't die Chad. Please don't die.
I Love You,
Mom

E-mail Home
1/29/2005 1:30 AM

Hey Mom,
Same ol' same ol' around here. Freezing on the bridge, but that's a constant. Got to guard some detainees last night. One guy pissed himself and the other two were crying. Good time. We're sadistic bastards, you might think, but they detonated an IED on Pokorny (he's fine) so fuck 'em.
Hope the cold snap stops back home. Bet you guys are ready for some spring by now.
Love,
Chad

Instant Message Conversation between Chad and Rob
1/29/2005

It's Rob: Hey! I have to go downstairs to share Bunnymac with Lori.

a random soldier: Que pasa?

It's Rob: But I just wanted to say hello.

a random soldier: Bunnymac?

It's Rob: Organic Easy Mac.

a random soldier: OK well hello… ha-ha-ha-ha-ha-ha-ha… omfg… you just made my day.

It's Rob: That's right… there's a bunny on the front. Hence, bunnymac.

a random soldier: It's organic… Oh man you guys are like parodies of yourselves… college kids.

It's Rob: I know. It's awful.

a random soldier: Eating organic food.

It's Rob: It really is.

a random soldier: I love you anyway.

It's Rob: When you take into account the fact that we go to Kenyon, it's even worse… no QRF tonight?

a random soldier: No. Tell Lori my new band name… It's called Pieces of Chad. I'm going to be a rocker. The front man.

It's Rob: An ex marine emo pussy… who eats bunnymac.

a random soldier: I don't want your bunnymac… I have standards… steak is so punk.

It' Rob: Lori calls. Please, be safe and good morning/night/whatever.

a random soldier: Byes you too.

It's Rob: This away message is for you.

a random soldier: Weee! I love away messages.

Auto response from It's Rob: bunnymac

a random soldier: Yes!

Journal Entry
January 29, 2005 11:46 AM
Things I Really Like

I was up on post trying to shoot people this morning (it didn't pan out) and I thought of a partial list of simple things I really, really like. Here it is;
5) Sleeping for more than 5 consecutive hours.
4) M249 SAW whenever I get to play with it.
3) Cuddling with someone cool.
2) Cookie dough before it gets cooked, but warmer than the fridge.
1) Hot Chocolate when it's freezing outside and your hands are turning blue under your gloves.

That concludes my list. Tune in next time for the Top 5 Things To Do On Post.

Journal Entry
January 31, 2005 11:53 AM
Blah...

Okay, so not my most creative title effort, but who really cares anyway? Right. No one.

So I can't wait to get back, as usual. Pretty much in the home stretch, you could say. Finally close enough to start planning what I'm doing when I get back. First night on the 96 hr libo we're going to LA, getting wasted and then going to a strip club. I don't usually like those but damn, I've been around all guys for seven months... I need a break. Then a new tattoo. Yeah.

I'm out.

Sitting here in the dark of the Iraqi night, writing by the light of a small flashlight, I'm wondering where you are and what you're doing. I wonder if you ever think of about where I am.
Probably not.

This recent burst of nostalgia is killing me. I close my eyes to find some solace in sleep and again I think of you. Maybe if I had stayed on the East Coast. Maybe if I had been better looking or more deceitful about my intentions. Maybe if I hadn't joined the Corps. But maybe you were the reason why I ran away.

I'm listening to my CD player to cover the sound of mortar fire near by. I wish I could show you this. The passion, the violence, and lust. I wish you could know this feeling. Helplessness because the thing I want is 8000 miles away surrounded by guys who wouldn't kill and die to see your smile. I'm here surrounded by guys who kill just to stay alive.

I want to taste your lips again. Feel your body pressed close to mine. For one night to feel something other than my own loneliness. One more time just to tell you I'm sorry for the way things turned out, and I can't go on living this way. This is killing me slowly with desire.
I just want you to know.

<u>Faust</u>
Circles endless circles
Here I am again
Down another bottle of poison
Clear the demons from my mind
Take another shot at cleansing
Pour my veins, the thoughts to dream

So I can close my eyes
Without the nightmare close behind
What stalks my waking hours?
My shadow my reflection
Circles endless Circles
I die a little more
Every time I wake up alone with him
The killer in the mirror
The son in the mirror
Who the fuck am I to decide
Which came first, who's to blame
I lost my soul, running from the pain

E-mail from Home
1/30/2005

Chad,
What's a little sadism between enemies? It's not like they make your life
a day at the beach, right? No, we haven't thawed out. In fact we are under
a winter storm advisory for tonight and tomorrow. Snow, sleet, freezing
rain. I just go with it. What can you do? Maybe we will get lucky and
Charleston will be warm. Of course 55 would be toasty to us. Just to mark
the days, we leave here the 15th and get home late on the 21st. We'll have
our phones with us of course. Do you remember the numbers?
     Dad and Jimmy have gone to pick up the doors and windows we
ordered for the studio. I guess we really are building this thing.
     I'm getting ready to make a grocery run. Should be a blast. Well, not
literally. I do live in a better neighborhood than you...
     Stay Safe.
     Love, Mom

E-mail Home
1/30/2005 8:57 AM

Hey Momma,
     Good luck with the weather getting warmer. Today hasn't been that bad
but our weather is freakish. I've got your phone numbers for Charleston,
so don't worry.
     Haven't see Jimmy in a long time. How's he doing? Tell him I said
what's up.
     Mmm... Grocery run sounds good. We got dates again of when we're
coming home, and the rumor is that we're not being told the "optimistic"
dates because they want us to focus on the election, and the Corps is a
giant rumor mill. But the official date is March 15 back in the states, and

rumor date is that we'll be back to the US by the end of Feb. Don't know what to believe, but either way we're shorter than a half sized midget.

Sending some pics your way, in a couple of emails. Hope you get them.

E-mail from home
2/1/2005
Subject: Don't be alarmed

Hey,

Situation stable, but PP Clifton had a heart attack. He's in the hospital but we don't have any info on prognosis or anything, just thought you would want to know. I'll send any new info as I have it.

Love, Mom

E-mail Home
2/1/2005 11:08 AM

Whoa.

Okay. That sucks. A lot. How's Dad? Mom-mom a wreck or is she coping somehow? Let me know what happens. That was certainly unexpected. I'm fine. My mind seems calloused. I don't know what to say. I'm so used to ugliness it's hard to get my head around it. If there's anything (I don't know that there is) that I can do, let me know.

Love,
Chad

Journal Entry
February 1, 2005 9:24 PM
Best Chorus Ever!

So Mike was writing this song on his acoustic last night and was trying to come up with words for it, so we pulled a collab' and came up with a song in progress about the old cliché of a soldier coming home from war with all this baggage, but it's not cause the war haunts him, its because he'd rather be back there than the home that's changed since he left. We'll finish it one day, but until then, the chorus makes a bad ass running cadence because it's so deceptively simple. It's put to a really slow style so it flows nicely. Not really my style at all but the image of our dog tags being the chain (literal and figuratively) is a concept I really liked.

All my sins
Hang around my neck
When I'm in the war

Its home I can't forget
So I come home
And it's the war I miss
All my sins
Hang around my neck

Nothing special but we thought it was cool. I don't usually write things with other people. I'm actually kind of shy about my personal work. It's hard to expose yourself like that, you know?

Iraq remains Iraq. Another day and another mission down. Found out my grandfather had a heart attack today. I don't know what happened, I should call and find out. It's weird having something like that happen out here. You don't know how to react. So I'm just not reacting at all.
Word.

§

The last time I talked to Chad was February 1st. He had called to see how his grandfather was doing. He sounded very tired and there was something in his voice I had never heard before. The last thing I said to him was "I love you."

"I love you too, Momma. Don't worry. I'll be home soon."

§

Terri's Journal Entry
February 2, 2005

I'm so glad you called yesterday. I almost didn't tell you about your Grandfather because I didn't want you distracted.

I've never heard you sound so tired. I'm willing you to hang in. I know you will. You're the strongest person I've ever met. I can't wait to see you smile again. Everything will be alright. We can both do this. Just come home, Chad.

Love,
Mom

Part III
Everything After

"Regard your soldiers as your children, and they will follow you into the deepest valleys; look on them as your own beloved sons, and they will stand by you even unto death."

Sun Tzu

Chapter 14

Back Home

Back home
Where my thoughts wander every day
Ten thousand miles away
Back home
They don't know the struggle
To wake up, suck it up and smile
They'll never see me get mortared
They'll never watch me under fire
Never get to see us laugh at each other
Or bow our heads for a fallen brother
Back home
They don't know what its like
Mom and Dad can never know
How it feels to take a life

No, Mom, I'm fine…
I hear it all the time
The phone calls home are all the same
I'm still alive; I got your package,
Yes we're staying safe

Back home
They never know what to say
"Keep you head down, son"
And don't bother to tell them
Keeping our heads up is what we do

We're Marines
They wouldn't really like the truth
Back home
They don't see the cuts and bruises
They don't see the tired eyes
Growing old before their time and
The aching joints or the
Exhausted killer, soaked in sweat
Back from a 7 ton ride

Our lives are the sacrifice,
Our freedom is the price
So that back home
They'll never have to know
What being a Marine is like

§

Every morning I had the same routine. I'd start the computer, then the coffee. On good days there would be an e-mail from Chad and I'd know that just a few hours ago he was safe. I would go down the checklist: Department of Defense, CNN, AOL news search for Ramadi. First thing in the morning and last thing at night, I checked on Chad.

There were days at a stretch with no e-mail and no phone calls. Days spent fighting back a creeping fear, searching for any information I could find. Holding my breath.

Then came the morning that I woke up and the world was somehow altered. It wasn't the one I had gone to sleep in. I turned on the computer. I went to make the coffee. There was something wrong. As in just not right. I took my coffee back to the computer. No e-mail from Chad. I hit the search. Two Marines had been killed in Iraq.

I got dressed and tried to overlook the unease, but found Rich wasn't able to focus either, so we ran an errand, grabbed a coffee, normal things. It wasn't working. We went back home. At one point we were both walking aimlessly through the house. Were we searching for Chad? I don't know. We hadn't put it into words. I had an odd nesting sense of preparation not unlike what I had felt at the end of my pregnancies. I started cleaning the house. I couldn't speak the words that had entered my head. The Marines are coming. It made no sense. I had to be rational.

Rich settled in to work on a painting. We would be heading to Charleston to the Southeastern Wildlife Expo just after Valentine's Day and he needed to finish. Function. Create normalcy. Why wasn't it working?

I sat back down at the computer. Nothing new. Still no e-mail from Chad. No news on the two casualties.

Without thought, I was on my feet. The Marines were coming. Now. Go put the rugs back in the bathroom. Get ready. I did.

I walked into Rich's studio. He was painting and didn't look up. I looked past him out the window, down the road. A dark SUV was coming closer through the dreary February afternoon. I couldn't tell him. I couldn't stop it. I walked away and into our bedroom, pushed the curtain aside and peeked out. There it was. It slowed at the drive but rode on. I saw the government tags. The driver was in uniform. My heart was racing. I was working to breathe. I had to tell Rich.

Far across the fields, I saw Ryan's bus coming. The phone rang. I picked it up. Caller ID said Marine Corps. "Is Rich there?" Just a second. I took him the phone. I tried to tell him, but I wasn't making any sense. No one was on the line. "The Marines are coming." I had said it. I told him about the words in my head and the government vehicle. He didn't want to understand, but he did.

Ryan came in the back door and straight down the hall. He hadn't taken off his shoes or even dropped his backpack. "What's wrong?" He'd felt it too. I was trying to tell him. My lips and arms were going numb. "The Marines are coming." I headed for the back door.

There are no words to convey what it was like to have the Marines pull up into the driveway. My feelings went far beyond fear to a place I didn't even know existed. The horror was absolute. We were suddenly in a place where there was no hope, no chance. It was over. The months of war we had spent hoping and praying, sending him all our love just helping him hold on to who he was in the face of the ugliness all around him, were over. The years of raising him, teaching him and encouraging him to live life, were over. We found ourselves standing in a whole new world, a world without Chad.

Rich wanted to run and never stop. Never let them say the words that would change our family forever. There was no where to run. And he could barely walk.

By the time they reached the driveway, I was almost out of the house. I saw the vehicle through though the living room window. It was actually happening. I heard a sound behind me but didn't stop. It was only later that I found out that Rich's legs had almost given out when he saw them. He had stumbled but somehow kept going. I don't remember reaching the door or going outside. I was standing there watching the two Marines get out of the SUV. "He's dead isn't he?" I asked, knowing. No answer. They were walking towards me.

"Mrs. Clifton?" Yes. Rich was beside me. "Richard Clifton?"

"Yes," almost a whisper, almost a plea.

"He's dead isn't he?" I repeated the useless question.

"Could we go inside please?"

I looked up. When had I sat down on the bench?

"I know he's dead. He died this morning."

They exchanged worried glances, an unspoken how-could-she-know. I had my answer.

Rich opened the door for the Captain. The Gunnery Sgt. helped me to my feet and inside. I couldn't have moved on my own.

Inside I looked at Ryan. I had to be the one to say it to him. I didn't want the words to be from anyone who didn't know him, hadn't known Chad. "Chad's gone, Ry. That's why the Marines are here."

"Two of them?" he asked pointlessly.

Of course he had seen them through the window too. I was looking at him, willing him to hang on, but watched his eyes falling away as if at a great height, falling back to a place in time, just a moment before. Before I had told him his brother had died.

The passage through the house was reversed. Everything was slower. We sat in the living room.

We regret to inform you. Capt. O'Brien, pale as the death he brought us. Carrying it with courage and respect, honor for a fallen brother. A Marine he had never met. A Marine he would never forget.

"LCpl Richard Chad Clifton was killed in action today as a result of hostile fire in Ramadi, Al Anbar Province, Iraq."

I spoke the words along with him, quietly. Somehow, I already knew them by heart.

I've been told that I am strong. I can't claim that. In those first moments and days, I was doing what had to be done. Simply that. I am the mother of a Marine. Duty, Courage, Honor. Loyalty Always. They aren't just words if you live them. Never leave the fallen behind. I would bring him home. It was my turn to walk the valley.

One of the first things I said to Captain O'Brien was, "Oh god, he's so sorry."

I know how much Chad loves us, and how well he knows us. What his death would do to us was Chad's only weak point. He accepted the consequences of his life choices as they applied to him. His only worry would be what he had done to us.

I had to stop him. "Excuse me," I said. "I know you have to tell us things about Chad. But, please, let me tell you about him. I know you have to tell us about his death, but I have to tell you who he was, alive. Please?"

He nodded. He and the Gunny Sgt. listened. I told them how brilliant Chad was, how full of joy. I told them of his love of music and fast cars, lacrosse and paintball, and books and good friends, a great party. His brother. They had never met him. I needed them to know. For a second he said nothing, and then Capt. O'Brien looked at Ryan directly. Tears were in both their eyes, "I am so sorry," he said.

We all were.

The Captain continued. Chad had been killed instantly by a mortar strike. He had inadvertently saved the lives of several other Marines. The edges were starting to blur. The pain was setting in. Rich asked if it could be written down. We wouldn't remember. "It's okay," I told him. I looked at the Captain, "They'll keep telling us until we understand. Won't you Capt.?"

"Yes ma'am."

They stayed while I made a couple of phone calls. They made arrangements to return the next day, and then were gone.

Ryan dove for the CD collection. I knew what he was looking for. Seconds later "Paint it Black" was playing in Chad's room. That's where it loses cohesion for me. I've been told what I did, but I have only vague snatches. I was highly functional and remember almost nothing. I made calls. I sent emails that contained one line: Chad was killed in action. On the other side of the world, people who loved Chad, people I had never met, were dealing with his death as well.

"In war, there are no unwounded soldiers."

Jose Narosky

Chapter 15

The loud explosion rattled the building. The first one hit close. Everyone was on autopilot grabbing helmets and flacks. BOOM, the second one hit even closer, the third, fourth, just when you think it's all over the fifth and sixth hit.

"Give me accountability now," I ordered.

My Platoon Sergeant, Staff Sergeant Hodges, was already done. My heart sank as he looked at me and said, "One is not accounted for, Top."

It's that deep sinking feeling that only a parent knows when the phone rings late on a Saturday night and your kids are late for curfew.

Forty-nine days earlier, 21-year-old Corporal Lance Thompson, one of my radio operators attached to Weapons Company, was killed in action. The three other Marines that were in the same vehicle never felt a thing when a suicide vehicle born improvised explosive device hit them. Cpl Thompson was the second Marine out of my platoon that was a Purple Heart recipient for a wound in action in Ar Ramadi, Iraq. I thank God the other Marine survived. I guess 50/50 are good odds when you are talking about 5000 pounds worth of explosives.

"Top! Top!" As I come out of my daze to the face of my Platoon Sergeant. "Top, it's the Platoon Commander!" My Platoon Sergeant yells to bring me back to reality as he hands me the handset of the field phone.

"This is Top," I say in a voice to let every one know to keep their mouths shut.

The Platoon Commander says in a voice I didn't recognize, "Top, I need you to meet me at the Battalion Aide Station now."

"Yes Sir" I replied. I was out the door before the phone could be hung up. As I ran to meet my Platoon Commander my flack jacket, helmet, M-16, 9-mm and full combat load of ammo didn't even slow me down. As I got close, his eyes told me I had just lost another son.

"Clifton's been hit, Top."

Corporal Thompson had been killed in action on the 15th day of

November 2004. After the news had gotten around the Platoon, they all knew that someone had to replace him at Weapons Company. They are the Company that has taken the most casualties in the Battalion. As I was walking back to my office there were three Marines standing in front of my hatch to take Thompson's place. Lance Corporal Frazer, Lance Corporal Sutton, and Lance Corporal Clifton. Before I could even start talking Clifton looked at me and said, "I am your man, Master Sergeant."I looked at this young man. He could not have weighed more than 140 pounds soaking wet. All I am thinking is, how in the hell can he carry his ALICE pack, weapons and full combat load. I looked in his eyes and saw more wisdom and pain than a nineteen year old should have to bear. That was the moment when the decision was made to give this kid his chance. Forty nine days later, on 3 February 2005, Lance Corporal Chad Clifton was mortally wounded when our base camp came under a barrage of mortar fire. He was the third member of my platoon to receive a Purple Heart. Did I make the right decision? Only God knows. But for now I will live with the decision that I made.

They say that time heals all wounds. But, I don't want these wounds to be healed. Every time I kiss my wife and kids; every time I have a BBQ; every time I jump on my Harley and go for a ride; every time I am just sitting out on the back porch and enjoying a cool breeze, I want to remember. Not just for my personal brothers but for all the service members who gave their life so we could have the freedom that so many take for granted. It's like the old saying goes "freedom has a price the protected will never know."

MSgt. Ken Etherton
USMC

§

I met Chad when we came back from 13 Area Combat Town. There was a party that night at one of the Sgt's houses for all the people who were getting out. Chad was one of three guys who had just checked in. I rolled up in a HMMWV with my guys and got out ready to unload the gear. Chad was standing by the bay door.

As the end of work got closer everyone was in a scurry to get to the party and have a few well deserved drinks. I made sure the new guys were set up with guys that had cars to get them there to welcome them. We ended up getting drunk and talking.

Throughout the next weeks I got to know Chad better. We had field exercise in the backyard (the area behind the Comm. Shop) where we would go out with all the supplies to put up the OE-254 antennas. Chad was on my team. He was a quick learner, very determined and had a great work ethic.

A while later we started working with Gunny Chavez learning everything about High Frequency. We learned a lot and with Gunny pushing us only helped us out more. I was prone to trouble and making mistakes when I first got to the unit. Chad being new and me needing to be good and teach what I learned, they stuck us on a team. I remember at first being mad because I thought it was a punishment, but no matter how shitty the detail was or what we had to do, if Chad was there we'd get it done.

We arrived in Yuma in March. That month I really got to know Chad and see him in many different stages of attitude from cranky to happy to sad to hyper.

Once we got to Iraq, I got put on watch and Chad went to combat outpost. After a month, he came back. My Dad had died on October 2nd and I got sent home. When I got back, I remember the smile on his face when I brought him a pack of US Newports.

He had gotten in trouble with commo, Lt. Tsirilis, for going out on a patrol with Fox Co. Chad was getting yelled and screamed at with his head down. Commo turned his back and Chad had the biggest smile on his face. A few minutes later he proceeded to tell us of his adventure.

They made Chad come back to Hurricane Point where he was doing talk-ons to land the helos. They were gonna keep him there to keep him out of trouble. We were supposed to be on the same retrans team to go to the Gov't center. Then Cpl. Thomson got killed in a vehicle borne improvised explosive device. I remember going back to HP and finding out that Chad went to Weapons. As soon as I heard I felt sick. I had a bad feeling.

I started staying at the Gov't center for weeks at a time only coming back for a day or two to shower and go to the PX. I'd see Chad and we'd eat chow or bullshit for a few minutes here and there. One day I was talking to Capt. Pastor and he requested that Chad or I teach him one of the radios again. The next morning I was on phone watch and Chad walked into the comm. shop. I had someone take my watch for a few minutes so I could talk to him. We talked for about a half hour about life, liberty, and the pursuit of action. We arranged to meet Capt. Pastor at 13:30.

I stopped to talk to Chad about 12:00 to see if he wanted to get some chow, but he was working with 81's mortar section, weapons co, and declined.

About 13:05 we started getting incoming mortars. I was leaving the chow hall and saw the ambulance at BAS. We were told someone in the platoon got hurt. I knew right there it was Chad.

I know that Chad had God in his heart, no matter what he said about religion. He was one of those people who, no matter how shitty it was, he'd voice it, and deal with it. The ever glowing smile on his face was contagious, no matter what. I consider him, as well as my father, my battlefield angel.

Flannigan, I miss you bro Thank you for everything you taught me and helped me with Couldn't have asked for a better friend. Through all the bad times in whichever hell we were stuck... you will never be forgotten. Your brother, Lucky
Joe Sutton
USMC

§

As I rounded the corner Cpl Sebena was coming toward me. Blood was pouring from underneath his left arm and shoulder. He was talking, but I don't remember what he was saying. I grabbed him, putting his other arm over my shoulders. I heard what sounded like Doc Tamarin say we needed a body bag. I wondered who had been killed.

We carried Sebena a few yards and he said he couldn't walk anymore. We were at the door of one of the hootches so I sat him down there and told him he would be okay.

I rounded the corner again, and ahead in the sand I could see LCpl Clifton laying by the door of the FDC pit. His back had been ripped open by the mortar. He was lying face down in the sand. Everything else disappeared. I went straight to him and knelt at his head. There was sand all over him. His blood was all over the ground. It had mixed with the sand during the blast and made a unique substance that was all over the wall of the pit and everything nearby.

The body bag came. We rolled him into it. As he rolled over I saw his face. It was him, but it was not. I sensed he wasn't there. It was so strange because I was looking into the eyes of a young man that I lived with everyday, but I could not see him there. I gently placed my hands over his eyelids and closed them. Strangely, I didn't want him to get sand in his eyes. I know he couldn't feel it but for some reason, somewhere inside of me, there was something that was worried about my friend having sand in his eyes.

I knew he was gone, but it didn't matter. Looking into his eyes, I had mumbled some farewell that I can't remember. I can't remember the words, but I'll never forget the way the sunlight looked on his eyelashes.

We carried him to the ambulance, which was a Frankenstein high back humvee. I rode with him to Battalion Aid Station, and stood outside the humvee guarding him. From what, I do not know, but he was a Marine who could no longer guard himself. I was a Marine who could. I guess that's how we've always done it. We take care of our own. We have each other's backs.

I went back to the mortar pits to clean up and remove any serialized gear. There was blood and bits of flesh all over the ground. There was nothing to do but kick sand over them. I remember how guilty I felt, but there was nothing else to do. It was some thing done many times, in many

battles, for many friends: kick sand over the blood of their comrades. I suppose it's as honorable as any horse-led funeral procession, to have your fellow warriors take care of the only parts of you that are left to take care of in a way only a warrior could understand. You can't imagine how much love and respect was in every kick of that Iraqi sand.
Sgt. Philip Northcutt
2/5 Weapons Co. Whiskey 3
USMC

§

When Chad was killed, he had an ever present writing tablet with him. Much of it was blood soaked and not recoverable, but a friend found a poem, and tore the page:

my fingernails are dirty
my hands are cut
my mind is colored
my face is worn
my tired eyes betray my soul
the morning is warm with yesterday
but the memory is vague
all my day dreams are tired repetitions of
the ugliness of who I've become
the things I've seen
the things I've done
this broken record is growing so old
show me something beautiful
show me something beautiful
to keep me safe against myself
as I walk my consequences like empty roads
alone
show me something beautiful

"The paper is spattered with his blood. The blood is mixed with the Iraqi sand. He is now an inseparable part of whatever happens here..."

§

"I hope it is true that a man can die and yet not only live in others but give them life, and not only life, but that great consciousness of life."

Kerouac

Chapter 16

The sun set on the day of his death muted and cold. As darkness fell, and the house became filled with candlelight, friends and family poured in.

There were ten days between the day Chad was killed and his services. I remember almost none of it. Visits by Capt. O'Brien stand out. I know I talked to the media and dealt with all manner of arrangements but it's all snatches and half memories, and those I've yet to fit in any chronological order. The house was full from early morning till late at night.

That first night after everyone had gone there was nothing left to do but go to bed. I remember climbing in. From the way we moved, it was as if we were suddenly a hundred years old. Rich and I always slept tangled together; the comfort of having each other to hold hadn't lessened from our early days of falling in love. This night we lay facing each other, holding hands, alone for the first time since hearing the news. Seeing for the first time the pain reflected, seeing the devastation. We didn't talk, we didn't sleep. We closed our eyes and held on and waited for the night to pass.

On Friday, the day after Chad was killed, Capt. O'Brien called to check in. I told him we wished to meet the plane that was bringing Chad's body home. Dover Air Force Base is the point of entry for our war-dead and it is only a half an hour away. We had been told it could take awhile to extract his body from a combat zone, so I was surprised when the Captain told me he hoped it wasn't too late and he would call me back.

In the meantime we had received a condolence call from Senator Joseph Biden. I told him we were hoping to go to the Air Base and asked if he would accompany us. He said he would be honored. I had no idea my request would be controversial and would require the Senator to be given a one-time dispensation by the Pentagon in order to go with us. It just seemed that our fallen soldiers should be accorded the honor. The Senator and the Marines and the Command at the Air Base made it happen. I'm glad I was largely ignorant of the politics being played out. I would have been very angry.

There wasn't much time for much political shuffling. Chad's body would be arriving that very night, and there was much to do. Rich, Ryan and I would be accompanied by a family friend, John, to drive us and he needed to be cleared for security. We were to meet our escorts at the Base at eight.

I hadn't thought about it before, but now I worried this would be too difficult. Rich had been barely able to speak since hearing of Chad's death. Ryan had withdrawn inside to deal with his loss, and I? I was functioning at a controlled remove. This could very well be more than we could handle, but Chad was coming home, and we would be there. I had told him I would be there when he came home.

We arrived at the proper gate and were met by Captain O'Brien, Senator Biden, and escort personnel from the Air Force. We boarded a shuttle. I was afraid. The Senator held my hand and talked quietly to us. What he shared was personal, a gift of himself, human to human. I value it still.

We were taken to a waiting room near the mortuary to await the plane. The staff from the base were gracious and attentive, but it seemed they didn't know what to say to us. I didn't know how often the families of the fallen came here. We were offered refreshment.

Senator Biden knew several of the airmen and did his best to set us all at ease. I was surprised and touched when he began telling them about Chad. I remember smiling at him in gratitude. We talked about Chad a bit and then turned naturally to the subject of Iraq. He told us what it was like there, having visited several times. He described the steep descent and ascent of the planes as they arrived and departed from Baghdad Airport in efforts to thwart anti-aircraft weapons that may be attempting to bring them down. He told us some of what the troops said to him about the war. His voice held respect, his eyes, sorrow. Then it was time to go. We boarded the shuttle and headed to the plane.

I was braced for a world of pain. What I got was unexpected. It had snowed the night before and it was cold, but mostly still. The only noise a soft hum from the idled plane.

There were rules. We had to stand next to the shuttle. We were not allowed to approach the casket at anytime. A flood light lit the side of the plane and tiny blue lights surrounded the tarmac. We stood in the darkness and watched as the flag draped coffin was lowered down. No one spoke, but soldiers moved forward, saluted, and bore the casket to the waiting vehicle. There had been a soft silent beauty to the whole thing. Even then, in my pain, I remember being awed by it, and grateful that each time one of our own came home this way, they were met with Peace. Just a few moments and it was over. I knew they would take care of Chad.

The hands that held him were full of care. The grace of it will be with me always.

We were escorted back to the gate. We said goodbye to Senator Biden. He had been the second surprise of the night because I had experienced in him the humanitarian and the statesman, and I never once caught a glimpse of the politician.

The phone rang constantly. Our community was stunned. There were calls from those clergy who wished to come pray with us. My answer was always the same. I could hear the silent shock when I answered. "You are welcome to come, to learn about Chad, meet those who loved him, or just to mourn him. But I don't wish to hear any prayers for Chad's soul or any beseeching of God on Chad's behalf. Chad is fine. He and God have things well in hand. We have no doubts, no fears for him. Our faith is not shaken. We are hurt, but we are not lost."

I never saw any of them. Thinking about it now, I'm sure they were offended. Did they ever wonder if perhaps they had offended me with the assumption that their beliefs were the only valid approach to God? Probably not.

I have always been a child of God. No one can take that away from me. I've tried to pass that on to my boys. And though I venerate books I've never found one worthy of worship and that is what religions too often do. They attempt to reduce the very essence of God down to one volume, as if that were at all possible. That which is complicated, they simplify. That which is simple they complicate. I have never been afraid of God, but I have been curious. I read the Bible, several versions, and also the Koran, and the Torah. What I found has been a worship of the messenger. Not the message. I do not belittle religions, but for me, I find they belittle God.

My whole world had been rocked. My faith held solid. It was the one thing in my whole life that remained the same. I have never had a need to have all the answers about God. I'm quite sure I'm not capable of ever knowing more than a small bit of the Truth. But I trust. God loves me. God loves Chad. Just do your best and trust. Thy will be done. Trust.

We had a closed casket to give Chad his privacy. His body was made perfectly viewable due to the care and skill of the mortuary attendants at Dover Air Base. We saw him a few days after he was brought home. A Marine met us at the funeral home to present us with Chad's personal effects that he had with him when the mortar struck. In a red velvet bag was his watch, minus the band. It was still running. It was set to Iraqi time.

When the door to the viewing room was opened, I practically ran to him "Oh Chad," I cried. "Oh baby…" I kissed him. I touched his hair and laid my hands over his.

It was real. He was lying there looking perfectly at peace. Something of the little boy remained, his long eyelashes maybe, but the rest was a young man in his prime. It was the first time I'd ever seen him in Marine Dress Blues, other than a photograph. He was so handsome. Should we have decided differently and let everyone see the dashing young hero he had become? Perhaps. But we chose instead to give him Peace. He had earned it.

We left him with tokens of love and life, a pagan notion Chad would have approved of. Among them, his grandfather's Purple heart from Korea and a plastic Army man.

Hundreds of people turned out to pay their respects to Chad. We had chosen the largest funeral home in the area and it couldn't contain the crowd. Those who couldn't fit inside stood in the cold, grey afternoon, wind off the ocean whipping dozens of American flags, and listened to his service over loudspeakers.

Inside, Marines in Full Dress uniforms stood at attention next to Chad's flag draped coffin. They silently changed guard at regular intervals. Along the walls were displays of resolutions from the Delaware House and Senate, Chad's Purple Heart, and some of his writings he had sent from Iraq.

We had a close family friend officiate at Chad's services. Sergio had known Chad most of his life. His son Mike was considered by us to be our "middle son." Mike and Ryan had met the first day of kindergarten and hence our families blended. We went trick-or-treating together and watched the fireworks on Fourth of July. They were our kid's emergency contact. This seemed to qualify.

"How proud we are of Richard Chad Clifton." said Sergio. "A young man of nineteen years, so valiant, so mature and so courageous. He always talked about becoming a soldier, a United States Marine. He developed a strong sense of duty to protect the values we hold so dear: freedom and the pursuit of happiness. There is an old Celtic proverb that says 'Don't give a man a weapon until you have taught him how to dance.' A soldier must deeply care. Chad felt the same love and compassion we all feel. Chad held a weapon, but he knew how to dance. He gave an entire lifetime of love, laughter and affection to those he knew. Chad developed a strong sense of duty to serve and to protect."

Charlotte was one of Chad's closest friends and the girl I had secretly hoped he would marry. Accompanied by Colleen she sang an Eve 6 song, Here's to the Nights. She had chosen it because of a summer night they had been riding to the beach listening to it. Chad had turned to her, smiling and said "I feel so alive right now." It was haunting and beautiful.

Rob walked to the microphone. Chad's coffin was just to his left. Rich, Ryan and I were just to his right. I knew he was dying inside, but he held up. This was a moment they had talked about. Chad would have been so very proud of him.

"This is the second draft. The first was full of fireworks, and I discarded it with great regret. Anger is a fantastically explosive, phosphorescent thing, full of shiny convictions and potent pops and whistles; it would have been a good show. But last night, after the viewing, I found myself exhausted and wandering about the kitchen in a stupor when I remembered the opening lines of Vladimir Nabokov's poem Pale Fire:

> I was the shadow of the waxwing slain
> By the false azure in the windowpane,
> I was the smudge of ashen fluff- and I
> Lived on, flew on, in the reflected sky.

In these lines, a bird, a waxwing, mistakes the reflected sky of a windowpane for infinite space when it is, in fact, a wall; it impacts, dies a quick, quiet death, but somehow survives in the reflection, a mirrored bird flapping its wings in a mirrored sky. And there it was, for me: clarity, for the first time in a week. This is not the place for my anger, and you are not the audience to unload it on. I am a civilian, and next to the men here who have served or are presently serving in the armed forces, my anger is trifling, paltry and almost insulting to the memory of Lance Corporal Chad Clifton, my best friend. We're not here to be angry. We're here to mourn, and in the process, commit him to the afterlife of memory. It is my task, and the task of all present, to be the tenants of the false azure. Over the years, we will contribute to his survival, and my contribution begins with this; not anger, but kindness, and love, which I am best qualified to give.

The most frustrating thing about him was, by far, his intelligence. He was an impenetrable debater. One would think they were informed, and of reasonable mental muscle, and then they would meet Chad. Thus ended their illusions of having actual opinions- or should I say, thus ended my illusions. He made me smarter, if only because he made me realize that there was more to intelligence than a report card. True, he never threatened anyone's shot at valedictorian, but of the class of 2003, he was undeniably the smartest.

But intelligence, like most other words in the English language, is a dull sentiment, and ultimately fails to describe the deepest, most integral and compelling part of Chad Clifton: his will. Frederic Nietzsche wrote about the will; he pondered what man was capable of in the absence of god, religion, social code or any artificial fetter that could prevent him from fulfilling his full human potential. This was his Superman, his pinnacle human. This is Chad. Whereas the rest of us willingly shuffled off to college, to learn dead languages and read dead books, Chad willingly faced the worst this world can offer. He wondered to me, in conversation: would he run? What good, what evil was he capable of? How would he react, and what would that mean? Well, he faced it. He faced it with both eyes open and he never ran. He pushed every threshold, pushed the limits until he stood on the brink and saw… nothing. To his questions- Human nature, love, war- he found no answers besides the deep echoing void, throwing his questions back at him. But he made his peace, made peace with the void and peace with the war, and I guess in that he found that there is no answer, and that there would never be. He understood this. He was 19; tired, worn far beyond his years and sick of Iraq, but he had the knowledge that most of us will spend our lives pursuing.

Chad was brave. Chad served while we studied, he fought while we slept. But he was, above all, a human being. He realized this in a way that very few in this room ever will, and he lays under the flag a Nietzschean superman: a pinnacle.

But we should also remember that throughout most of middle school, he sported, shamelessly, a mullet. In fifth grade he founded a paramilitary organization called F.A.R-Forever A Rebellion- and appointed me Vice President. In seventh grade, weighing less than most travel luggage, he joined the wrestling team. Upon his return from boot camp, he accidentally stabbed himself in the hand with a Ka-Bar while talking to me online. Last summer six or seven sheets to the wind at his going-away-to-Iraq-party, he used his intoxication to cuddle with my girlfriend, and mock me about it. And in Iraq, after a three-hour firefight at the government center, he returned to his OP to play monopoly with his friends.

But he is gone, and we are left here as the survivors. We assemble our photographs, we write our paragraphs, and find, with sadness, that they are only shades of Chad. This, unfortunately, will never change, but perhaps we can make the best of it by being faithful to our memories and never making him seem better or worse than he truly was. Chad, always the uncompromising realist, would have it no other way. Though the photographs and paragraphs will never be as alive as we might wish, perhaps they will be sufficient. Until then, we can do no better than exist, necks craned upwards, staring at the reflected sky. "

Aaron, another close friend, was next to speak.

"It seems like I have a thousand memories of Chad. Most of which, I will be decidedly selfish and keep for myself, but I wanted to share a few with all of you, to share some of the smiles that our friendship has brought me. When I first came to Cape Henlopen High School in 1999, Chad was one of the first people I met. He was very intelligent, out-going, yet soft-spoken, quick-witted, and humorous. He was quick to laugh, but never quick to judge, and always had time for a friend.

I remember going ice skating with Chad and a couple of other friends. Chad and I were, to say the least, not Wayne Gretzky. A fact that was quickly realized by the giggles of the girls watching us. We learned a few things that day, as we had plenty of time to think while picking ourselves up off the ice. The first is that, when ice-skating, or attempting to at least, avoid small children at all times. Another important lesson was that no matter how fast you got going, the wall was your friend and would always be there to stop you... suddenly if necessary.

I remember when Chad got his Cougar. He loved it! At the time, I had a Mustang, and what does one young American male with a fast car do when he gets together with another young American male with a fast car? Why they race each other of course... down Route One... right in front of the State Police barracks. No, no one got ticketed, but looking back, maybe that wasn't the brightest idea we ever had.

I remember going to Grotto's after rifle team practice. If you ever went to Grand Slam before the smoking ban, they used to give out packets of matches with their name on them. So what do two young males do with this sudden ability to create fire? They flick lit matches at each other. Until one of the matches stays lit in the air, landing on Chelsey's shoulder, and the smell of burned hair wafts through the parking lot. No, she did not end up with the Demi Moore crew cut, but again, looking back, maybe that wasn't the brightest idea we ever had.

I remember a lot of late night talks with Chad, especially when he was working a Java Byte Café. Here I will be a bit selfish, and besides, the topics are too numerous to list, but believe me that sometimes the wisdom shared between two youths has more impact than anything you have ever heard from an adult. Looking back on those late night talks, I believe that those would rank in some of the brightest ideas we ever had, and if not, definitely some of the most memorable conversations I have had.

Chad was a poet, and a writer at heart, so I have a poem that I wish to share with you all.

> The young Marine stood and faced his God,
> Which must always come to pass.
> He hoped his shoes were shining,
> Just as brightly as his brass.
> "Step forward now you young Marine,
> How shall I deal with you?
> Have you always turned the other cheek?
> To my church have you been true?"
> The Marine then squared his shoulders,
> And said, "No, Lord, I guess I ain't.
> Because those of us who fight the wars,
> Can't always be a saint

I've had to work on Sundays,
And at times my talk was tough.
And sometimes I've been violent,
Because the streets were awfully tough.
But I never took a penny,
That wasn't mine to keep.
And I've worked a lot of long hours,
When we got in just too deep.
And I never passed a cry for help,
Though at times I shook with fear.
And sometimes, God, forgive me,
I've wept unmanly tears.
I know I don't deserve a place,
Among the people here.
They never wanted me around,
Except to calm their fear.
If you've a place for me here, Lord,
It need not be so grand.
I never expected nor had too much,
And if you don't, I'll understand."
There was a silence all around the throne,
Where the saints had often trod.
As the young Marine waited quietly,
For the judgment of his God.
"Step forward now you young Marine,
You've borne your burdens well.
Walk patiently on Heaven's streets.
You've done your time in hell."

In closing, I have always been a huge fan of music, as was Chad. I would like to leave you with my favorite quote of all time, one by Mr. Jim Morrison of The Doors. I think it fits Chad nicely. "I see myself as a huge fiery comet, a shooting star. Everyone stops, points up and gasps 'Oh, look at that!' Then – whoosh, I'm gone… And they'll never see anything like it ever again… and they won't be able to forget me… ever."
God bless you Chad. "

Sergio then read a letter I had written to Chad.
"Nineteen Years. Of course we wished we'd have much more time with you. But it was very clear the path you walked. You were a soldier from the day you first stood on your own two feet. A soldier's blue blood ran strong in your veins.

It was our honor and privilege to help prepare you for your journey. The pride, love, and fear were always there. The road you had chosen was so difficult we struggled with how to teach you what we thought you needed to know and to still find laughter and silliness and joy. And the whole time you were teaching us. About courage. About strength of convictions. About being Truly alive. And we were so blessed to know the blessings as we lived them.

And here we are at the moment of our greatest heartbreak. We have to let you make the next part of your journey on your own. We have no fear for you now. Have none for us. You did well Chad. You are our hero for more reasons than anyone will ever know. We will carry you with us for the rest of our lives and we will find you at the oceans edge on perfect blue sky days, in the storms of summer, the starry night sky, frosty mornings when the geese migrate back and the first soft snowfall of winter. And we will love you always. Go in peace. Godspeed."

The power point presentation came up on the screen. Ryan had stayed up all night creating it. "Paint it Black" filled the room as images of Chad flashed on the screen, from Parris Island to Iraq. It was surreal to sit there and watch those images. His life and death had come full circle. None of it was a surprise. All of it hurt. We we're all just doing the last, best things that we could.

Tim and Mike from the band ended the service with an acoustic version of Green Day's "Time of your Life."

The love and the grief and the pride that filled the air that night were unbelievable. I knew how much we loved Chad. I suppose it shouldn't have surprised me so many others did too.

We left the funeral home and headed to Chad's wake. It was to be held in the Baycenter in Dewey Beach, the same complex Chad had worked in during high school. As we turned onto Route One my niece Kelli pointed out the window of the limo. "Look," she said. For the next few miles, sign after sign, on billboards, restaurants, stores, were dedicating a message to Chad. We will never forget.

The next day was Valentine's Day. It was time to take Chad to Arlington. Rich had given me my Valentine's Present. It was an amethyst pendant cut in the shape of a heart. "It's a purple heart, because you were wounded in the war, too." he said.

We left Lewes with a Delaware State Police motorcycle escort and headed west across the Chesapeake Bay. Through the front window of the limousine I could see Chad's coffin in the hearse in front of us. Behind us stretched a line of cars and charter buses as far as I could see.

When we reached the Maryland State line, State police from there joined the procession and took us to Washington. There were more direct routes, but they took Chad into D.C. and past the U.S. Capitol. At each jurisdiction, officers joined as others peeled off. They were giving Chad every honor they could.

Section 60 is where the fallen from Iraq and Afghanistan are laid to rest. The Honor Guard carried him through the rain. I felt like I was in a very bad dream. My mind went back to that spring day we had walked here with Chad. I was so numb I never flinched when the twenty-one gun salute was fired. I heard small gasps as every one else did. Taps was played and then it happened. The Honor Guard was folding the flag. An officer brought it over to me and went down on one knee. He offered his sympathies on the loss of my son.

"He was a brave Marine, Ma'am. He will never be forgotten." He placed the flag in my lap.

Oh God, Oh God, Oh God. I picked up the flag. I held it to my chest. I had taken the damned flag. Good job, Momma…

"Semper Fi ," I managed to whisper.

"Semper Fi, Ma'am." he said quietly, tears in his eyes, and added "Oohrah."

"Human dignity has gleamed only now and then and here and there, in lonely splendor, throughout the ages, a hope of the better men, never and achievement of the majority."

James Thurber

Chapter 17

05 Feb 05
Dear Mr. and Mrs. Clifton,

I am writing you in these difficult times to express my deepest sorrow, and to offer my condolences, to you and your family on the passing of your son, Chad.

Lance Corporal Clifton, fondly referred to as Clifford by his friends and fellow Marines, was one of the finest Marines I have ever had the privilege to command. I had the pleasure of knowing your son for only a few months, he joined the platoon in mid-November and his impact was immediate. He was a wonderful person, and we all quickly became very attached to him. His warm smile, humor, and intelligence was a breath of fresh air in these difficult time. Even at such a young age, his maturity and dedication set him apart from his peers. He was truly a special young man.

As part of Weapons Company, the platoon is always in the thick of things, and this is where Chad's star shined the brightest. He was not only the platoon radio operator, but he was the driver for the platoon sergeant. These two roles required multi-tasking, and he relished the challenge. Professionally, he was superb at his job as a communicator, and he learned the new responsibilities quickly. As a Marine he was a true Warrior, fearless in battle, and he performed to the highest standards and traditions of the Corps. I was extremely proud of him, and his actions, and hopefully you can take comfort in the fact that your son conducted himself as an outstanding combat Marine.

On the day Chad died he was performing his duties as a radio operator, having a good time with his fellow Marines. We were all laughing, and he was his usual self with a wide grin, and was making fun of some of his friends. Without warning, a mortar round impacted our position, and he was killed instantly. Please believe me when I tell you it was instantaneous, and that he did not suffer at all. He was surrounded by his friends and was laughing just prior to his death.

Clifford was always smiling, laughing, and concerned about the welfare of his fellow Marines. He was a true inspiration to myself, and the rest of the platoon. We are all better men for having known him, and we will cherish his memory and keep him in our hearts for the rest of our lives. While I know that this letter can do nothing for your loss, your pain is shared with the Marines of Third platoon and the Communications Platoon. He will be sorely missed.

With deepest sympathy,

Paul W. Callahan

1st Lt, USMC

Third Platoon Commander

Dear Terri,

I have served in the Marines for almost 21 years and this is by far the most painful thing I have to do. My heart is breaking as I type this letter and every time I think of Chad's smiling face. What a great kid. I love him as I do my own son. I can not fathom what you must be going through as I am a father of five children of my own. A son, four daughters and one grandson. I write this letter not knowing what to say but as one of your humble servants.

I don't know if you watched the 60 Minutes special a few weeks ago. CBS did a special on 2/5. The focus was on Weapons Company and there Company Commander, Capt Rapicault. The last week in October the Capt, his driver and his radio operator were killed in action. That same day Chad was right there to volunteer to take over for Cpl Thompson the radio operator for Weapons Company. As I looked at this skinny young kid I was wondering if he had what it took to take over this senior billet. I thought about it for about that long and knew he was ready. Even though he had only been in the Battalion for less then a year he was the man for the job. When I gave him the nod his grin was priceless.

In an infantry Battalion only a few are selected to be assigned to a Company. Chad was one of my best operators. All through our work ups before our deployment he was always working to be assigned as a company radio operator. If he didn't know something he didn't wait to be taught or told what to do. He figured it out on his own or asked. He was always looking for knowledge. I watched this kid land helicopters for wounded Marines. I do have to smile as I think of the first time he did this on his own. He was so excited and I can hear his voice as he told me "I got it Master Sergeant, No problem". As I stood off in the distance and watched this young Marine, with his radio on his back talking to the pilot to bring him in to the landing zone I knew right then he was going to do great things. He proved himself over and over again that he was a great warrior.

I am so proud to say that I served with a man of Chad's caliber. He was so fun to be around. I don't think he ever had a bad day. No matter how tough the job he was never to be out done by anyone. I just wanted to say thank you for raising a young American Hero like Chad that really made my job easy!!! Its great families like yours, that give our boys the morals and values that founded this great nation of ours!! It's young men like Chad that make me want to stay in the Corps. The Nation and the Marine Corps were lucky to have him.

Last night we got the whole Comm. Platoon together and we talked for over an hour about Chad. We laughed and we cried. We held hands as we prayed for Chad and his family.

Before I close, I went over to see one of my friends that boxed up all of Chad's personal effects and he said that he personally put his note books and all of his writings in the box to be shipped to you.

One day I hope to meet you so I can shake your hand, give you a hug and thank you for bringing Chad into my life. He will never be forgotten. He was a true hero.
MSGT Ken Etherton

2/24/2005
Dear Mrs. Clifton,

On behalf of my entire family, we are deeply sorry, and please accept our condolences. As for me personally, my weeping heart goes out to you. I know that my words can not soothe the pain that you must feel. I only wish I could mend your broken heart, but I know that I possess no such power. It took me sometime to think what to say to you. I would like to share with you how I saw, and what I thought of, this bold and gallant Marine. I am grateful to God that He gave me the honor and privilege of having such an awe-inspiring American working with me.

Chad, came to me as a Private First Class, very young and brand new to the Corps. At that time, we had been back from Iraq for about six months. I was in charge of the battalion's Tactical Air Control Party (TACP), which consisted of communicators and pilots/aviators. Our sole mission was to drop bombs on the enemy. Cpl's Thompson, Cook, Bishop, and LCpl's Webb and Plaisted did an outstanding job for me during Operation Iraqi Freedom I. I knew upon returning to the U.S. that I was losing three Marines due to their end of service to the Corps. Therefore, I waited for us to get our new batch of Marines from 29 Palms. As they came in, I screened them thoroughly. I needed people who not only had guts and intelligence, but also possessed good character, integrity, honor, loyalty, esprit de corps, and unselfishness. Chad, not only met my standards but exceeded them. I will never forget the day that I tested him, I felt good about this new PFC; he truly impressed me. The rest of the team felt good having him join us. He was the last to join the team. I thought to myself, "Now I've got my missing piece to the puzzle."

We commenced training, not wasting any time, for we knew that the battalion would redeploy back to Iraq. TACP also was designated to help develop and establish a new concept that was being mandated from 1st Marine Division to all of us in the infantry battalions, to communicate data over long distances through the High Frequency medium. Many Marines throughout the Corps had little to no experience with this idea, some never believed it could work, but these Marines of mine were on the forefront of this concept and your son helped me tremendously with this effort to make it a proven and worthy concept. Hence, he was part of history for us communicators that are in an infantry unit. No other infantry battalion in the division accomplished what we did. I really appreciate what Chad did for me. He was really someone I could rely on. I am very precise whom I trust and whom I can rely on, but Chad had my full trust and confidence. I will never forget his devotion to learning about these new radios. He really picked things up quickly. He was never the person who said, "I can't do it:" or "this is too hard" like you hear so many young people say today. He would always say to me with great zeal, "Roger that, Staff Sergeant!"

What I really remember about him the most is the times we had in Yuma. He really made us laugh. He was our "heart and soul" in the team. Sometimes the team would go out on liberty and go to a restaurant. On the way to the restaurant, in the van, we would turn up the radio and enjoy the music. There was a radio station that would play an advertisement for an 18 and under dance club. The ad went something like this, "Come out tonight, and represent your local Jr. High!" Since Chad was the baby of the group, we would tease him, "Hey Clifton! There you go; we'll drop you off at the club after dinner!" He would say, "Yeah! That's right, I have to go and represent. Drop me off guys!" And we would all laugh. Oh God, those are the moments I cherish. Your son put a lot of hard work out in the desert in Yuma. Coming out of that training exercise in Yuma, Chad grew up so much. He showed me unlimited potential. By the way he acted; I could tell that he came from a good family. I have come across Marines from all over this country and from other countries of different races, of different creeds and religions, some came from broken homes, some came from good homes, some came from the poorest of families, and some came from the richest of families. Some Marines should not be in the Corps and are unworthy to wear our uniform. But your son was worthy. He earned the title Marine and the rank that he bore. He was one of the few that possessed good moral values that a lot of new Marines lack. I assume that you are to thank, so Thank You. He is my hero, not because he has fallen in battle, but because he chose to join our Band of Brothers after a tragic event in American history. We hear how Tom Brokaw tributes the generation that fought in World War II as the "Greatest Generation." I say that this generation of Marines that took the duty of a Marine with a free mind and without any reservation, to help defend their country from these terrorists, are the 21st Century's Greatest Generation. We owe a lot to them; we must remain grateful and above all, never forget their sacrifice.

Your son demonstrated a steadfast devotion and a dauntless approach to duty that I only wish more young Marines will follow his example. He always gave me his best and never showed fear. Theodore Roosevelt wrote:

"It is not the critic who counts; not the man who points out how the strong man stumbles or where the doer of deeds could have done better. The credit belongs to the man who is actually in the arena, whose face is marred by dust and sweat and blood, who strives valiantly, who errs and comes up short again and again, because there is not effort without error or shortcoming, but who knows the great enthusiasms, the great devotions, who spends himself for a worthy cause; who, at the best, knows, in the end, the triumph of high achievement, and who, at the worst, if he fails, at least he fails while daring greatly, so that his place shall never be with those cold and timid souls who knew neither victory nor defeat."

Your son, my compatriot, was no timid soul. I am always proud of him, my fellow citizen and Marine brother, Lance Corporal Clifton. In the last verse of the Marine's Hymn it ends like this:

"If the Army and the Navy ever looked on Heaven scenes,

They will find the streets are guarded by United States Marines!"

I say to you that God has received one more outstanding Marine for that Guard Detail. If He would ever need Close Air Support, Chad will be the man to get the job done. I am glad that he is buried in Arlington where great heroes of U.S. history lie to rest. I say that not only does Chad lie there with them, but he now walks amongst giants. I agree with you, his journey is complete. He will always remain alive in our hearts and minds.

You and your family are in prayers. If there is anything you need from me please feel free to ask. May God bless you all. Take care.

For Ever At Your Service,

Jose I. Chavez

3/22/2006

Mr. & Mrs. Clifton,

I hope this note finds you and your family doing well. MSgt Etherton has been keeping me abreast of things and I have to say I was deeply moved by the excerpt I had read for the book. It is difficult to put into words how I feel about your loss. Many times I have wanted to write to you and express my sorrow but always felt it was better to let you mourn without any interference.

After being home for a while and settling into "life", I have had the opportunity to spend some time with my family and truly reflect on things. I know the value of life and how profoundly grateful I am to spend it with the ones I love and care about. I know that I am fortunate in many things. While loss and strife is not foreign to me it has always been marginalized by faith in God and belief in the duty I have sworn to uphold. For me, leading Marines had and will always be the most important thing I could do.

When Chad checked into my platoon he, like his fellow Marines, was expected to perform at a high level of proficiency and conduct. Some miss the mark, some struggle and some excel and fly. Chad was the latter. Quickly he was shown to be dependable in all things. He volunteered when others would not and displayed a high aptitude and intuitive way of figuring things out. Because of this, he was selected to learn more sophisticated equipment and given more responsibility. His abilities, positive can do attitude, and work ethic were and are what hallmarks great Marines.

Let me just say a bit about why Chad was selected to go to Weapons Company. The Marines I sent to the line companies are simply the best junior Marines in the platoon. They are given a lot of responsibility and are critical in mission success. The only reason Chad was not sent there earlier is because he had some special skills as a TACP (Tactical Air Control Party) Marine that needed to be located with the Battalion Air Officers. When Cpl Thompson died and we needed to send another Marine to Weapons Company, we had several volunteers. The platoon staff pared it down to three and I interviewed each Marine. Chad had made it very clear about him wanting to be a Company RO for a long time. SSgt Gomez would often comment about his desires to go to one of the line companies. When I sat down with Chad he was not my first choice to go, but it was his demeanor and his bearing that caught my attention. He simply articulated that he could do the job and would not fail in the execution of his assigned duties. I made sure he understood the dangers and he fully accepted the risk. Weapons Company took most of the Battalion's casualties up to that point and had just lost their Company Commander and radio operator the day before.

This little episode was indicative of your son's character and courage. He never saw himself doing anything but the most important work regardless of the risk to himself. He was that kind of Marine. A couple days before he died I ran into Chad on my way to the CP, when he was cleaning some vehicles. I asked him directly if he was taking care of Weapons Company. He shot back "Don't worry Sir, they are all taken care of" ...I knew his answer. I had gotten nothing but glowing remarks about his work. I swelled with pride every time I heard those reports. I will never forget your son.

When Chad died, I had been only about 100m away and saw the impact of the rounds. I ran to where the impacts were and saw Chad and the Marines and Corpsman trying to help him. I want you to know that I stood by him and prayed for him. I along with the Weapons Company 1st Sgt. carried his body on the helicopter out.

I can only imagine this past year has been difficult for you. Holidays, birthdays only make it tougher. I pray that your loss is lightened over time and that God heals your pain. As you think about Chad please know that his life, although cut short, will have positive impacts in all those who knew him and his memory will be carried by those who will continue to wear our country's cloth.

Sincerely,
Chris Tsirlis
Captain USMC

Dear Mr. and Mrs. Clifton
2/6/2005

First I want to say sorry for your loss, I was one of Chad's friends, his passing was a loss to us too. Not only was he a great comrade, but he was also a great friend. I remember the first time I ever got drunk, was with him. He didn't drink but he made sure I got out of trouble and didn't go out to make a fool of myself. He was always motivated, and he always had a smile on his face, a smile that I'll never forget. And even though he went to another company, he always stopped to say wassup to us when ever he saw us. When I heard what happened to him, it brought tears to my eyes, I kept asking God why. I have never lost a friend in my life, so it was really hard for me. I'll never forget Richard C. Clifton, a really great friend. He will always live with us, and it was an honor to work with him and to be a friend of his, a brave American hero.

Robert Ordaz

Hello Clifton's Family,

I am a friend of Clifton's and I wanted to tell you about him.

I had been with 2/5 for over a year before Clifton joined up with us. I personally didn't pay much attention to him because he was so small and I didn't work in his section. I do believe I joined in a drunken celebration for his promotion to Lcpl though. Anyways… I wanted to let you know what kind of man he was, from my eyes. Clifton has won the human race before us and we are left with great memories of his time with us.

Clifton was in no way a pushover or a pussy. On first impression his stature stated that he could not hold his own but if you tried to play games on him or trick him he saw through damn near everything. On top of that he would let you know in a very bull dog like way. He took shit from no one. Needless to say I was very impressed. He was a smart-ass through and through. Well my first real working experience with him was a 18 mile hike. A hike I had never seen before nor have ever seen repeated. Eighteen miles really isn't that much, but this hike went over a mountain and half way up another, back down and back over the first mountain again. (I believe this was his second hike with 2/5 so that's not the best way to start.) Well anyway, I had the privilege to have Clifton hold on to my pack when we started up the second mountain, which was about four miles up a steep incline that did not level out. He made it over the first mountain just fine but it seemed the second was wearing his body away. While he was holding on to my pack I felt something hit my heels; it was Clifton. He had face planted right behind me. He was blacked out for about 30 seconds as I scrambled to get his clothes off and water on him, trying to wake him up. No one was around to help because so many people had passed out before that all the Doc's were busy. All of a sudden Clifton came to, and was mad at me, saying I had pushed him down. He was talking nonsense and was delirious. Either way he refused to give up and wouldn't stay down. When a Doc came by he told the Doc he was fine and had just tripped. I protested but Clifton wouldn't listen. We had made it to the turn around point and caught up with our platoon. Well the trek back was real bad. Clifton's body was obviously shutting down on him but he would not give up. We were maybe two miles behind everyone else but he wouldn't stop. Right before we got to the final mountain, Clifton's body gave out once again. This time I stayed for three or four minutes or so and he never came around. The Doc's had to put him in the vehicle and put IV's in him. Clifton would never give up. He always stayed in the fight until his body gave out. This is what he showed me and it was a great first impression. That's when I truly started to see what kind of a man Clifton truly was.

To this day I feel very privileged to have ever known Clifton. I don't know if you know this or not but Clifton volunteered to go to WPNS CO. He might have told people differently, but I know he was a warrior and was more than happy to go. Even with the knowledge that WPNS CO had lost the most people and was in constant contact with the enemy, Clifton still went. Once again Clifton proved to me that he was a fighter and would never give up.

I just want you to know that Clifton was more of a man than most people I have ever met in my life. I am so honored to have known him as a warrior, as a man, and as a friend.

I was at the ceremony in April and I was also at the ceremony in February. I, like many others, did not fare well in either. I was not emotionally able to meet any of Chad's family and friends at the time. I just recently started dealing with the issue and was so happy to see this e-mail on our board. I stood in formation at his memorial in Ramadi and when they played "Dust in the Wind" for Chad, I lost it. I couldn't breathe

and it felt like the ocean running down my face. Chad was a passionate individual. I now have that song on CD and listen to it whenever I can handle it. I also have some pictures from his ceremony in Iraq if you would like them. Chad was awesome and it kills me just wondering why Chad and not someone else. We had but short months to share our lifetime with the men we work with, we share so much its uncanny, and to loose one feels like you lost a part of your life. And when I held his dog tags lightly in my hands for the last time I realized what he did; he saved the lives of at least 10 Marines. I recently, last Thursday, learned how grateful those Marines are. You never get a second chance at life, yet Chad gave them a second chance.
Steven Arterburn

March 1, 2005
Dear Sir and Madame,
My name is Sgt. Zach Fierros. I served with your son here in Ramadi. I want to share with you that your son had a beautiful personality. It was refreshing to meet a young man like him in today's Marine Corps. I used to stand COC watch with him as his supervisor. Although I did not let him know, I enjoyed hearing his conversations about air support with the officers. He was very intelligent and down to earth. At least more intelligent than I. I would like to let you know from my heart that he was a great young man and could have done anything. I am sorry to have to introduce myself to you this way. I have been stationed on the east coast and I will return there to visit Lance Corporal Clifton. Maybe I could make a trip to meet you all. God Bless and Take Care,
Sincerely,
Zach Feirros
"Semper Fi"

§

In mid March, Capt. O'Brien arrived with several large boxes. They contained Chad's effects. Some had come from California. The others came from Iraq. Everything he owned had been gone through and sanitized. Before being brought to us, it had all gone to Aberdeen Proving Ground to be gone over by the Army.

We unpacked the boxes and lined everything up in the kitchen floor. We had to review the contents and sign forms. Everything was categorized and put in plastic bags. I lifted one bag that had been labeled "Last Letter to the Family." Capt. had seen me pick it up. Our eyes locked. He nodded. I put it aside. There were bags for everything. I was looking for his writing tablets. There were a couple tablets with some writing, but nothing substantial. The factual journal Chad had been keeping was not there. His creative writings were not there. Nor his camera and ten roles of film.

I was stunned. One of the first things I had done was contact his MSgt. about getting those writings. When I emailed him about it again, he assured me that they had been put in Chad's seabag and master locked. "Was his seabag still locked when you got it?"

No Sir. The seabag was cleaned and folded and sent empty.

§

Dear Mom, Dad and Ryan,

If you are reading this letter, that means I wasn't lucky this time. Everyone chooses their path and mine has led me here.

I just want you to know that there is nothing I can write to express how sorry I am to have put this on you. I know you love me and this will hurt you. I love you guys more than anything. I want to thank all of you for being there when I needed you to be.

So am I in a better place? Who knows. The concept of heaven is childish, but I do believe that the point of life is simply to feel and exist, and that we keep going through different consciousness until everything we need to do has been done. Time has already happened, we're just moving through it. There's no need to wait for anyone. We will all instantly be together, one way or another. The world has already ended, we just don't know when. Fate and free will coexist. You have already made your choices. I have made mine. No regrets.

I want to be buried at Arlington National Cemetery, not because it matters where you are buried, really, but it's a nice place. If you can, get me in a pair of dress blues with a ka-bar or something. It's just an old pagan tradition…

When you go through my old writings, don't get blinded by the darkness. Those were only the times I wrote to release emotion. Most of it was semantics and delusions and some of it absolute shit. "If you stare too long into the void, the void also stares into you." That quote was on my helmet. Don't let depression and your own self awareness rip you apart like it did me sometimes. It took me a long time to realize that.

I don't want everyone to forget Me. I don't want you three to develop the same sugar coated memory that most people will get. I am not that person. I was brilliant to the point of self destruction. My own self awareness was tearing me apart, slowly. Like being two people. But I was still kind. I hated cruelty. It's a mix.

Ryan, you are not joining the military unless we get invaded. And then only the Navy. I'm serious. It's not your path, so don't walk mine. I love you and I'm proud of you. You don't need to prove anything to me or anyone else. Enjoy something everyday. It's better to regret something you did than something you didn't.

Dad… I'll never forget all the mornings we spent, just us, in some boat or blind, freezing my ass off but sucking it up because I wanted to hang out with you. I know it was hard to understand my choices sometimes, but I always wanted you to be proud of me in the end. What you did with your life will always amaze me… it takes more guts than I will ever have. You really are my hero.

Mom… there is nothing I can say that you don't already know. You understood me better than anyone, even though I protected you from seeing my worst sides. But you caught glimpses and knew anyway. My dreams were not as empty as my conscience. You and I were best friends and I love you. I'm sorry things had to be this way.

That's it, that's all I have. I'm crying and writing time is over. I love you guys and I hope and know you'll find happiness in life again. Don't give up anything cause of me. It was my path to walk and I knew the consequences. I love you,

Chad

*"And I will die, and you will die, and we all will die, and even the stars will fade
out one after another in time."*

Jack Kerouac

Chapter 18

In the beginning of April, 2/5 came home. A few days later we were on our way to California for the Battalion Memorial service. We left Philadelphia Airport through the same security gate where we had last seen Chad. For the whole trip I had the sense we were walking in his footsteps. When we reached San Diego the feeling intensified. I could almost feel him watching as we made our way through the terminal.

He had loved Southern California and it didn't take long to understand why. I tried not to think about the life he could have had here. We reached our hotel in the dark, exhausted. The next morning I saw the Pacific Ocean for the first time.

The drive to Camp Pendleton was the next part of the journey. It was a beautiful day and the drive was bittersweet. At the gate we were directed on by young Marines who obviously knew why we had come. Their voices held respect and their eyes held sadness. They too, knew the cost of war.

I stepped out of the rental vehicle. I smoothed my dress and turned to walk towards the large tent set up on the asphalt parade ground. I had only taken a step when I registered the Memorial display erected just beyond. It was a line of rifles, point down amid fifteen pairs of combat boots, helmets hung on the stocks. The Soldier's grave. I had known it would be there but it didn't lessen the powerful emotional blow. It somehow knocked my breath away. I truly felt the impact in my abdomen. Tears sprang to my eyes, but I was drawn. We checked in at the registration table, gave our names. The young men were very polite, but subdued. We were given programs and small American flags, escorted to the seating area. We were the first family to arrive. "Is it alright if I walk over there?" I asked. I nodded toward the memorial. "Oh yes ma'am," responded the Marine. It felt as if the air had thickened. I had to force through, press forward.

At the base of each memorial was leaned a photo. Although I had read each name as they were released from the Department of Defense, it was the first time I had been able to put a face to most of them. There were fifteen KIA's from 2nd Battalion, 5th Regiment. Chad had been the last.

It was the first time I saw Chad's death as part of the whole. I had experienced our personal loss, that of our friends and family, even that of our wider community. This was different. This was Chad's other family. These were the people he had gone to war with. He had been there when these fourteen had fallen.

At the end of the row was Chad's picture. It had been taken at Christmas and he was smiling. Above it, his dog tags were hanging from his rifle. I couldn't help recalling the image of him passing through airport security, slipping them over his head.

During the services in February I had been protected by the shock. There was no such protection now. How could I be standing there? How could this be real? This wasn't how it was supposed to be. I was supposed to be here when 2/5 came home and Chad came home with them.

One by one, Marines started to introduce themselves. "I was a friend of your son's." I could see their uncertainty. Did we blame them for coming home alive?

We took our seats and the program began. Each family had an escort, a friend of their Marine, and that escort gave a personal eulogy for their comrade. Ours was LCpl. Mike Abaloe. He had also given Chad's eulogy at the service in Ramadi. I can't recall much of what he said because I was paying so much attention to his face and voice. They were full of pain. I knew then that this second family felt the loss as keenly as we did.

Afterwards, there was a reception in the recreation center. The guys started to approach us. They wanted to talk about Chad, and we very much wanted to hear what they had to say. For the next two hours we were surrounded by dozens of young men. We laughed and cried. The stories they told rang so true. They had known him well. They missed him too. They would never forget.

Mikey told me he had something to give us, but had to go to the barracks to get it. When he returned he gave me an invaluable gift. Two of Chad's journals. He had used them when he was working on what to say at the Ramadi service and they didn't get packed. So they didn't go missing. He had just handed me the means to keep the promise. If I ever believed in guardian angels it was then and there.

Too soon, we had to let them go. I looked up and we were the last family there. Time had stood still, and for a little while Chad was almost close enough to touch. Was he there, smiling through his tears as we were?

Back at the hotel, we took a walk along the beach and collected rocks, feet in the ocean.

"We'll find you at the ocean, on perfect blue-sky days…"

I sat on the balcony and listened to the waves crash and read the words he had left me. I understood for the first time what the war had cost him. Perhaps that's why he couldn't come back. He had died so suddenly, without warning. He was surrounded by friends, laughing. In an instant the war and the pain and the ugliness were gone.

We walked down to watch the sunset. It had cooled off, so I pulled on Chad's leather jacket. I found a stick that had washed ashore. I knew I had to let him go. I wrote "We love you Chad" in big letters in the sand.

"It's okay, Chad. You're free. There's nowhere you can go our love can't follow," I whispered. "Fly. Your war is over. 2/5 is home. You brought your best friends home alive. Peace."

We sat there and watched the sun sink into the ocean, and as the first stars came out, the sea washed the words from the sand.

Acknowledgements

Writing this book was a journey, one that I did not navigate alone. My thanks forever to Mike Abeloe for bringing Chad's words safely home. To Rob for the trust and the belief. To Heather who did what no one else could have done. To Ryan for being my one-man tech department, and to Rich who stood quietly to catch me if I fell.

To the young men of 2nd Battalion 5th Regiment, I have been honored by your care and humbled by your courage. Tho I walk the valley, I have one hell of an escort.

And to Capt. David O'Brien for leading us thru the horrors of war.

Chad, thank you for every minute. This is it, all I have. I wouldn't change anything if it meant changing you. No regrets, Anam Cara. I'll see you in forever. Blessed Be.

Glossary

BAS- Battalion Aid Station
BWT- Basic Warfare Training
Commo- Communications Officer
DI- Drill Instructor
FDC Pit- Fire Direction Center
FROC- Field Radio Operator Course
HF (Radio)- High Frequency
IED- Improvised Explosive Device
MCT- Marine Combat Training
MEPS- Military Entrance Processing Station
MEU- Marine Expeditionary Unit
MOS- Marine Operation Specialty
MRE- Meals Ready to Eat
NVGs- Night Vision Goggles
OCS- Officer Candidate School (Quantico, Virginia)
Opsec- Operation Security
PFC- Private First Class
PFT- Physical Fitness Testing
PT- Physical Training
QRF- Quick Response Force
RO Radio Operator
RPG- Rocket Propelled Grenade
RTF- Recruit Transport Facility
TACP- Tactical Air Control Party
VBIED- Vehicle Borne Improvised Explosive Device

Suggested Listening

Throughout Chad's journals he made note of what music he was listening to at the time. He saw music as a reflection of his feelings, but also a cultural and generational marker. As I put this book together I purposely listened to his CD collection. His love of music was huge and this is in no way a comprehensive list, just a few more words he left behind.

Albums
  Dead Letters by Rasmus
  Dizzy Up The Girl by the Goo Goo Dolls
  The Essential Johnny Cash
  Ultra Dance #5 by Various Artists
  Franz Ferdinand by Franz Ferdinand
  New Miserable Experience by the Gin Blossoms
  Welcome to the North by The Music
  Night on Fire by VHS or Beta
  Vietnam: A Musical Retrospective
  Give Up by Postal Service
  Life for Rent by Dido
  Annual 2004 by Ministry of Sound
  I Miss You by Blink 182
  Pink Panther's Penthouse Party
  Vol. 3, Subliminal Verses by Slipknot
  13 Tale from Urban Boheme by Dandy Warhols
  Transatlanticism by Death Cab for Cutie
  Turn on the Bright Lights by Interpol
  Room for Squares by John Mayer
  The Places You Have Come To Fear the Most by Dashboard Confessional
  A Rush of Blood to the Head by Coldplay
  Californication by The Red Hot Chili Peppers
  Synergy II: The Story Continues by Various Artists
  Hot Fuss by The Killers
  I'd Rather Dance by Kings of Convenience
  Absolute Affirmation by Radio 4

Artists

Black Sabbath
Bjork
Creedence Clearwater Revival
Rob Zombie
Petey Pablo
Eminem
Fatboy Slim
Fall Out Boy
The Clash
The Animals
Reel Big Fish
No Doubt
Rammstein
Paul Oakenfold
Portishead
The Rolling Stones
Tricky

Suggested Reading

The following books are suggested reading because they are at some point mentioned or referred to in Chad's writings, or are the source for a political, theological, or philosophical opinion expressed by him. The exception would be Gunny Tracy's book which was written during 2/5' tour in Iraq and published after their return. It gives a realistic day-to-day accounting of what life in Ramadi was like.

The Faded Sun Trilogy by C.J. Cherryh
Howl and Other Poems by Allen Ginsberg
The Sword of Truth Series by Terry Goodkind
Desolation Angels by Jack Kerouac
On the Road by Jack Kerouac
The Things They Carried by Tim O'Brien
Human, All Too Human by Friedrich Neitzsche
Jarhead by Anthony Swofford
Generation Kill by Evan Wright
Vietnam; A Reader Edited by David Zabecki
They Marched into Sunlight by David Maraniss
Ripcord by Keith Nolan
Rites of Passage by Robert Peterson
13 Cent Killers by John Culbertson
Warrior Politics Robert Kaplan
The Art of Warfare Sun - Tzu
The Prince by Niccolo Machiavelli
Street Fight in Iraq by GySgt Patrick Tracy